SCHOOL POWER

Implications of an Intervention Project

James P. Comer

*With A New Preface and Epilogue, and
a New Foreword*
by Marian Wright Edelman

THE FREE PRESS
New York   London   Toronto   Sydney   Tokyo   Singapore

The Free Press
A Division of Simon & Schuster Inc.
1230 Avenue of the Americas
New York, N.Y. 10020

First Free Press Paperback Edition 1995

Printed in the United States of America

printing number

1 2 3 4 5 6 7 8 9 10

Library of Congress Cataloging in Publication Data
Comer, James P.
　School power.
　Includes bibliographical references and index.
　1. Education, Urban—Connecticut—New Haven. 2. Yale University. Child Study Center. 3. Community and school—Connecticut—New Haven. 4. Motivation in education. 5. Public schools—Connecticut—New Haven. 1. Title.
LC5133.N37C65　　　　　　370.19'31'097468　　　　　　80-757
ISBN 0-02-874053-x

Contents

Foreword

Originally published in 1980, *School Power* is, tragically, as true today in its analysis of the problems all our children face as when it was first written. If anything, the problems Dr. James Comer addresses in this powerful work have only grown in the intervening years. Too many of our children are still growing up without hope, without opportunity, and without a sense of their future.

There is no time for pointing fingers and assigning blame for these problems. As Dr. Comer shows us, when parents, schools, and communities work together they can make truly miraculous changes in our children's minds and hearts. Dr. Comer stresses the need for children to learn how to manage their stressful environments by exercising critical thinking and social skills. With parents, teachers, and community leaders participating together in this process, children are empowered and are able to learn.

In 1968, Dr. Comer walked into the inner-city Baldwin School in New Haven for the first time. It was a school with boarded up windows and a playground strewn with glass. A school where teachers often didn't show up for work and where students ran out of control up and down the hallways. A school where, as Dr. Comer notes, "you could feel the hand of hopelessness." But through the School Development Program forged by James Comer and his colleagues, the teachers, parents and community came together in new and innovative ways to turn Baldwin and several other New Haven schools around. *School Power* is an account of this remarkable change. It is also a profound statement on the nature of power itself. Through Dr. Comer's work, we understand that real power does not lie in fear, threats, or punishment, but in the willingness and ability to listen and make change.

Dr. Comer's pioneering program in the New Haven schools has become a model for countless districts across the nation seeking to improve their schools. Dr. Comer also has much to teach us beyond the classroom on how to best understand and care for our children.

MARIAN WRIGHT EDELMAN

Preface

In 1977 I searched long and hard for a publisher for this book. I was repeatedly told that there was no interest in education. It was finally published in 1980 by The Free Press almost as a favor to me, and because the publisher was intrigued with our work. But subsequently, education—and particularly the education of children from poor families—has been recognized as one of the most important issues facing the country. What happened?

The answer is that nationwide recognition, coming slowly, has begun to snowball. Many parents have long understood that a good education would help their children maintain a good life, or obtain a better one. Several books published in the 1980s—*A Nation at Risk, The Right Schools for the Right Kids, Investing in Our Children, A Nation Prepared*[1]—helped us

understand that education and the economy had become inex-
tricably linked, that most American children (but particularly
poor children) were underachieving in school, and that the
greatest population growth was among the poor.

Then it was discovered that African-American, native
American, and Latino groups, who for historical reasons are
disproportionately poor, will make up about a third of the work
force by the year 2000. Business, government, and political
persons and groups eventually recognized the implications of
the situation—limited economic competitiveness with other
post-industrialized countries and burdensome social problems—and promptly moved to put education on the front
burner.

In the last five years the concern has sometimes bordered
on hysteria. Political action, so-called "new ideas," recrimina-
tions," and "solutions" abound—from researchers, interven-
tionists, business people, politicians, and people who believe
that they know what schools should be like because *they* once
went to school. A high-ranking military officer, now deceased,
called me and criticized my concern about the limits of merit
pay (after all, it worked in the military), and slammed the
phone down before I could further express my opinion. Many
of the would-be problem solvers have not been in a school in
forty years, particularly a school serving poor children.

Fortunately, many—not all—are beginning to realize that
there is no "quick fix" and that we must look at what works
and why, and make success possible at every schoolhouse or
academic setting. But school success is a lot like democracy: it
cannot be mandated or imposed. It is the product of people
working together in a representative, fair, and cooperative way.
The process of creating such conditions in schools must be
understood before it can be repeated efficiently and consistently. At present, there are but a handful of school improvement programs with documented success in low income areas
that have created, described, disseminated, and sustained such
programs.

In the earlier edition of *School Power* I described our tortu-
ous journey at two low-achieving schools, from frustrated,
angry, disillusioned parents, staff, and students in 1968 to
greatly improved relationships and rapidly improving acade-

mic achievement by 1977. There was still much to be done in those schools at that time. Many doubtful observers suggested that the improvement was due to the presence of our Child Study Center group—psychiatrist, social worker, psychologist, and special education teacher—a presence that was expensive and impractical. We attempted to demonstrate that the improvement was due to the theory we set out with, and subsequently enlarged and applied (with the insights and help of parents, teachers, and administrators)—not merely our presence; and that the theory applied through a similar process anywhere—east, west, north, south; big, little, or middle-size schools and districts; different racial and income groups—could make school improvement possible.

We have had some successes, and as a result there is some renewed interest in *School Power.* For this reason I have been asked to update and share our experience with groups now taking a serious look at school improvement. I am delighted to be able to do so.

Before proceeding, however, I would like to thank again all the parents, teachers, administrators, and students in the original project who took a chance, and helped us to demonstrate that all young people can achieve at an acceptable social and academic level, sometimes an exceptional level, under appropriate conditions. I would like to thank the many superintendents who invited, accepted, and supported our approach in their districts at a time when doing so was a significant risk. I also thank the many district coordinators and their staffs for their dedicated, determined efforts. And there is no way that I can adequately thank all the members of our Child Study Center School Development Program staff. But I thank you nonetheless. I hope that our combined efforts will help improve schools for all our children.

Introduction

The United States Public school system has been a leading carrier of democratic values and traditions for at least the past seventy years. Universal, as defined by each state based on society's acceptance of a Jeffersonian tenet,* the American public schools have also been expected to take leadership in the correction of every national inequity our federal government has addressed in the past generation. This has included the inequities associated with poverty, racism, and sexism. At the same time, the public schools have been viewed as a leading vehicle for correcting or modulating the problems created by drugs, violence, the sexual revolution, and the impact of major disruptions in our society.

The confluence of these structural and symptomatic problems in the 1960's forced a (begrudging) openness to help from

---

*If a nation expects to be ignorant and free in a state of civilization, it expects what never was and never will be.

other resources, and to innovation. However, the material and psychological costs were very high, and experience in negotiating what needed doing was very low.

Our political, social, and economic institutions tended to expect the public schools to take on these missions without adequate back-up of resources or the priorities necessary for such innovations. Educators, viewing their primary tasks as enabling children to acquire the methods and content of learning and socializing, frequently have been concerned that these additional social, political, and psychological objectives of schooling will impair the school's capacity to achieve its primary mission.

Nonetheless, genuine collaboration and systematic change were necessary for the public schools in the 60's, and are so today. Conflicting interests, lack of knowledge and skill, and inadequate school structures resulted in the late 60's and 70's in a growing skepticism about collaborations that were not authentic. Parents also learned painfully and bitterly that "change" or "new" is not necessarily better. Often such changes were an exchange of one burden or disadvantage for another. It became clear that there were risks as well as opportunities when schools were also expected to redress the wrongs for their children that the non-school part of the community has imposed on them and their parents. The importance of examining serious, successful efforts in this area is self-evident. This book describes and evaluates one model of collaborative undertaking, that between a private university center, a public school system, and a community of teachers and parents.

The university is a community of scholars at various levels of questioning, extending, refining, and disseminating knowledge about people and their world. Our understanding of men, women, children, and their world can be pursued and refined in many ways and in many different settings. Scientific and clinical knowledge about humankind cannot be pursued, as can mathematics or philosophy, with a blackboard and a piece of chalk, or by thinking alone. Clinical understanding, by definition, is "of or pertaining to direct observation and treatment of patients"* and implies the function of providing diagnostic and therapeutic care, a responsibility for helping and for doing no harm.

*New College Edition, The American Heritage Dictionary of the English Language, Houghton Mifflin Co., Boston, 1976.

Academic medicine and the social sciences also depend on empirical observations as the basis for collecting data to which they bring an analytic intellectual process and instrumentation in order to apply, test, or refine theoretical propositions. At such times empirical data becomes the basis for new hypotheses and for theory-building construction that in turn becomes the basis for new applications and for improved services to patients; for more satisfying educational experiences for students and teachers; and for a more useful method of understanding and making predictions about social institutions and their functions.

Thus, theoretical and clinical knowledge in medicine and many of the social sciences requires a mutually satisfying relationship with patients or clients and others being studied to ensure their cooperation and to comply with ethical standards. This clinical relationship promises understanding and services in exchange for the opportunity to observe and study the patient or other subjects, to test hypotheses that will advance and refine our knowledge. Usually, it also provides a basis for collaboration in which each group needs the cooperative involvement by the other group in order to carry out its functions and achieve its satisfactions.

The distinction between clinical and educational is an important one, though there are fuzzy areas where they overlap, and where it is productive to tolerate the ambiguity of not knowing precisely which is which. In education the teacher provides a service "imparting knowledge and skill."* It is the teacher's obligation to facilitate the cognitive and social learning which the children's parents and community have delegated to him or her. However, education is designed primarily to advance development, not to cure a deficiency. Thus, education enables children to harness their curiosity and exploratory energies into mastery via symbolization and symbolic communication in the context of a social group. Each group actively learns at the same time as each one is a socialized member of a group of peers with a qualified teacher. This adult leader teaches and helps each student learn from others, as well as learning from the instruments and knowledge set forth in the curriculum by the teacher.

In 1966, after more than fifteen years of providing periodic consultation and in-service training in public schools, as clinical

*Ibid.

and educational scholars we planned to establish a systematic long-term collaborative exchange between a clinical center and two primary schools. We planned to learn together and from each other by allowing clinicians to work together with teachers and educational administrators in the school setting, with the agreement and involvement of the parents. The clinicians knew that being able to observe children in the public schools would expose them to learning about a large sector of child life that otherwise they usually heard about only in an indirect fashion. The educators knew that clinicians used certain dynamic constructs and observational methods to understand the ailing child, which, when translated into an understanding of healthy or normal children, could be useful to teachers in their work with children and their parents. Both groups spoke of adding a clinical dimension to the educational setting and process.

It had become clear in our experience over the years that such a collaboration would be more valid and more useful if there was a quid pro quo—a service offered in exchange for the opportunity to observe, record, and study children in the school, especially in Head Start and elementary school settings.

The services included consultation with teachers about individual children, seminar discussions of child development literature, meetings focused on child-rearing patterns and group activities on psychological and child development issues in curriculum planning and evaluation. There were clinical and theoretical explorations about the relationship between child behavior at school and in the family. With permission of the parents, children could also receive appropriate diagnostic and therapeutic care in the schools.

We referred to this process as bringing a clinical dimension to the schools as we increased the scope and depth of our knowledge about children, teachers, and parents in educational settings.

As we were planning our long-term collaboration,* encouraged and supported by the Ford Foundation, we were aware that in the United States in the 1960's there was the impulse for a quantum jump in education and in democratizing our society,

---

*That special relationship in which all engage directly in a common enterprise, assuming roles not only appropriate to training, and skill, but fashioned cooperatively to serve the "general welfare."

which at times seemed to rudely jar the sheltered classroom. The apparent dangers attending the direction and application of scientific-technological discoveries had directly and indirectly jolted the once quiet profession. For good reason, therefore, teachers were in need of help. In a general sense, they needed help to grasp the nature of the new problem(s) confronting them, to fashion diverse ways of responding to problems, and to develop the skills appropriate and adequate to their task and their daily demands. It was a rare teacher who felt her college preparation was sufficient. Too many felt, often justifiably, that their college teachers were themselves lacking in knowledge, understanding, and skill. A major theme of teachers was that they were too remote, just could not know. All they knew was theory; their fellow teachers showed them the ropes. This distorted, somewhat denigrated view of theory left teachers disarmed in the face of the cascade of unordered phenomena, of the unpatterned facts they encountered daily. The experience of this project confirmed again and again that teachers learn best when scholars are colleagues rather than instructors. The bond between scholar and teacher grew as they worked together through very trying times. It was this bond which made possible the subsequent "unity of theory and practice." Nowhere in this book is that unity more clearly illustrated than in the effort to bring stability to the school.

In the process, teachers learned to respect scholars and their importance in new and concrete ways. Working together to solve problems, it became clear that the scholars had no prescriptions, but they did have analytic methods that were useful in working toward solutions. American teachers tend to be intimidated by scholars as they simultaneously tend to mock them as "just a bunch of theorists." Understandably, they insist a bit too much about being "down to earth" practitioners. In this program teachers searching for solutions learned to "theorize," to seek patterns and the deeper meanings of overt behavior. They became more skillful in recognizing subtle cues from students and how to respond to them. The collaboration enabled teachers to grow in confidence and professional skill. Under current pressures, even veteran teachers tend to become too dependent on kits and manuals around which to build a curriculum, rather than to base curriculum development on imaginative ideas stimulated by working with and understanding children in their learning behavior, a context in which kits and manuals have a useful place.

In such collaborations, teachers must be able to exert substantial control over the rate at which mutually agreed upon changes take place. In practice, this requires a fine sensitivity and mutual awareness by the participating collaborators. Perhaps the turning point in such situations comes when scholars and teachers know they need each other and why, and know that the "others" know the same.

The matter of control adds an ethical feature of its own. When it evolves through a democratic process as we know it in the United States, it not only infuses the relationship of those immediately involved, but it extends to other relationships. Teachers and scholars become more open to children and parents. The quality of the collegial relationship transfers to relationships with others. Hence, an environment is created in which all can find supports and the strength of others. The important transformation that occurs is the conscious creation of an environment which fits its members, rather than unconsciously accepting a static environment.

This book describes, discusses, and evaluates what seems essential to us, and seemed essential to the Ford Foundation,* how a private university child study center, a public school system, and a community of teachers and parents could establish a long-term collaboration which would primarily benefit the children in the schools. As additional yields from this collaboration, we have been concerned with a more satisfying and progressive professional development for the teachers involved; and for an appropriate and prideful participation and sense of ownership for the parents of our students. Also, we were committed to an evolving program, one that would go beyond the novelty effect, with self-critical and self-change capacities that were not artificially distorted or "psyched up" by funding crises. It could not succeed if it were totally dependent upon "outside" funds, or if it were so expensive it could not be useful to other school systems or to other schools in our system.

This book will introduce professional and nonprofessional readers to these issues and to the mutuality of our sense of own-

*We are grateful for encouragement, criticism and suport from Mario Fantini, Douglas Ferguson, Richard Lacey, Marjorie Martus and Edward Meade.

ership, pride, and openings to future careers for the teachers and parents involved. It emphasizes the acquisition and refinement of knowledge about children and their families for the university and public school personnel involved.

The wisdom of our colleagues in the Ford Foundation made explicit the mutuality and complexity of our collaboration. They insisted that the Foundation award be divided in half, just as the responsibility and accountability for the Baldwin-King Program was divided. Also, they knew it would take time (the grant was for a six-year period) and that the program could succeed only if eventually the useful yield was supported by the operational budgets of both institutions. This book describes the development of our collaboration and its results as we continue this program into its second decade.

SAMUEL NASH, M.A.
former Director, Special Projects and Program Planning
New Haven Public Schools
Research Associate, Yale Child Study Center

ALBERT J. SOLNIT, M.D.
former Sterling Professor of Pediatrics and Psychiatry
Director, Yale Child Study Center

PART I

1
Things Have Changed

One rainy day when I was in elementary school in the mid 1940's, we assembled in the hall during the lunch break rather than outdoors. The noise and excitement reached a feverish pitch. Our principal walked out of her office into the hall, banged a yardstick on the table, and there was instant and absolute silence. She did not have to use any threats. She did not wonder whether we would obey. We knew that she would not call our parents. Our parents expected us to obey the principal and the teachers, and we did. That was power.

In 1952, during my first year in college—enacting the "look at me, I made it" ritual—I returned to my elementary school. One of my favorite teachers, Miss Cross, whom I and my classmates all respected, was being "sassed" by two ten or eleven-year-old children. She noticed my surprise and discomfort and said to me in a resigned tone, "Things have changed since you were here." Indeed they had, but that was only the beginning. The disrespect for authority in the 1950's escalated to the serious authority problems, violence, and vandalism in the schools today. Many school staffs appear powerless in the face of troublesome student behavior.

Are these problems as pervasive as commonly believed? The evidence suggests that disorder, disruption, and disrespect for rules and authority are indeed widespread. In a 1977 report the Deputy Superintendent of Schools in Chicago, Dr. Manford Byrd, told a congressional subcommittee investigating juvenile delinquency (including violence and vandalism):

> The losses resulting from these incidents (violence and vandalism) cannot be measured solely in terms of dollars. No one has measured the immediate and longterm effects on the education of children resulting from a climate of fear generated by these conditions. Many hours of education are lost because of false fire alarms and bomb threats. Much harm is done to educational programs when classroom windows are shattered, teaching material destroyed or stolen, and schools damaged by fire and other acts of vandalism. When students and teachers are fearful of going to school—terrified by assaults and other acts of personal violence—a healthy environment for learning is lost. These losses affect us all. When educational programs of schools are disrupted, when much needed educational funds are diverted to building upkeep and security personnel and devices, the children lose and society loses now and in the future.[1]

In one less troubled urban middle school it was found that 10 percent of the students took 65 percent of the administrators' and counselors' time.[2] Most of the teacher complaints about these youngsters were about disrespect for teacher authority. Ten percent is a small part of the whole, but 10 percent probably represents a fivefold increase over the number of youngsters who were excessively troublesome to school staffs in the 1940's. In addition, school problems today are more serious, disruptive and time consuming than ever before. Beyond a certain level of disruption, a school cannot successfully carry out its educational mission no matter how skilled and committed the staff happens to be.

School crimes today include homicide, rape, robbery, assault on teachers, assault on students, burglary, larceny and substance abuse. Between 1970–73 drug and alcohol abuse in schools increased 37.5 percent and weapons seized increased 54.4 percent. Assaults on students increased 85.3 percent and assaults on teachers increased 77.4 percent.[3] It is believed that there is significant underreporting of school crimes and that these estimates do not represent the full extent of the problem. But the burglary and larceny rate increased only 11.8 percent and the dropout rate increased only 11.7 percent.[4] These data suggest that youngsters are not eager to leave school nor do they simply want more material things. The problems appear to be personal and interpersonal—individual dissatisfaction and difficulty in getting along with others. These problems are reflected in student attacks on themselves (abuse of alcohol and drugs), their peers, school staff, and property.

Every community has cause for concern. The congressional report went on to say, "We should emphasize that this is not a problem found exclusively in large cities solely involving less affluent school districts. Schools voicing a concern over the escalating rates of violence and vandalism along with the often attendant problems of weapons, drugs and rampant absenteeism, can be found in any city, suburb or town regardless of geographical location or per capita income. Simply put, while not every school suffers from serious violence and vandalism problems, no school can afford to adopt the smug attitude that 'it can't happen here.' Unfortunately it can, and has been happening at all too many schools."[5]

In an affluent suburban school district in Washington state the cost of vandalism in the 1974–75 school year was estimated to be $55 per student.[6] This was due to two very costly acts of arson and thus unusual, but indicative of the pervasiveness of the problem. The usual range for the cost of vandalism in the large urban school systems is five to eight dollars per year per student. In Los Angeles, for example, over $7 million was spent in a single school year (1974–75) for such efforts.[7]

Why did these problems not exist in yesterday's schools?

Largely because principals and other authority figures had more power than they have today. Prior to the late 1940's, a school principal was often an autocratic ruler—powerful and feared. Teachers were on the second tier in the hierarchy of school power and authority. Principals and teachers together could establish and reinforce desirable student behavior. Most parents, students, and teachers accepted absolute principal power as the way things were and should be.

The benefit of such absolute authority and power was clear expectations. Parents generally reinforced the behavior and academic expectations, rewards and punishments of the school. Violence and disrespect for authority figures were not tolerated. As a result, teachers were under less strain and could give their full attention to teaching the academic subject matter. Under such circumstances, students who were prepared and motivated to learn could do so.

During the 1950's, principals and other authority figures began to lose their power. Today most teachers, students, and parents no longer give principals total discretion about how schools will be run. Teachers, students, and parents expect to be heard. They will sabotage the efforts of a principal they believe to be unfair, uninterested in their ideas, or otherwise unacceptable. The tactics range from passive non-cooperation to active opposition or attack. Even very personable and able principals, and other administrators, cannot dictate school policy as their predecessors once did.

With less power, principals and teachers are less able to promote desirable student behavior. Parents are not routinely reinforcing the bahavior and academic achievement expectations, rewards, and punishments of the school. Students—with limited life experiences and emotional immaturity—make many more decisions about their conduct and purpose in school than they did in the past. Now able to challenge and reject the right of adults to influence their social and academic performance, many young people develop school attitudes, values, and behavior harmful to themselves, their peers, and the overall school program.

Of course the good old days were not all good. Many school administrators abused their power. Poor children, minorities (whether they attended integrated or segregated schools), women, and the less gifted often did not receive the attention and encouragement needed to support a high level of learning. Highly authoritarian and precisely structured programs often crushed the creative spark, imagination, and independence out of students.[8] Many bright, creative but independent and sometimes rebellious youngsters were forced into line or eventually pushed or dropped out of school. A society with too few independent thinkers is vulnerable to control by disturbed and opportunistic leaders. A society which wants to create and maintain a free and democratic social system must create responsible independence of thought among its young.[9]

Changes in curriculum, student-staff relations, and other aspects of the education process in the 1950's were designed to make schools more democratic, more humanistic. Have these efforts gotten out of control? If not, what did happen? Are there obvious answers?

Some believe that Dr. Spock and others like him led us into an age of permissiveness allowing children to get out of control. Others blame leaders, and all adults, who lost their right to establish moral standards as a result of American involvement in the Viet Nam War and other immoral social policies. Some blame television or classism or racism. Some claim that administrators and teachers are simply out to earn a living and do not care about their students; that union power is more important than teaching. Some argue that teacher colleges are not doing a good job. Still others view poverty, decaying neighborhoods, and cities as the cause of today's school crisis. In one way or another, at one time or another, in one place or another, all of these factors contribute to school difficulties.

The problem with each of these explanations is that it is like coming into the theater in the middle of a play. One observes a bit of action but does not know the dynamic forces which led to it and cannot predict what is likely to happen next. The relative importance of any given bit of action cannot be understood until enough of the drama unfolds. The problem of today's schools is the result of a more complex dynamic than any one of the several given above.

I propose that in order to understand the problem schools face today we must examine the bases and use of power in our society and the way they have changed in the last forty years.

Power accrues to those who meet the economic (food, clothing, shelter, health care, and safety) needs of people. Thus employers, union leaders, or others who can influence employers are powerful. Government or political leaders who establish and enforce the laws for living in a society, who protect and provide order are powerful. The primitive witch doctor was powerful. The modern physician is powerful.

Power also accrues to those who meet the spiritual, psychological, and social needs of people—a sense of belonging, value, purpose and direction, and emotional comfort. Power accrues to those who provide individuals with useful skills and information that enable them to earn a living and find a niche in the world—parents, teachers, friends and mentors of one kind or another. Mentors can be the people who help us learn how to do a job successfully or the people who give us a model of behavior or those who give us a way of understanding and managing our individual worlds.

From childhood through young adulthood, parents and teachers are critical mentors for children. Without them the young could not survive and grow. This is the basis of a powerful emotional bond between parents and children first and most important, and between teachers and children second, but still important. This is the major source of parent and school power.[10]

In complex societies with large subsystems (racial, occupational, regional, etc.), leaders fighting for the rights and needs of their subsystem's members in the total society are also powerful. The same or other leaders providing for the needs of members inside their subsystem are powerful. This may be one of the reasons why congressmen who are censored and convicted by the larger system are often reelected to Congress by members of subsystems which they have been representing, protecting, and providing for in symbolic and real ways. The more rejected and alienated people in a subsystem feel the more likely they are to support their embattled representatives. They perceive their representatives, as they perceive themselves, to be unjustly under attack from the larger social system.

Power in a society is neither equally distributed nor constant among the leaders of various organizations and institutions. Today those who control the economic destiny of large numbers of families and individuals are most powerful. This is so because a job is so important in enabling heads of households and individuals to meet their basic needs. People who are able to work can acquire a sense of purpose, adequacy, worth, value, and belonging and can meet other social and psychological needs.

Prior to the age of affluence—and even today for those who feel closed out of the economic mainstream—individuals who met the spiritual, psychological, and social needs of people were more powerful than those in control of economic functions. That is why even today a minister who is serving a low-income congregation is likely to be seen as a much more important and powerful figure than an employer who provides only marginal or inadequate income, or government officials and politicians who do not provide them with a sense of well being.

While it is true that people and policies beyond local social or religious networks influence the lives of individuals more, local leaders are *experienced* as the most influential. It is through the local minister that individuals relate to God and religion. Through the precinct committee person, labor representative, friends with contacts with those who are able to provide a job, housing, and other essential needs, people relate to the larger system. While better educated and more affluent people have a greater range of job and other need providers they can relate to, they too meet their economic, spiritual, social, and psychological needs through a variety of people and institutions, and in the process the need providers acquire or are granted power.

Given these bases of power, societal conditions prior to the 1940's made it possible for a small group of need providers—parents, ministers, employers, politicians, principals, teachers—to be very powerful. The rapid application of science and technology in the post–World War II period greatly changed the nature of American life. These changes brought concomitant changes in the structure and allocation of power across all institutions and among their participants. The evolution of this social power change is important to explore.

Pre-1940 America was a nation of small towns and rural areas. Travel was slow and difficult and there was relatively little movement in and out of these areas. Rapid and mass communication was still in its infancy. Television was still in the laboratory as late as the 1930's. Most information about the world was filtered through and censored by local leaders—employers, labor representatives, ministers, politicians, parents, teachers, principals—or information sources such as newspapers, schools, libraries. Even in major cities and at every level of government and business, small-town conditions and attitudes persisted to a great extent.

These authority figures, because they were local, often interacted with each other and the general public in one way or another.[11] The school teacher sometimes helped the farmer keep his financial record. The widow did domestic work for the judge, and he helped her out when one of her sons got into trouble. The school principal was a deacon in the leading Baptist Church in the town. A child might see the mayor or the mayor's wife in the grocery store. On a given day, or every day, a child might walk hand in hand with his teacher to the schoolhouse.

Although the rules that governed these relationships were often unjust, these were intimate interactions among institutional authority figures of the society—political, school, church—parents and children. This was the basis of a sense of belonging or community, often including trust and respect. With limited travel in and communication with the outside, authority figures were the holders of truth, spoke with almost a "common tongue" about expected behavior, meted out jobs, justice and injustice, and met the spiritual, psychological, and social needs of community members. In so doing, local authority figures acquired great power.

In the town of yesterday, tight-knit networks of people, in general agreement about what was right and wrong, significantly shaped the development and behavior of children. When I was about eleven years old, a teen-aged cousin took me to a house of prostitution managed by a friend of his. We only talked to the women present. In fact, I did not realize that it was not a regular family home. But by the time I got home a "sister" from my church who lived next door and had seen me go in had called my father and informed him. I was not spanked. My father pointed out that if I wanted people to respect me there were things I could not do and places I could not go. Being respected in our tight-knit church community was important. I did not go back.

Tight-knit social networks of approving and disapproving people are more effective determinants of a child's behavior than laws, policemen, security, and surveillance equipment. Eventually the attitudes, values, and behavior of the adult authority figures become a part of a child's character. Because parents and friends belonging to church and other social networks before the 1940's were related in one way or another to larger community networks, most people reinforced the accepted community standards. The school, the principal, and the staff were an intimate and highly respected part of the social networks of most families. Their authority was an extension of parental authority. Even the school building was hallowed ground.

In addition, because the American economy was relatively simple, there was less institutional—family, school—stress. Most people could make or bake life's essentials or live from the surplus of others. Jobs were, more often than not, available for even uneducated heads of households. Recreation and social life—church, club, community organizations—was largely based in family and social networks. Even though many people had trouble meeting essential needs, survival was possible without an elaborate and impersonal bureaucratic system. Because of limited travel and information, people had little reason to challenge or question the power distribution and rules of local community living. In general, since parents did not do so, neither did their children. The most victimized—minorities, women, the poor—had too little power to effect change. So complete was the control of leaders, largely male, that many women did not appreciate the ways in which they were being victimized.

Child rearing was less complicated.[12] Parents reared children as they themselves and generations before them had been reared. Because life conditions changed very slowly before the twentieth century and social mobility was rare, parents had experienced the kind of world they were preparing their children to live in. Children had relatively few choices about their future personal lives or society. As mentioned, many community members other than parents guided and shaped their development. Thus, family stress was less, and in turn school stress was less.

These were the good old days that many people long for today. In fact, such conditions still exist, to a limited degree, in isolated sections of the country. Information gleaned from television has less impact in isolated areas than the attitudes, values, and ways of local authority figures or important need providers. For the vast majority of Americans, and all technology based societies, these conditions will never exist again.

Profound scientific and technological changes have taken place. We have moved from a horse-and-buggy era to a car, airplane, jet, and rocket-age level of technology in about seventy years—within the lifetime of our senior citizens. This is more change and more rapid change than ever before in the history of the world.

Scientific and technological developments have promoted metropolitan living, high mobility or rapid transportation, and massive, rapid, and visual communication of information.[13] It is now possible to have breakfast in New York City and lunch the same day in Los Angeles. We are now a nation of people in daily contact with strangers. Thanks to mass transportation school administrators and teachers now often live many miles from the neighborhood schoolhouse. They are no longer in daily and informal contact with parents, ministers, and other institution leaders. The school staff and the school program are sometimes strangers and foreign bodies in the neighborhood—subject to distrust, rejection, and attack. In many schools the staff is no longer a natural extension of parental authority.[14]

Radio and television now bring rapid sound and visual communication of events, attitudes, and values from around the world.[15] No longer are a few local leaders the holders of all truth. The "common tongue" or general agreement among local authority figures about what is right and wrong no longer exists.[16] It is possible to hear differences of opinion expressed about the most basic issues—for example, what constitutes freedom of choice, life, death—almost every half-hour over radio and television newscasts.

Scientific and technological discoveries have explained many of the former mysteries of life. Medical science has made it possible to cure once dreaded diseases. Religious or spiritual explanations are less useful to many people. Thus religious leaders are less influential for many people. For many, recreation and social life are outside of the family. Much of it is now commercial and carried out with and among strangers.

In addition, basic survival needs can no longer be scratched from the ground, forest, rivers, lakes, and streams. Food, clothing, and shelter come to us through complex production, marketing, and distribution systems. Because of these complexities, temporary and sustained unemployment exist for many side by side with highly visible affluence for most, wealth and power for some. Sustained unemployment not only denies parents the opportunity to meet the food, clothing, and shelter needs of their children but also denies them the sense of adequacy, belonging, and worth which being able to do so provides. This increases the likelihood of family problems and decreases the chances of many children to be adequately prepared for school.

The leaders of business, government, religion, education, and other institutions and organizations have made little effort to help family and community development keep pace with scientific and technological development. Even today there is no coordinated, comprehensive body of legislation and programs that could be called a national family or community development policy.[17] Where development programs exist the concentration is on "bricks and mortar" rather than governance mechanisms and community programs to reduce distrust and alienation among people and permit a sense of community.

Instead, exclusionary policies and practices—exclusion from the political and economic process for some groups, irrelevant qualifying examinations, and inappropriate education—which affect the ability of people to acquire money, employment, and meet basic needs have spawned civil rights and opportunity movements among blacks and other minorities, women, etc. Exclusions, action, and reaction have resulted in widespread distrust and alienation among groups. As a result, in some places the school staff is "the enemy."[18]

At the same time scientific and technological miracles have raised the hopes and expectations of almost *all* people. Functioning on a job in order to realize the high level of expectations many people hold today requires the highest level of social and psychological development ever needed. For example, fighting or swearing in response to frustrations, delay, disappointment, and the like—in an age where these conditions are commonplace—is usually unacceptable. An impulsive or poorly organized air traffic controller is intolerable. But such a person might have fared well as a longshoreman, a disappearing occupation. Families excluded the most in the past and thus under the greatest economic and social stress today have the greatest difficulty promoting the level of social and psychological development their children will need to function well in the world of today and tomorrow.

While the poor hurt more, the well-educated and affluent are not unaffected. Because of raised expectations and pervasive negative attitudes toward people who are not able to care for themselves, there is intense school and workplace competition. School losers—less than the best academically and socially—often drop out even though they remain in school. Many young people capable of high academic achievement wonder whether the psychological and social stress of competition is desirable. In addition, as the late anthropologist Margaret Mead pointed out, the young observe the news before their parents and adult leaders can censor it. They know more about cheating, lying, and stealing by irresponsible adults than they know about the legitimate, useful, humane work of many responsible adults. Disillusionment, uncertainty, confusion, anger, and apathy are widespread among many young people from affluent families.[19]

In addition, affluence may increase the possibility that families and individuals will be able to meet their basic human needs, but there is no guarantee of this. Many affluent children experience neglect and rejection at home and in their communities in a way that makes it just as difficult for them to experience a sense of belonging, value, and worth as many poor children. In fact, many poor families are involved in social networks such as church and social groups, which provide these needs better than in some affluent families.

Many young people respond in ways harmful to themselves and society as they try to make it in a complex world with insufficient emotional, psychological, and social support systems. Alcohol and drug abuse are but two of the many harmful ways that young people and adults are responding to life's complexities. In many poor and drug-ridden communities, extra-legal economic systems have popped up—traffic in stolen goods, prostitution, etc. In many cases these responses are defensive reactions or rejections of the mainstream social system in response to a sense of being rejected or not being able to function well in the mainstream system.[20]

All of these changes have weakened or destroyed the sense of community and the tight-knit social networks that once served to promote social order, outside and inside the schoolhouse. All of the once powerful authority figures—no longer the unchallenged holders of all knowledge and truth, with control of jobs and income, and less the dispensers of spiritual solace—are less powerful. School principals and their staffs are but one group among the leadership that has lost power and authority as a result of the forces described above.[21]

In spite of the profound changes in power relationships over the past forty years, the structure and operation of school programs has changed very little. Even though teachers, parents, and students have the power or potential power to resist, many principals and teachers try to work in the same autocratic, authoritarian way they did in the past. Administrators view resistant staff behavior as insubordination, while the staff views resistant student behavior as insubordination rather than a consequence of an ineffective school structure and operation.

Children who clashed with authority figures or who did not learn or enjoy school would have dropped out in the past. But with the decline in jobs for unskilled people, many of these now remain in school. As the level of social and academic requirements needed to obtain a job increases and the social and academic performance of many students declines, concern among employers, public officials and parents mounts. The problems of education are no longer being left to educators.[22]

A major strategy in the attempt to improve education over the past fifteen years has been to try and involve parents in the work of schools.[23] In some places desperate and determined parents have decided that their hopes for a better future ride directly on the success or failure of schools; these parents have taken power to control the schools into their own hands. There is a special emotional intensity where the future of children is at stake. In perhaps more affluent places, parents and community members have not taken power directly but believe that they have the right to question school practices, oppose some of them, and prevent others.

Schools—highly visible and open for scrutiny—are often the target of anger diverted from social agencies and conditions which are less accessible and responsive. In addition, school problems—underachievement, violence and vandalism, racial disturbances—are "good news" to some, like those politicians, reporters, scholars who advance their own interests and careers on the backs of school problems and people. In too many instances, the more complicated the problem the more simplistic the explanation given and solution proposed. School people are often the bad guys and the solution usually proposed is that they simply care more or work harder.

School staffs that are already frustrated and feeling a sense of failure because of their inability to help many children now feel under unjust attack by students, parents, consumer groups, politicians, and the media. In self-defense, administrators and teachers are now more organized. Through their professional organizations and unions they are often at war with their communities. In relatively few places are there helpful, cooperative, collaborative relationships between parents, community, and schools.[24]

Without cooperative, collaborative relationships, school problems are not going to be easy to address. Schools are being asked to solve social problems they did not create. School people are not responsible for the effects of persistent unemployment on many American families; societal attitudes about race, class, and sex; neighborhood and housing decay; and the disillusionment and uncertainty among youth. It is true that in response to overwhelming problems the behavior of some school people perpetuates and aggravates these problems. Yet most educators I have met recognize that a high level of teaching and learning cannot take place unless the most harmful psychological and behavioral effects of these and other conditions are reduced.[25]

The innovative teaching and curriculum programs created over the last two decades were designed in response to the broad societal changes and problems described above. The objective of most has been to develop and educate the whole person—the social, emotional, moral, psychological person and not just the intellectual person. The methods include opportunities for children to express themselves through arts and athletics and with the aid of mature adults, explore values in an open, receptive environment. But few communities have accepted such programs easily and most object to them outright. As a result, the ability of the arts and athletics to enhance academic achievement as well as social and psychological development has never been fully appreciated. Arts and athletics have been incorporated in public school curricula but they have low status.

Some people cite the teaching time given to the arts and athletics as the cause of declining scholastic aptitude and achievement test scores, the low level of basic academic abilities among today's graduates, the inability of many to get and hold jobs, the very low achievement scores of poor children (a disproportionate number of whom are minorities). Superficial media coverage, politics and educators acting like politicians—giving answers without asking questions about the complex forces interfering with educational achievement today—are confusing the issues.

Confusion has led to a cry to a return to highly authoritarian, highly structured academic programs emphasizing the teaching of basics—reading, writing, and arithmetic.[26] We have forgotten that this approach never worked for many youngsters even in "the good old days." Also, the highly structured, authoritarian approach never really disappeared. In addition, most schools that tried to address moral, social and psychological develop-ment issues over the past two decades never did or ever intended to stop trying to teach basic academic subjects.

Most importantly, is it true that an alarming number of Ameri-can students are not achieving today at the high academic level of the past? Is the crisis in education today in academic learning, or in behavior? If it is behavior, will continuing to try to teach basics in an authoritarian system improve disorderly school behavior?

I have found no evidence at all that schools are not produc-ing enough highly motivated, well-trained students for Amer-ica to remain a world leader in science and technology. There are as many students achieving at a high level as in the past, perhaps even higher. For example, the aptitude scores and gen-eral educational development of students accepted to, and even denied admission to, professional and graduate school programs today is higher than a decade or two ago. The educa-tional development of most students seeking careers in the most intellectually demanding occupations is far above the threshold level needed for them to be able to perform well.

Most occupations are not as intellectually demanding as they are generally thought to be. It is estimated that 65 percent or more of today's and tomorrow's jobs can be held by people with average (or slightly less) intelligence and a good ninth grade education![27] While most of today's jobs do not require great intelligence, they do require greater frustration tolerance, personal discipline, organization, management, and interper-sonal skills than were required two decades and more ago.They require greater problem-solving skills. These are precisely the skills that many of the young people who are staying in school today, as opposed to two decades ago, lack. (Again, because of the disillusionment and confusion among affluent young, these problems exist in affluent and poor schools alike.) Yet very lit-tle attention is given to the systematic development of such skills, and the school climate necessary to do so.

The crisis in our schools only partly involves academic achievement.[28] Young people in the complex social setting of the schools, expected to learn and get along well socially without adequate social and psychological development to do so, act up.

Rejection of school goals, commitment to anti-school goals and ways (drugs, alcohol, and the like), apathy, etc., are but some of the acting-up behaviors. This makes it difficult for teachers to teach and for other students to learn.

A schoolhouse and staff made up of strangers, perhaps "enemies," serving young people under increased social stress, is a potential powder keg. The relationship of caretakers—parents, teachers, etc.—and their charges is a two edged sword. The young love and cherish people and places from which they receive the skills and emotional support which enable them to make it in the world or to meet their basic human needs. The same people and places are often the first and major recipients of the frustration and anger—violence, vandalism, disrespect—of young people who are not making it well in the world. I suspect that this is the reason that personal and school property violence is increasing more rapidly than school burglary and dropout rates.

Giving more time to the teaching of basics will not begin to address these problems. Effective teaching of the basics (one part of intellectual development) will not be possible for many students until the social, psychological and moral growth, interpersonal skill development, and social climate conditions are adequately addressed. In addition, raising achievement and intelligence test scores a few points can be of little value. The achievement and intelligence test scores of people in jail today are probably higher than they were forty years ago. Raising achievement and intelligence without improving the ability of people to function well in the world will not decrease the crisis in our schools and on our streets. I am not suggesting that academic skill development is unimportant. I am suggesting that moral, social, and psychological development of the young should receive equal emphasis or greater emphasis for now, if that is the front-end cost of returning attention to academics in the near future and long term.[29]

Out of concern for school problems, in 1968 the Yale Child Study Center initiated an intervention program in cooperation with the New Haven School System. We did not pretend to understand the source or extent of the problems I have discussed above, nor to have solutions for them. The only thing that was clear to us was that all of the parties involved in the educational enterprise—parents, teachers, administrators, students—were unhappy and at war with each other. The exercise of power was chaotic and conflicting, paralyzing people and programs. Whatever the underlying problems were, they could not be identified and addressed in such an atmosphere. Our strategy was to be in and learn about schools for a year, and then, with parents, teachers, and children, design an intervention program based on social and behavioral science principles.

Part II of this book will describe the program we designed. The rest of this chapter, and the other two in the first part of this book, will look at the problems we found, our understanding and assumptions about their source, and the context in which the problems were set.

The paralysis of power in the schools was the most pervasive and troublesome problem we found and had to address.

In addition to the societal forces already described, the complexity of the school itself and its mission renders many people powerless. The management demands of a school are analogous to those of a hospital. The day-to-day school operations usually do not include life or death matters, but like the hospital, the school is frequently staffed by people with different levels and kinds of training—administrators, custodians, teachers, social workers and clerks of varying races, income groups, regional and religious backgrounds; different education disciplines, and different educational philosophies; personnel trained in colleges of varying prestige and styles. A school staff must relate to parents and students whose backgrounds are equally diverse. Where there are people who are different in many ways trying to work together, the social system they are working in must be well managed. Otherwise, conflict and chaos is very likely.

Carrying the analogy further, when the patient enters with a generalized complaint, the diagnosis is often a long test and retest process, and the problem is often elusive. When a fifth grader is reading at a second-grade level, the process of finding out why is similarly elusive and elaborate. Is the child's underachievement due to some organic or physical problem? Is it correctable with a pair of glasses? Is it a motivational problem? Are teachers poorly motived or rejecting? Is the child not learning to read because of developmental or social problems? Are there too few models of readers in the child's home, neighborhood and school environment? Is the school climate chaotic, preventing the child from concentrating? The causes of such a problem are more difficult to diagnose than most lay people would imagine.

Knowledge and resources must be mobilized and coordinated to care for patients and treat their disease and to make it possible for students to learn. The doctor has the authority to do so and is the leader of the care and treatment team. But here an analogous situation between the hospital and school begins to break down. Principals should operate, with the assistance of school staff, in a similar fashion. They should serve as the leader of the child development team. Principals should be able to lead the team in the identification of problems, planning, and in developing problem-solving teaching and learning strategies, facilitating adequately harmonious relationships among diverse groups, evaluating and modifying programs to make them better address the school's task of child development. A principal who can operate in this way has a chance of being a powerful person in today's schools and can better acquire staff, parent, and student consensus and cooperation.[30]

Only a few principals have been trained in personnel management or trained to help their staff promote psychological, moral, and social development of children. Training programs for principals have concentrated on administrative procedures, including organizational development and fiscal management. Some programs have incorporated human relations training, but few, if any, have offered systematic field-based supervision. In the absence of experientially based training, few principals are prepared to serve as educational leaders in today's complex schools.

A similar problem exists in teacher education. Teachers in training need to have in-depth training in child development, supervised exposure to children in schools for several years, and career guidance before beginning to work as full-time, licensed teachers in schools.[31] In fact, supervision and support of new teachers, licensed or not, would be helpful. But it is still possible to become a teacher with a year or less of prior supervised contact with children. The supervision future teachers receive is usually related to teaching academic material and not to promoting the moral, social, and psychological development of children.[32]

Some student teachers, who are not offered practicum experiences early in their training discover that they are uncomfortable with children. As seniors nearing completion of an expensive college education, it is often too late for change. They enter classrooms measuring the hours of each day, the days until the next vacation. Some survive, by whatever means necessary, often at the expense of the pupils. Some leave defeated. Some enter administrative positions to escape the classroom, without realizing that skills needed to be a good teacher are necessary, in even larger amounts, to be a good administrator. Those who do not possess the essential expertise, but seek refuge in administration, severely compound the problems of the school.

Over the last twenty-five years the number of social and behavioral science courses in teacher education programs has increased. But most are limited to theory with little attention to application. Thus it is possible for very bright, credentialed teachers to understand the principles of "fight or flight" in the face of danger and fear, but observe a frightened transfer student kick a staff member, and respond only to the "bad" act but not to the cause of that student's fear. Most importantly, it is rare that an education program prepares a teacher or administrator to identify personal, other staff, and school practices which contribute to the problems of children.[33]

Most teachers do not receive training that will permit them to use supportive staff—social workers, psychologists, health professionals—when support staff is available. Support personnel are usually trained in separate programs and never meet with teachers they are to support before they try to do so under the stress of an on-going school program.[34] There are few universities where school human service professionals and teachers have a common core curriculum from which they can develop a shared perspective, a common professional language and learn to appreciate what they can contribute to one another. Many dollars available for support staff are not well used because the professionals are not prepared to work together efficiently and effectively.

Preparing school professionals to work with parents and people from communities surrounding schools received almost no attention until very recently. Nonetheless, government and private consumer groups are calling for, even mandating, maximum feasible parent participation in school programs. There are few in-service programs that prepare parents to work in schools. Few school systems have developed programs to help parents, administrators, and teachers blend agendas and work cooperatively.

The absence of in-school training and guidance for parents, teachers and administrators is one of the reasons that PTAs, parent-teacher councils, and other groups have been minimally effective. When people are asked to work in a way they are not trained to work or address problems they are not trained to address, one can expect resistance at best, and at worst, floundering, inappropriate, ineffective programs.[35] In fact, the resistance to all of the innovative programs of the past two decades is, in part, related to the fact that administrators, teachers, and parents were not trained to expect a changing society, a changing curriculum, or to understand changing relationship patterns.[36]

It would be easy to fault the higher education professionals—the teachers of administrators and teachers. But the decisions that led to the structure and content of higher education programs in the 1940's, much of which is still in use today, appeared to be reasonable at the time. The response to technology and change in the 1940's was an effort to upgrade the teaching profession. College and university based education programs rapidly replaced teacher apprenticeship programs and all other non-college pathways to becoming a teacher.[37] Degrees and licensure became important. Advanced training and degree granting followed. These developments paralleled and were influenced by changes in other professional areas—law, medicine, psychology.

After World War II, money for research in all disciplines and professions became more readily available. As a group, researchers in education grew enormously in number, visibility, and respect, especially those in the social science disciplines. At the same time, social scientists were attempting to develop a more rigorous, more scientific research model. Outcomes which can be quantified are thought to be "hard" or more valid scientific data. Research projects that measure the outcome of a particular "treatment" or teaching method, learning model, behavior control method—while controlling all other conditions (variables) that might affect outcome—best lend themselves to quantification. Such data are favored for publication. Publication is a major consideration for academic promotion and reward.

The preference and reward for quantifiable research affected education in two important ways. First, this situation removed powerful academic persons from intimate involvement in the delivery of educational services. Second, it contributed to the notion that there is some single "cure" for educational problems, if only it can be found, packaged, and delivered.[38]

Doing research and/or teaching on a college campus, and perhaps making periodic forays into schools to obtain research subjects, became prestigious activity. Supervising student teachers in off-campus schools, or involvement with school systems in the direct delivery of educational services brought little academic reward for college faculty.

Practice came to be thought of as a less intellectual undertaking. Practitioners often regarded research and academic institutions as operating in a make-believe world, not very helpful with real world problems. This tension grew and eventually made collaboration between colleges and universities and off-campus schools difficult. As a result, college faculty had relatively little exposure to the day-to-day problems of schools. There was little opportunity to see and adjust teacher and administrator training programs to the changing relationships among parents, teachers, administrators, and students.

The preference for research which measured the impact of a single "treatment" slowed the growth and obscured the significance of comprehensive system analysis; the study of the interactions and impact of people, programs, and procedures among and upon each other. In the single, specific "treatment" approach it is implied that one group—students, parents, teachers, or administrators—is the locus of problems in education. It often ignores the fact that human problems are the result of multi-determined, interrelated factors. The single cause and treatment approach suggests simplistic solutions such as urging teachers to have higher expectations of students, without trying to neutralize the forces that lowered the expectations in the first place; suggests a cure-all like open education without considering the administrator, parent, teacher, and student development necessary for it to be successful. Even when researchers indicate that their findings do not suggest a single problem or simple solution, this is often the interpretation in practice.

In our work in schools we found trying to isolate and measure the impact of a single educational "treatment" like trying to measure the effect of a fan on a feather in a wind tunnel. Social forces—civil rights movements, neighborhood deteriQratrion and family residence changes, unemployment, teacher turnover, community attitudes and organization—acting in the society at large, a particular city, neighborhood, family, and school often affect student behavior and academic achievement as much as or more than a particular education "treatment" being studied. Indeed a successful program based on a single "treatment" research finding and applied in a well-managed school setting may not work at all in a poorly managed school which appears to be quite similar from an income, racial make-up, size, or staff training standpoint.

There are research and study approaches that could be more helpful. System analysis, naturalistic study methods used in anthropology and human ecology, clinical diagnostic methods used in medicine, and the case study methods used in business would permit a qualitative analysis of the interacting, interrelated forces at play in a school.[39] For example, it is much more useful to a school staff for a research program to help them understand that a young student who has recently been transferred into a strange new school setting may respond by kicking his teacher or other acting-up behaviors because of genuine anxiety, rather than to simply document that the kicking episode was one of twenty-seven disruptive acts in the classroom that day. It is much more beneficial to the school to look at how its transfer-student admission procedures, principal and teacher attitudes, student preparation for a new arrival, the arriving student's preparation, acting together, can increase or decrease the anxiety and acting-up behavior rather than to measure the effect of any one of these factors alone.

I am not suggesting that studies which attempt to measure the effect of one "treatment" have no place in education. I am suggesting that a harmful imbalance in favor of quantitative, controlled research needs to be corrected. There is a time and place for both types.

The perception of a school as a dynamic, continuously changing system which clinical, naturalistic, systems analysis and case study research can provide, would take the emphasis off of the search for a single, all-powerful solution to school problems. It would put the focus on the need to prepare principals to manage the complex forces at play in a school. Such a focus could lead to changes in administrator and teacher training which would give trainees the skills needed to help students learn to cope with the many behavior options, career, and life opportunities which modern society presents. Principals with such skills, supporting and supported by teachers with such skills, could be more powerful and successful.

School staffs, parents, and students accuse each other of not caring. We have found that, more than anything else, teachers and principals want to be effective and successful. The apathy, rejection, and low expectations that they have for many students are usually defenses against a sense of failure as professionals. Similarly, the lack of interest in schools shown by many parents is defensive. Indeed, the same is true of the behavior of students. The great majority among all three groups would make the personal changes necessary to be successful if the training, mechanism and support for doing so existed in and outside of schools. But many factors make it difficult to provide the needed institutional changes.

Inertia or resistance to change—often generated by government, higher education, union, and school system activities; by personal investments of time, money and psyche in current arrangements; and by the security of the status quo, tradition, certain attitudes and values—is massive. Also, there are no quick and easy solutions to school problems. Improving schooling is a complex, gradual process and it is almost imperceptible for a significant period of time even with good managers carrying out effective programs. Schools are under pressure to reduce problems and improve test scores, yesterday. Thus, many schools are more willing to try quick cure-all techniques and new materials than to engage in the careful planning, implementation, and evaluation of school programs needed to bring about significant and sustained change.

Most importantly, change is difficult because it goes against our psychological grain. Some of our fondest memories are of tough, authoritarian parents, teachers and friends—people who were and are important to us and are a part of our psyche. In addition, the cooperation and collaboration needed to build this nation has not been romanticized and highly valued in the way that our authoritarian, individualistic past has. Thus we are inclined to highly value and try to hold on to and use the latter, even in the face of massive problems which these styles help to create. At one level, changing the way we work would require rejecting an important part of ourselves. This makes it very difficult to achieve wide acceptance for the changes needed in the training of educators and in educational practices required to respond more appropriately to the conditions of our times.

Massive, entrenched inertia and resistance in schools cannot be met head on and quickly overcome by anybody, including elected officials, appointed officials, or education experts and the application of expertise. In addition, inertia and resistance feed and grow on the distrust and confusion they create among the actors in the school enterprise—administrators, teachers, parents, and students.

As a foundation for the schools project described below, we felt that it would be helpful to bring these actors together into a governance body for the school, calling the group a Steering Committee. This, we reasoned, could restore the sense of community, accountability, and trust similar to that which existed in a natural way in schools of the past. Most importantly, it could permit the effective exercise of power and authority by the principal, with the advice and support of teachers, parents, and professional and non-professional support staff. With this mechanism some of the abuse of unchecked power of the past could be avoided. In turn, this could reduce some of the conflict between the major actors in school programs and permit the kind of program planning, implementation, problem-solving, and evaluation needed to successfully address the complex problems of the modern school at a change rate the participants could tolerate.

Before describing the program we designed, it is important to explore the forces, functions and management of power in today's schools in more detail. It will also be helpful to describe in some detail the setting of our program.

2

School Power

Students, not principals and teachers, are the most powerful people in many of today's schools. Massive technological change greatly contributed to this development over the past several decades by decreasing the power of authority figures, including principals, and increasing the information young people receive today. Decreased principal authority has made a struggle for power a frequent reality between community, home and school, within school staff, and between staff and students. Often, to their own detriment, students sometimes win the struggle. When this happens many students continue to function adequately in such schools. Nonetheless, a sharply increasing number exercise negative or veto power—the power *not* to learn, *not* to attend, *not* to behave well.

Because of good transportation and rapid, massive, visual communication, many more children are exposed to undesirable models of behavior today than ever before. Many more children observe attitudes, values and ways different from or in conflict with those of their families, social networks, and institutions. Yet today's young people are no more mature or capable of handling the increased conflicting and often stimulating information they receive than were young people of the past, who received less information and had more adult control of and advice about the information they did receive. Today a higher level of personal psychological, social, and intellectual development is required than ever before to be able to cope successfully with the increased information and the complexity it reflects.

There has been very little or no change in school structure and management to accommodate these massive technological, social, and relationship changes and needs. The response of educators has been to develop largely technological solutions—new math, new machines, new buildings, new curricula—for what are essentially personal development, interpersonal, and intergroup problems. The launching of the Sputnik rocket by Russia in 1957, the success of our own space program in the late 1950's and 1960's, and the rapid utilization of high technology by our society only fueled the scientific and technological emphasis, as opposed to a human development emphasis, in our schools.

A few programs were created in response to the increased need among children for versatility, social skills, and expanded intellectual activity—in the arts or values clarification, for example.[1] But for the most part these programs are not designed to effect change in the child's school and home. Some new programs were influenced by technology. Behavior modification, for example, is often used in schools with mechanical precision and without adequate attention to the feeling or relationship issues involved in behavior. Because these programs generally fail to address the quality of relationships in the entire school environment they are usually less effective in positively influencing the development of children than they could be.

Today's young people are more in need of mature and emotionally important adults, working together in a good relationship climate, who can help them learn to manage the increased stimulation and confusing behavior choices they have, than were their counterparts a generation or two ago. Without such help many will act in self-destructive ways or will undermine the school's mission. Such behavior cancels out the benefits of staff training, and the time, energy, concern, and efforts of teachers, parents, administrators, and taxpayers.

When children do not learn or behave well in school, many on a school staff experience a sense of failure and feel powerless. Parents and community—employers, politicians, taxpayers—become frustrated, angry, and unhappy, and everyone involved becomes accusatory and defensive. One natural response to a disruptive school setting is for the school staff, in self-defense, to blame the children and their parents; and the parents and local community, also in self-defense, usually see the problem in the school staff. Both groups generate and sustain demeaning stereotypes.[2]

Teachers may say, "Parents don't care. They are irresponsible, won't keep appointments, won't come to school programs, don't appreciate our efforts, drink Pepsi-Cola for breakfast, fight, drink, are no good." Often these angry accusations are generalizations and rationalizations for their own frustration and apparent failure. Such an environment can result in teachers responding to behavior and learning problems in angry and punitive ways or with helplessness and apathy. Parents in situations where the children are not learning well often say, "Teachers don't care about our children, think they are better than us poor people, black people, poor white people."

Out of a sense of frustration, disappointment, and anger, parents and consumer groups often mobilize to attack school problems—usually seen as the school staff. Administrators, teachers, and other school staff often mobilize power to acquire new resources—money, materials and additional personnel—to address school problems and to protect themselves against attack. These efforts often lead to a chaotic and episodic movement of power to the groups most able to mobilize at a given moment and to the achievement of relatively unimportant, sometimes counterproductive individual and respective group goals, while teaching, learning, and school behavior do not significantly improve. Rather, apathy, anger, and conflict are often the final product.

In an unrewarding or negative environment people often lash out at one another. The fighting is often subtle and on occasion even at an unconscious level. Being late to an assembly when a highly controlling principal wants a teacher to be on time is one of the ways to get back at or undermine the higher authority person who demands performance but does not provide adequate leadership and support. Not participating in school programs is one way that parents express alienation, anger, and objection to the operation of the school program.

Sometimes the fighting is overt. The open disagreement and expression of anger among parents, teachers, and administrators—and sometimes deliberate opposition to management decisions that would be useful to the children in order to spite one another—is troublesome and confusing to students. Just as children in a family can take advantage of a situation of conflict between parents to achieve their own ends, so too can students take advantage of conflict between home and school.

Children in home-school conflict situations often receive a double message from their parents: "The school is the hope for your future, listen, be good and learn" and "the school is your enemy." The latter message can be driven home in a very subtle way: "Mrs. Jones yelled at you because she doesn't like us." On the other hand, in a school in which the staff and community are in harmony, the parent's response to the same complaint might be, "Mrs. Jones scolded you when you didn't finish your work because she wants you to do well in school." Children who receive the "school is the enemy" message often go after the enemy—act up, undermine the teacher, undermine the school program, or otherwise exercise their veto power.

The specific factors causing parent, staff, and student struggle and estrangement may be quite different from place to place—particularly if middle and upper income schools are compared to low income ones. But the existence, not the causes, of a negative struggle for power is the issue here. In a school where parents, teachers, and administrators are struggling for power, the principal most likely has little. But while the parents and teachers have more power, it usually cannot be used effectively. The power of all involved is amorphous, fragmented, and tenuous. Thus nobody is able to address the school mission in a cooperative, systematic, sustained way, and the conditions contributing to student veto power grow and, in some schools, prevail. Administrators, teachers, and parents are paralyzed and powerless.[3]

Administrator, teacher, and parent needs contribute to the troublesome dynamics I have described. But it is the unfulfilled needs of students which initiate the process. The most helpful approach then is to look first at the kind of skills children need to enter school and the preparation they receive at home to be ready for school. These skills, of course, are the *positive* power children have. An understanding of the reaction to the absence of such skills will help us visualize the way the behavior and learning problems—negative power—we see in schools today develop. Such an exploration will suggest the kind of structural and management changes schools need and the kind of skills school staff need to better cope with students in modern schools.

In order to learn and behave well in school, students must be able to listen to instructions or receive information from their teachers and other responsible adults and other children in a group. To be a learner, a student must be able to tolerate the frustration and disappointment of trial, error, losing, delayed rewards, and waiting without becoming unusually disruptive. Learners must be free and spontaneous enough to be able to use their existing knowledge in the initiation of activities or projects which can bring them new knowledge. They must be able to invest themselves in activities long enough to carry them through to completion and experience the intellectual and psychological benefits of having done so. To be able to work, learn, and play with others, a student must be able to appreciate and respond to the needs and feelings of others and must have the interpersonal skills necessary to negotiate respectful and helpful responses to his or her own needs and feelings.[4] There are other characteristics that competent school learners need, but these will suffice here.

For a student to arrive on the school's doorstep adequately prepared to learn and behave well at five years of age, the caretakers (usually parents) and others in the child's environment should have stimulated early development along important developmental lines—speech and language, thinking, emotional, social, and moral—and have taught and modeled the required behavior in a way that was helpful and rewarding. The stimulation of such development starts with holding, patting, squeezing, cooing, "bye-bye's," "da-da's," feeding, helping to sit, crawl and walk, playing patty-cake, finding the missing pacifier, relating the word "potty" to the urge for a bowel movement, and on and on, through paths of ever increasing complexity, as the maturing nervous system and muscles permit.[5]

Several examples will convey the way in which social skills are taught and modeled and the way desirable psychological and moral development begins to take place.[6]

When Mary, the two-year-old, wants a glass of milk and the caretaker is busy feeding Jon, the new baby, the caretaker tells

Mary why it is necessary for her to wait just a little while and then he or she will get the milk. The two-year-old's frustration tolerance is low. Children of this age want what they want *right away!* They may try to intimidate with a temper tantrum. But because the caretaker is so important to them, they will generally wait. If the caretaker ignores or discourages the tantrum and praises the ability of the child to wait, the child will feel it is worthwhile to wait, feels rewarded, and is prepared to wait again for a longer period. In this process, Mary increases her capacity to tolerate frustration, to wait, understand the needs of others, receives verbal communication, sometimes uses language to express her needs and feeling, learns the behavior which will meet her needs and bring her approval. Success is addictive! She will use these ways again.

Billy wants Betty's ball. Because he is two years old, he may just walk over and try to take it. If she resists he may scratch, bite, or hit. The wise caretaker does not scold, spank, or banish him to another room. He has never been here before and he does not know the rules of the social game. The caretaker is more helpful if he or she explains that he must ask for the ball, maybe share it with her, or wait until she is through, or do something else: "Come, let's play with the blocks until Betty is through." The caretaker may have to help Betty decide whether she wants to keep the ball or share it. Through these interactions both children are gaining control, negotiation, and problem-solving skills.

The caretaker puts Sammy to bed with a story. It's a quiet and very intimate time. He is curled on the protective body of the caretaker—warm, safe, and nice. The story is about little people making it in the big, dangerous world. Because that is an important concern, he wants to hear it every night. "Again, dad." He hears words, the rhythm of speech, punctuation; observes left to right and top down reading movements and he hears the story so often, he memorizes it. He then "reads" it to everybody interested. All are proud of him. Everything about this situation is positively charged emotionally. Reading receives a positive charge, becomes a good, rewarding thing to do. In addition, communication and reading skills are being learned in this process.

A five-year-old at a basketball game with his father started off to a refreshment stand without asking permission. In a bantering style, the father called him back. They discuss whether the stand is upstairs or downstairs, where his seat is located, the fact that he should not walk away with anybody and what to do if he became lost. Planning, organizing, anticipation, problem prevention, and problem solving skills are being transmitted. These and many other similar incidents that occur in the course of daily life with parents or other caretakers develop habits of thinking and behaving that are needed for good academic and social performance in school.

Children who grow up in stimulating, emotionally supportive, highly verbal, and protective environments where the caretaker teaches and models skill development are usually ready for school. When the child is able to meet expectations, he or she receives praise or a positive feedback in school. This also compliments the caretaker—a child-rearing job well done. The caretaker or parent and school people feel good about each other. The child receives a message from parents that the school program is good. The positive emotional bond between parents and child is extended to the school. The school staff can then serve as parent surrogates. This facilitates learning.

Academic and social learning by young children is motivated and directed largely through the influence of important persons in the life of the child. This is even true of older children and adults. But for young children, the outside influence is critical. Children learn much on their own. But they have not reached a stage in cognitive development that would permit them to appreciate the need to acquire, nor do they know how to acquire, skills which prepare them for academic or school learning.

Learning the meaning of "A" has as much significance to children as learning the meaning of *, a nonsense symbol, has to us. Children only learn "A," how and when to use it, because important people want them to do so. It is true that a certain amount of innate intelligence and psychological and cognitive development is needed before they can learn. But by the time they enter school the vast majority of children have the mental equipment required for learning basic academic skills. What too frequently happens is that the relationship of community to school, within-school staff, teacher-to-child is such that too many teachers are not in a position to motivate all children to learn at an optimal level.

When satisfactory home and school conditions exist the caretaker and the school staff constitute an alliance and are both able to interact with a child in a series of social and teaching experiences in which the child can gain personal control, motivation for learning, a balance between individuality and cooperation, interpersonal and social skills, and a sense of responsibility for his or her own behavior. An average child with these experiences is able to learn at an adequate level in the average community-school-peer group environment.

Most children who get off to a good start in school continue to do well and to acquire the skills necessary to perform well in the society as adults. School is, after all, a template and a reflection of the larger culture.

Children who have had difficult or bland pre-school developmental experiences more often do not acquire skills needed for school and success in later life. Some children receive adequate emotional support and psychological development prior to school but acquire ways which are different and disturbing to school people. Most schools have an expectation level geared to the societal majority. Children who show social and academic skills different from that of the majority are often considered bad or "dumb" or of low intelligence. Punishment is often used to correct "the bad." Low expectations are established for those perceived as "dumb," and a self-fulfilling prophesy is set in motion.[7] Many such children are only underdeveloped or have developed in a way different from that expected in school but compatible with an environment or experience outside the school. Many could meet school expectations after additional preparation.

Psychologically healthy, able children who are underdeveloped or not prepared for the school setting will not be labelled and treated as "losers" without a fight. They will try to undermine or attack the authority figures who punish, put down their abilities, ignore their assets, or in any way lower their self-esteem and sense of competence. Academically and socially unsuccessful students often seize the chance to control and attack figures they perceive as threatening to their self-esteem and sense of competence. They often do this through disruptive or self-destructive behaviors.[8]

I once observed a group of first graders literally take a class away from a teacher who represented a threat. As the teacher tried to carry out a lesson, one youngster would act up on one side of the room. When the teacher turned to address that problem, another child would act up on the other side of the room, and around again. Five or six ringleaders worked together to bring off the take-over attack to the delight but detriment of most of the class, and to the despair of the teacher. Such behavior substitutes for success which they cannot have in acceptable ways. The other extreme is to withdraw from activities in which they are failing. They prefer the attention they receive through disruption, holding back on what is expected of them, and withdrawal to being ignored or failing without any area of success. Negative forms of success are as addictive as traditional success.

A child's school failure is often turned into a statement about the quality of child rearing by the caretaker. This is a major reason parents in some settings avoid and feel animosity toward school. Home and school are then not allies in their interaction with the child. The school staff is less able to serve as parent surrogates. Development is further hampered when the neighborhood and peer conditions are troublesome. Even youngsters who have good child rearing experiences and positive early school experiences can subsequently be adversely affected by powerful anti-school neighborhood and peer pressures, increasing pressures for poor school performance.[9] A chaotic school climate where adults are in conflict further limits the development of such children.

Children achieving poorly in school at an early age do not receive the skills—organization, discipline, capacity to complete tasks—needed for later school success. Poor school attendance and continued low achievement often follow. Disruptive and withdrawal behavior in school continues and escalates. These are the youngsters who more often drop out of school later on and are more likely to become anti-school gang members. These are the young people who, in or out of school, more often are involved in delinquent and criminal behavior.[10] Even without such severe outcomes, such youngsters often become marginally adequate or inadequate workers and heads-of-households, and poor caretakers for the next generation. They are usually unable to contribute to the well-being of their community or the society.

Wherever and for whatever reasons there is a disproportionate number of children who have had difficult pre-school experiences or experiences that are markedly different from those expected in school—school conditions are likely to be difficult. This is more likely to be a school where student veto power paralyzes educators and undermines their mission.

It is widely held that school problems in affluent communities more often grow out of a challenge, reinforced by peers, to established attitudes, values and practices. Thus school problems here develop more in pre-adolescence and early adolescence. Affluent parents and schools usually have more public and private resources to help individual children in trouble. Yet drug, vandalism, and other problems in affluent schools suggest that individual help is not enough; that the major problem is the difficulty young people have in coping with the complex and often poorly functioning school and larger social system. Even so, real opportunity for decent jobs and living opportunities in the future often limits the level and extent of acting-up behavior of young people in the average affluent community, and academic and social skills are usually achieved.

It is not uncommon for affluent youngsters to reject the attitudes, values and practices of the school or majority culture for extended periods of time and to accept and rejoin at a later date. This is possible because many had reasonably good early developmental experiences and remain exposed and tied to the major culture through friends and family. For most, it is not difficult to acquire any specific skills they missed during the rejection period. It is harder for a child who has had a difficult pre-school experience and who is less tied to the major culture to elect to function in it later on. It is still more difficult where such a person must overcome racial or other discriminatory practices to do so.

With the rise in human rights and opportunity expectations in the last few years, preparation for living and participating at a level in which one can feel respect is absolutely necessary. No groups or class of people will tolerate the denial of basic rights and reasonable opportunities which existed in the past. School—particularly public school—is the only place where society has the right and opportunity to promote such preparation. Thus schools should not declare that they cannot teach any group or class of students. In fact, given the need of the society for persons with good social and interpersonal skills, the schools cannot leave the development of these skills to parents alone, even parents capable of doing a reasonably good child rearing job. Parents, schools, and communities must become partners in this effort.

Motivation and development of children to the point that they are capable of desirable social and interpersonal behavior cannot be provided adequately through the provision of information or symbolic acts alone. Teaching material, curriculum programs such as values clarification and others are not enough. Nor is isolated ritual such as a pledge to the flag or a morning prayer enough. Social, psychological, and moral development is fostered in largest part, by the living experience of the child at home, in the neighborhood and in school—the way he or she is treated by parents, principals, teachers, and others. A child's experience is the model and motivation for his or her style and quality of treatment of others, people and property.

A significant body of literature suggests that the kind of academic and behavior problems I have described are due largely to limitations of the parents and children involved. A growing body of literature suggests that the primary problem is in the attitudes and behavior of school staff and the educational bureaucracy. A number of observers and research projects suggest that compensatory education, parent participation, and other programs designed to aid children performing poorly academically cannot do so.[11] Other observers and the results of research projects suggest that school staff and the eduational bureaucracy cannot or will not change in ways required to better meet the educational needs of children.[12] Some observers even argue that schools cannot change until racism, poverty, and other social problems are eliminated through political and economic restructuring of the entire society.[13]

As always, there is an element of truth in all theories and analyses of a phenomenon as complex as schooling. I certainly agree that there is need for political and economic changes that will reduce the deleterious effect of racism and poverty on neighborhoods, families, and, in turn, child development and preparation for school. The failure of the society to develop social policies that would enable a sense of individual and institutional relatedness needed to offset the opposite effect of technological development has adversely affected both affluent and poor communities. But I am highly suspicious of the motives and wisdom of a conclusion which suggests that children cannot learn and behave well in school at a reasonable level until the social system is radically changed.

Low-income and minority group children would be the greatest victims of a "wait to the millennium" policy. At best, such an argument may represent an overcommitment to an abstract theoretical position without adequate consideration of the real-world consequences. There may be no millennium. It may take adequate learning and social development of a sufficient number of minority and low-income students to make the millennium possible. At worst, a conclusion that nothing can be done to improve the education of poor and minority children may be a thin, more palatable veil for a policy of benign neglect and maintenance of the status quo in educational practices.

The Yale Child Study Center–New Haven School System project rejects the notion that low-income parents cannot adequately prepare children for school and that the children cannot perform school tasks at a reasonable level. It rejects the notion that school people cannot and will not develop operation and management approaches, attitudes, interests and skills needed to better develop more chldren educationally, socially, psychologically, and morally.

Our conclusion is that most programs designed to improve schooling fail because they do not adequately address the developmental needs of children and the potential for conflict in the relationship between home and school, among school staff, and among staff and students. They do not consider the structural arrangements, specific skills, and conditions school people need to address the complexities of today's schools. This is necessary to be able to cope with the kind of problems too many children present.

Many school problems stem from the first difficult contact between home, student, and school which initiates a process in which administrators, staff, and students begin to struggle for power. Undesirable behavior and poor learning eventually occur. But parents, teachers, and students really want good schools and do not want the power of the principal. They struggle for power when the school program is not going well.

A school response that recognizes different or troubling student behavior as social underdevelopment or development appropriate for another setting, and recognizes low achievement as reflective of cognitive underdevelopment—and establishes programs to develop children in a way that they can be successful in school—could eliminate the struggle for power and limit or reverse the downhill social and academic performance of many students who have had pre-school experiences that did not adequately prepare them for school. A school that recognizes that it must develop a program which enables staff and other people important to youngsters to interact with them more intimately over a longer period of time in order to help them learn to cope with the complexities of the modern world could be more effective for all students.

But the authoritarian management structure and style still present in many schools makes it difficult for the school or school staff to address the problems which lead to poor student and staff performance. A less authoritarian school management structure could make it possible for administrators, staff, parents, and students to work together to create desirable school behavior and academic achievement.

A principal has the best chance of being successful and powerful in today's schools when he or she can lead a representative management group—teachers, parents, and students when they are mature enough—in a coordinated process of planning, identifying school problems and opportunities, establishing goals, mobilizing resources and developing problem-solving and skill development programs, evaluating these programs, and modifying them in response to evaluation findings on an ongoing basis. To be able to do this, principals must understand child development and human relations principles and be able to apply them to every aspect of the school program; must have good organization, management, and interpersonal skills; must understand instructional theory and methods and be able to apply them to the curriculum program.[14]

Some principals can achieve the same without a cooperative effort. But this requires unusual personal qualities and does not permit adequate leadership skill development in other program participants. Such programs often decline sharply after the departure of an effective but authoritarian leader. Students in such a system have less opportunity to become good independent thinkers and personally responsible actors.

A representative management group gives a school the flexibility to adjust to the needs of parents and children in a community rather than holding up a single standard and judging those who do not fit as deficient. The sharing of insights and ideas can give school people a better understanding of local community needs and opportunities and give parents and children needed cultural majority skills—technology related, and not middle -income or white. Children from culturally different backgrounds can develop skills that give them a choice of future roles and opportunities. Many are now limited to life opportunities consistent with the social skills they developed in communities that are marginal, excluded and reacting negatively to majority culture attitudes, values and practices.

A representative management group approach need not lower standards. The highest academic standard can be maintained for those capable of achieving at that level if all students have a sufficient number of success experiences in a variety of areas—academic, artistic, athletic, as persons with good social skills, as community service givers—and are not acting out in response to a sense of failure.

A representative management group can reduce the distrust, alienation and acting-out behavior between home and school and among staff and students which plague the modern school.[15] Parents and staff can again reinforce each other, enabling staff to serve as parent surrogates. The expectations and climate of a school functioning in this way can be changed from one of suspicion and conflict to one in which most people expect and work for the successful attainment of goals which they helped establish.

The representative management approach at the middle school (5th–8th grade) and high school can enable students involved to learn planning, organization, problem solving, and evaluation skills from the mature adults they participate with in the process. This would also give the students, and others they represent, a stake in the program outcome. The skills they would learn are those necessary to be able to participate in the larger society later on as relatively good and independent thinkers and responsible adults. It is the absence of an opportunity to learn such skills and the increased information and complexity young people face that is a major reason for acting-up student behavior. In the vacuum, immature peer group attitudes, values and practices emerge, become elaborated into gang, anti-authority, or veto behavior.

The problem, as pointed out above, is that most principals are not trained to work in this way. Most teachers do not have the training or experience to work on a school management team. Some parents not only do not have the training and experience to participate on a management team but are also sometimes uncomfortable in this role and are sometimes distrustful and antagonistic. There is little possibility that educational training institutions will change sufficiently to enable new teachers and social service support staff to acquire the skills to work in this way before they take jobs in schools. Even if they did, this would not affect the many staff people already in schools. But it is possible for school systems to develop programs which will enable parents, teachers, administrators—and in the upper grades, students—to work together in a cooperative and collaborative management arrangement.

Because behavior problems generally initiate the downward spiral for student and staff performance alike, the absence of training that will enable administrators, parents, and teachers to create a relationship climate which will reduce behavior problems is a critical though absent area of expertise. Once school staff acquire skills that enable them to manage a variety of child, staff, and community relationships successfully, negative attitudes about the social and intellectual potential of different children greatly diminishes, and school problems decrease. The staff is then able to give full attention to the development of the curriculum and teaching styles that work in a given setting. Successful change begets successful change and an uphill spiral is established and can be maintained through a continued representative management effort.

It was the child development and human relations expertise that our Yale Child Study Center staff brought to the program and shared with the school staff. In return, we benefitted from their expertise in education. Before describing our program, it would be helpful to discuss the setting and spirit of New Haven. The limitations and opportunities of applying the principles of our program to other places will be more apparent after such a discussion.

3
New Haven,
New Haven

New Haven and its surrounding suburbs is an industrial area with a history that mirrors national achievements, trends, and problems. But because it is middle-sized, with slightly more than 135,000 residents, the problems of living and schooling in this modern age are not as distorted here as in larger cities. Because it is an industrial and university city, it has more resources to study and address problems than many cities. Probably for these reasons, by the time we began our work in schools in 1968 it was already a social history legend—a Model City.[1]

Knowledge gained from studies in New Haven can have national application. Its physical and human development programs were the models for the federal government's War on Poverty and Urban Renewal programs. A decade ago people from everywhere trooped through the redeveloped downtown area, observing impressive new stores built around an indoor mall, a new hotel, a glassed-in overhead walk across the busy streets and a downtown parking garage that is an architect's dream. Several blocks away, toward the Yale Medical Center, two, then three, and now four upper-middle-income apartment buildings stand where some of the city's most run-down housing once stood.

Fortunately the city fathers had the good sense not to tear down all of the old.[2] They restored some of what was historic and structurally sound. During my first three years in New Haven I lived in a restored townhouse on Court Street. Court is a narrow, three block long street between the New Haven Green in the center of town and Wooster Square Park. The block closest to the park was the restored area. Complementing the restored houses were massive cement planters, pillars with ornate gates at both ends of the street, and small below-ground level terraces behind each townhouse. Some of the buildings were unpainted brick and others were in lively pastel colors. Ours was a restrained yellow and white. The variety of interior decor was a self-expression bonanza.

Each fall the street was closed and we held a block party to which all the neighbors brought home-made dishes. Everybody talked, danced, and commented about how much the children had grown over the year as we viewed home movies. The young children would point with glee as they appeared on the screen, exclaiming, "That's me!" The block party menu included Italian food, soul food, Irish and Jewish food . . . maybe some others . . . reflecting the different groups on the street.

Factory workers, doctors, housewives, lawyers, store clerks, interior decorators, bankers, teachers, students, and some "professions unknown" lived on the street. Each spring there was a clean-up party—more a "coming out from the northeast winter" party—less elaborate than the block party . . . almost unplanned . . . "Let's prune the hedges." When the weather was warm, people sat on the cement stairs and talked politics, health, death, and about each other—most of the time in a positive fashion, sometimes not so positive. I often had the feeling that this was the way America should be, maybe, just barely maybe . . . still can be.

Much of what we and others in New Haven enjoyed was the culmination of the dream of a tough, shrewd, friendly little man (small in stature only) by the name of Richard Lee. Dick Lee was the mayor of New Haven from 1953 to 1969. He grew up in the town and ran for mayor partly because he did not like the decay in "his town." He spoke of the problem during his 1951 campaign for the Mayor's office:

> I went into the homes on Oak Street and they set up neighborhood meetings for me. I went into block meetings . . . three and four in one night . . . and I came out from one of those homes on Oak Street, and I sat on the curb and I was just as sick as a puppy. Why? The smell of this building; it had no electricity, it had no gas, it had kerosene lamps, light had never seen the corridors in generations. The smells . . . It was just awful and I got sick.[3]

He lost that election by two votes. He won in 1953. Before being elected mayor he served on the Board of Aldermen and was the director of the Yale News Bureau. Town born, Yale affiliated, a long-time worker in the rough and tough New Haven political vineyard, without a college education, friend of the educational elite and the factory worker alike, and action oriented by personality, Lee turned New Haven around.

He gathered some of the best talents in the "city-saving business" as assistants and advisors. Before some other cities were fully aware of new federal funding programs for urban areas, New Haven was off and running. My memory of the city after my first visit in 1963 was that of a giant hole in the downtown section where the shopping mall now stands; air hammers, earth movers, noise, dust—going, building, booming, growing. Ahead of its time in the 1960's, it was only repeating its history as a city that plans and rejuvenates itself without losing its self-awareness as a city with deep roots in America's rich past. Rollin Osterweis, a student of New Haven's history, has pointed out that on three previous occasions the city fathers moved to restore New Haven, preserving some of the old as they introduced the new.[4]

One of the products of the 1960's renewal is the Park Plaza Hotel in downtown New Haven. You can sip a cocktail in its Top-of-the-Park Restaurant and look down on the New Haven Green, and if you are history-minded, slip back to the very origin of the country. It was from this Green on April 22, 1777, that Benedict Arnold, the young cavalry officer who was later condemned for treason, demanded the keys to the powder house in order to fight the British in Lexington. It was on this Green that Africans bound for slavery, who overcame their captors on the Schooner *Amistad*, only to be tricked and recaptured before they could return to Africa, were allowed to exercise while awaiting trial. Their leader was the African prince, Cinque. In one of America's most remarkable trials, these slaves were defended by ex-President John Q. Adams, acquitted, and the majority returned to Africa.[5]

Massive immigration is an important part of New Haven's history. Until the middle of the 18th century, New Haven had a fairly homogeneous population. The original settlers were English Puritans whose social and political dominance survived into the early years of the 19th century. Occasionally some French names appear in the town records during the period of the Napoleonic Wars, and there were some Irish laborers employed in the construction of the Farmington Canal in the 1830's. After 1830, with the onset of industrial revolution and the prospects of improved socioeconomic status in the new world, the rate of immigration began to increase.

In the late 1830's, German immigration to New Haven reached a peak. The Bavarian Jews were earliest of these German settlers. They established Congregation Mishkan Israel in 1840 and became prominent in the city's industrial growth, bringing piano, cigar, and corset manufacturing factories into the city. This group incurred animosity during their period of adjustment—not only due to religious prejudice but also because they remained German-speaking for many years. A second wave of German immigration occurred just after the Civil War (1865–1885), this time largely Lutheran and Catholic. The Irish immigrated to New Haven in great numbers during the middle of the 19th century.

Mass immigration of Italians began in the 1880's, although they came earlier in small groups. Farmers and laborers for the most part, they left the Old World to escape an endless cycle of poverty. Many were first employed as railroad workers when the New Haven to New York tracks were laid; others were brought to New Haven to work in factories as unskilled and semi-skilled laborers. Large contingents of Swedes, English, and Scots also arrived in New Haven toward the end of the 19th century. The Swedish Baptist Church was organized there in 1882; its Lutheran counterpart was founded in 1883. By 1900, 28 percent of New Haven's population was foreign born, as late as 1950 the foreign born accounted for nearly 16 percent.[6]

Most of the immigrants to New Haven were unskilled and without formal education. Many came as servants, working for those who paid their passage to America. Most faced rejection and hardship. As late as 1952 a first generation Italian-American teacher was turned down in a suburban school system until it was discovered that she had an "Irish connection" (her husband).[7] But most of the immigrants were able to earn a living wage in a late 19th century and early 20th century economy that could readily absorb unskilled laborers. Many in the next generation received a moderate level of education and training, achieved power in the unions, in the political arena, and in business, acquired many of the better unskilled or semi-skilled jobs and began to move toward professional and technical status jobs. With increasing power, control, and stability, many more in the third generation achieved professional, business, and powerful political positions. Through the 1980s, Italians had the greatest political stength in New Haven. Today, blacks and Latinos have significant political power, but little economic power.

Jobs, religion, a transplanted culture, unions, political, government, and business participation enabled the various immigrant groups to remain relatively stable in the face of discrimination and abuse. However, community workers in largely white, blue-collar neighborhoods are quick to point out that not all immigrants made it; that there have been many casualties of immigration, dislocation, and change of such magnitude.

Back to the Top-of-the-Park Restaurant. Looking away from the Green with a historical eye, one can look out across the entire Yale campus. Its eastern boundary—Yale's Old Campus—borders the New Haven Green. Many American leaders, while students at Yale, walked, played, read, and in general enjoyed themselves on the Green and in the courtyards within the Old Campus quadrangle. Several blocks beyond the Old Campus, at Yale's western boundary, Dixwell Avenue begins. Yale's Payne-Whitney Gym complex is on this corner. A Yale residential college is across the street. During the Revolutionary War a major skirmish in the battle of New Haven was fought on the site where Dixwell begins. Today Dixwell Avenue is the heart and soul of black New Haven. Dixwell runs to the northern townline. The city is bordered on the south by Long Island Sound.

Most blacks arrived in New Haven during the migration of southern blacks after 1940. Yet there were blacks in New Haven as early as 1646. There were 2,887 blacks in New Haven in 1900, 5,302 in 1930, 22,113 in 1960, and more than 47,000 or 36 per-

cent of the total population today.[8] The black "old New Haven-
ers" (pre-1940's) are proud; some are prosperous. Prior to the
mid-1940's the black "upper class" was a small number of professionals, church leaders, and Yale-connected workers—custodians, cooks, fraternity service personnel. Others held largely
marginal jobs in factories, small business, or did domestic work
in private homes. Black children attended racially integrated
schools as early as 1874. By and large, the old black community
was a stable, relatively secure but very, very small minority.[9]

Although blacks came late, the Spanish-speaking population came even later. Puerto Ricans began to arrive in the Elm
City (the name given to the city because of the large number of
elm trees that once lined the streets) in large numbers in the
decade of the 1960's. The census of 1950 lists only 162 persons
as having been born in "other America," but by the census data
of 1970 this number had grown to 3,020 persons of "Puerto
Rican birth or parentage." Today the number is 13,866.

The surge of black and Spanish-speaking newcomers was not
without some negative feelings on the part of blacks and whites
who arrived earlier. The white establishment had blocked efforts
to found a black college in New Haven as far back as 1831.[10] Black
professional and technical workers who came in the 1950's
reported a less than enthusiastic reception from blacks and
whites. But actually the educated and skilled black community
attracted to the several universities, business, and industry of the
area have had a relatively easy time making it in New Haven.
Things have not gone as well for other blacks . . . though life for
the poor in New Haven is not New York City or Chicago poverty.

Our program began in the Baldwin and King schools. Baldwin
lies midway up and two blocks west of lower Dixwell. King is on
Dixwell, three blocks beyond the commercial area.

If you had walked up Dixwell the year our program began,
1968, you might well have felt a peculiar mixture of joy and hope,
despair and hopelessness so often found in struggling black communities. Decay and promise were in competition everywhere.
Bars and churches, barber shops, beauty shops and funeral par-
lors, soul food restaurants and small clothing stores dotted the
three-block lower Dixwell commercial area, some owned by
blacks. A hardware store owned by whites did business as usual
behind boarded-up windows, a casualty of a disturbance the pre-

vious summer. A grocery store owned by whites was going out of business.

You would have heard moving gospel music from a church on one corner on Sunday and soul music from a record shop on the street on Monday. On Sunday, you might have seen a black bride and groom and their wedding party, resplendent and beautiful, leaving church after a traditional wedding ceremony, probably still including a pledge of obedience from the bride to the groom. On Monday you might have seen the numbers man (illegal gambler) and even the drug pusher doing business on the same block. The aroma of soul food from a little restaurant down the street from the hardware store would not be missed.·

Dr. Taylor, a black optometrist and an old New Havener, had his office on the second floor above what later became the home of the Black Panther party. Dr. Smith, a long-time black resident of New Haven, had his office in a new apartment building he had built to try to upgrade the area. Dr. Ince, a black dentist, shared this office space. From the dental chair one could see numerous children going in and out of the Elm Haven high-rise apartment project across the street. Over 17,000 people were crowded into the approximately 50 block Dixwell area.[11]

The Dixwell Community House stood aging with the promise that it would be rebuilt as an attractive modern structure. Empty lots where houses were leveled to make way for redevelopment stood gathering weeds, whiskey bottles, and tin cans. In the three blocks of lower Dixwell there were four major gathering areas or "stomping grounds" where men gathered, drank liquor, laughed, "wolfed" (bragged of their exploits, deeds, told tall tales, discussed the baseball pennant race and the white man). Some worked and some did not. In sharp contrast, young men from the Nation of Islam, well-dressed, courteous, serious, and with a sense of purpose, sold their newspapers on the streets. Youngsters—most looking happy, attractive and promising, some worrisome—passed on their way to three major elementary schools in the area, Winchester, Baldwin, and King.

In 1978 Dixwell was the same, yet different because many of the promised buildings had been completed. But most of the social problems still existed Construction of the Martin Luther King, Jr. School, an attractive modern building, was completed just as our program was getting off the ground. The Dixwell Community House, which houses various community programs, is part of an architectural award-winning complex. The Dixwell Avenue Congregational Church is a stunningly attractive structure in the same complex. Across the street is a new commercial complex housing a bank, Telephone Company office, a drug store, and a supermarket .

Dr. Taylor moved to a refurbished building down the street and the Black Panthers in his old building and the pool hall next to his new building have come and gone. So too have four or five businesses in the shopping center and elsewhere on Dixwell. The men are still on the corner. Children still stream in and out of the projects. Bars on the windows of stores and homes tell you that the old problems have not gone away. Angry graffiti are scrawled on walls here and there. I still get a feeling of joy and hope, despair and hopelessness as I walk up Dixwell.

The problems of the Dixwell area, and similar areas in New Haven and across the country, are numerous. But most importantly, they are economic. By the time poor blacks began arriving in large numbers in New Haven in the 1950's and 1960's, other ethnic groups held many of the living wage jobs that did not require a high level of education and training. Such jobs were not increasing as fast as the number of people entering the job market who needed them even in the early 1950's. Racial discrimination closed many blacks out of the living wage jobs that were available. Many were able to find only marginal income jobs, often not earning enough to adequately support a family.

Many blacks in New Haven came from rural North Carolina, South Carolina, and Arkansas, trying to find a quality of life that was not possible as low-paid agricultural workers or oppressed second-class citizens in southern communities. For many reasons—among them racism and resultant undereducation and training, exclusion from living wage job opportunities—some who had stable families, were hard working, religious, and responsible in the south, lost this stability on the hard, cold streets of New Haven and northern cities everywhere. Obviously most black families survived and thrived or there would have been complete chaos. But too many did not. Thus, the cause of the mixed feeling of hope and despair as one walks up Dixwell Avenue and other black communities in New Haven and across the country.

Public policies in New Haven, like public policies everywhere, complicated things. For example, a school community relations worker who once lived in the Elm Haven housing project pointed out a troublesome policy. Her family and other successful families were forced to leave public housing as soon as they earned barely a minimum wage. As a result, families with the most problems were isolated in the housing projects. As could have been predicted, this overwhelmed the project, entire neighborhoods, and schools. One elderly black woman living near a low-income housing project said of some of the children, "They crush my flower garden, cut a path across my lawn, break my windows . . . but I better not say nothing to them . . . they momma will come down and cuss me out. It ain't like it used to be."

Overt racial confrontation was not widespread in New Haven and even now it is less intense than the disruptive conflict and violence in many cities. There have been black and white student clashes occasionally. At the height of racial conflict in the late '60's and '70's, "white power" and "black power" slogans were scrawled on streets and walls in several communities. Recently a couple of black families have been harrassed to the point of moving out of a lower middle-income white area. But racial disharmony has been more subtle. A black civil rights leader who grew up in New Haven put it this way, "We [blacks and whites] got along O.K. But we went our way and they went theirs. We knew what was for us and they knew what was for them. That's why I probably never considered going to college . . . and why I can't get a better job today."

Over time, however, discrimination in housing and employment, undereducation, poor work and social skills, underemployment and unemployment began to complicate relationships between classes and races. Formerly white neighborhoods gradually became black or, in fewer numbers, Spanish-speaking, as whites moved to the surrounding suburbs. A number of blacks have also moved to the suburbs. Many middle-income whites and blacks who remain in the city send their children to private schools. As a result, while blacks and Hispanics are an overall population minority, black and Hispanic students are a majority of the school population, 75.1 percent in 1978. In 1978 70.6 percent of all elementary school students were black and Hispanic, 80.1 percent middle-school, and 78.5 percent high school.[12]

Just as New Haven was one of the first cities to face the need for physical renewal, it was one of the first to try and create a psychological sense of community and human well-being; to acknowledge that public officials had a responsibility to guide the process. Its Community Progress, Incorporated, a program begun in 1962 to help families, communities, and individuals in declining neighborhoods, was the model for the national War on Poverty program.[13] Program developers reasoned that the poor could and should be helped to help themselves, that developing a program to make this possible was the proper function of government. The schools in which we worked initially, Baldwin and King, were in CPI neighborhoods.

CPI programs included housing, child care, education, job training, leisure time, service to elderly persons, social and psychological professional consultation to various agencies, and other intervention efforts. A neighborhood service director in each of seven CPI neighborhoods was supported by two or more community relations workers to bring the community and the services together. Many of the community relations workers were nonprofessional residents of the community. Neighborhood service directors were liaison to service agencies. Many of the services were located or associated with newly developed community schools.

The community school concept had been a product of urban development. Federal, state, local government, and foundation funds were used to build these schools—mostly middle schools, grades five through eight, and elementary schools in low-income neighborhoods. The schools were to benefit individuals and neighborhoods in four ways; through improved education, recreational opportunities, social services, and an opportunity for community members to meet and work toward improving the community's political and social effectiveness. The program operated during and after the school day.

The massive community schools building program was barely off the ground in 1963 when the New Haven Human Relations Council pointed up the problem of racial imbalance in the schools. The viewpoint that segregated education—deliberate or de facto—was inherently inferior held wide acceptance at the time. The New Haven School Board members were responsible and intelligent. In short order—without court order—they developed a bussing plan to create racial balance in the schools. Bussing and community schools (the latter designed to strengthen neighborhoods) appeared to be inconsistent strategies. But supporters of bussing pointed out that the four major goals of community schools could still be achieved even if children were bussed. Bussing advocates pointed out that whites in suburbs had been bussed to New Haven high schools before suburban towns built their own with no harm to the children or to a sense of neighborhood.

All of the problems the nation faced with bussing in 1980 were evident in New Haven in 1963.[14] Much of the white liberal community was bitter in its opposition to bussing. Working-class whites threatened to use physical force to prevent bussing. Low-income blacks were indifferent. Black middle-income groups were disillusioned and became alienated from so-called liberal whites. Most people were more willing to bus blacks to predominantly white schools than to bus whites to predominantly black schools. Occasional verbal and physical racial conflicts erupted in schools along with some very positive black and white student experiences. Many whites and some middle-income blacks moved quickly to suburban, church, and private schools.

Another bussing effort called Project Concern was initiated at the start of the 1968 year.[15] The suburban towns volunteered to participate in this program in which over two hundred black children were bussed to surrounding suburban schools. Over 90 percent of the involved New Haven parents endorsed the program. Many suburban teachers felt that the New Haven children had developed higher aspirations and confidence levels than they might otherwise have done. A large majority of teachers felt that the presence of the New Haven children did not reduce achievement of suburban children. Yet all suburban schools have dropped out of the program.

Just as in other areas where bussing programs have been installed, the need for low-income housing in the suburbs—the only real way to assure racially integrated schools—was not raised in 1968, nor is it raised now. One effort to help middle-income blacks buy homes in the suburbs had limited success.

The New Haven School System itself developed a number of compensatory education programs. Head Start and Follow Through programs, designed to overcome learning lags, received considerable support. Title I programs, federal government supported programs for children from families below the poverty level, added extra staff and materials for elementary school age youngsters. Programs to provide exposure to the arts for low-income children were developed. Many student and adult volunteers tutored and supported programs in the schools. During my training in psychiatry at Yale, I worked in a low-income elementary school through participation in a CPI-related project, the New Haven Psychiatric Council.

The Council was headed by Dr. Albert J. Solnit, director of the Yale Child Study Center, and included a number of psychiatrists from the community who were concerned about social problems. The Psychiatric Council provided consultation to early childhood day-care programs, schools, work training programs, and other activities. Most Council members agreed that some of the most successful consultative efforts were in the programs for children. This observation was encouraging and was a factor that led to greater Child Study Center involvement in New Haven schools. Because of the work of the Psychiatric Council, the New Haven schools, and other consultation efforts of the Child Study Center, Ford Foundation officials suggested that involvement with schools on a more complete basis might be even more helpful. Plans for such a program began to take place in 1967.

But despite its position as a leader in concern for physical and human development, the problems of the nation caught up with New Haven. August 19, 1967, according to most accounts, a white merchant shot a Puerto Rican man during a dispute, and a violent disturbance was set off in several of the black districts and in the downtown area. Fortunately the model city had a model riot—none killed, only three persons injured, and according to police reports (disputed by some) not a shot was fired by police. Part of Mayor Lee's statement at the end of the emergency summed up the problem not only for New Haven but for the nation.

> We seek answers to age-old problems, but, tragically, they have not all been found, not nearly. In New Haven we have been at those problems for more than a decade. But in a decade we have been trying to solve things which have been wrong with urban America for a century or two.[16]

Across the nation and in New Haven, blacks began to mobilize as never before to gain political and economic strength in order to make the American system work for the black community. In the summer of 1967, black leaders—militant and moderate—gathered in Newark, New Jersey, for a black power conference only days after a devastating riot rocked that city and stunned the nation. In New Haven, a Black Coalition representing most of the black social, civic, and social action organizations was developed to resist division and speak to and influence the New Haven Establishment. Everywhere black leaders spoke of "control of our destiny," "local control," and "black pride and power." In part due to the times, smoldering discontent with CPI burst into full flame. A major criticism of the program was that it did not attack exclusions and denial of opportunity based on race alone. It was also criticized for not making the most of natural support mechanisms in the black community such as churches and lodges. Educated, higher paid white professionals and lower paid black nonprofessionals, the latter often having greater entre and rapport with the people in the community, was a situation often at the root of interpersonal and policy conflicts. While CPI is almost a nonexistent organization today, neighborhood corporations developed during its tenure are influencing political outcomes. Many blacks given a chance to hold management and leadership roles in CPI programs have parlayed these opportunities into management positions in business and appointed and elected positions in local and state government.

In the midst of national and local racial ferment, on April 20, 1968, Dr. Martin Luther King, Jr., the most visible, effective, and beloved symbol and leader of the black struggle for justice and opportunity, was assassinated. The dammed-up anger of blacks, the present and "many thousand gone," burst forth and again racial riots swept the nation. Feelings and concern among all ran very high.

It was against this backdrop—historic New Haven, a New Haven shaped by Yale and industry, by immigration, by migration at a time of great change created by the rise of science and technology, black and white action and reaction—that we initiated the Baldwin-King Program in September of 1968.

We were fully aware that an education program could not correct what was wrong with Dixwell Avenue or low-income communities throughout the nation. We also understood that problems in schools in low-income and affluent communities alike were, in part, due to forces beyond the local schoolhouse. But we felt that the best way to understand and to begin to cope with problems in and outside of schools, low-income and affluent alike, was to begin to work in and change at least some of the schools. We began.

PART II

4

The School Program

The Baldwin-King program was initiated in 1968 as a planned five year effort to improve the quality of living and learning in the Baldwin and Martin Luther King, Jr. public elementary schools in New Haven, Connecticut. In 1973, the Baldwin facet of the program was discontinued.*In 1975 we began to work in a school with a similar socioeconomic, racial profile, largely serving isolated housing projects, Katherine Brennan.

A plan to phase out the program in King School during the sixth year was changed because of parent and staff interest in continuing. In 1975, a program entitled "The Social Skills Curriculum for Inner City Children" was developed at the King School and is in place at this writing. These programs have led to other collaborative efforts between the Yale Child Study Center and the New Haven School System.

Our decade of experience, 1968-1978, spanned the full swing of the pendulum in modern educational thinking and practice. We began in the flush of excitement about open education and other

*The reason Baldwin was discontinued is explained in Chapter 5.

innovative approaches. We now operate in a back-to-basics climate. The former approach, like the latter, resulted from an incessant demand for a better education for all children. Neither extreme has lived up to the promise of its enthusiasts and promoters.

We came to center stage promising neither to rewrite history nor to relive it. Our lines had been written with a mix of tradition and innovation that we hoped would draw the enthusiasm of both actors and audience. We were not promising to solve all the schools' problems, but we hoped to help parents, teachers, and administrators reduce their problems and achieve greater success.

Having explained our stance and objective, the remainder of this chapter is a brief synopsis of the plot, and a bit of thematic analysis, with acknowledgments to the producers and the production staff.[1]

Financial Support

A. Baldwin-King Program
    Ford Foundation
    $100,000 a year for five years to the Yale Child Study Center and $70,000 for one year to phase out the program
    $100,000 a year for five years to the New Haven School System
    Title I (Federal Government funds available to schools with a high percentage of low-income children)
    $166,000 per year for five years to the New Haven School System
    New Prospect Foundation
    $50,000

B. Interim Period
    Yale Child Study Center
    $40,000 for two years
    Title I Funds

C. Social Skills Curriculum for Inner-City Children Program
    Center for Minority Group Studies, National Institute for Mental Health
    An average of $60,000 a year for two years, 1975–77
    An average of $155,000 a year for three years, 1977–80

Approximately 55 percent of all funds were allocated for professional salaries. Another 35-40 percent of the funds paid for parent and teacher stipends. The remainder supported educational consultants, outside evaluators, supplies, and travel.

Often program evaluators ask for a cost per student analysis, but I believe that would not be helpful in this. case. From the very beginning, we viewed the project as a research and development effort that would benefit more than the children and families served in Baldwin and King schools. Members of the Yale Child Study Center and New Haven School System staffs, including teachers and parents, have been consultants, program developers, and workshop participants in numerous school improvement efforts elsewhere in New Haven, in Connecticut, and at the national level.

Most of the money for the YCSC supported our staff—administration, psychiatry, psychology, social work, curriculum, and special education. Money for the NHSS supported staff specialists and training, as well as extended day and other nontraditional activities and arrangements.

Program Development

The program was suggested in 1967 by Mr. Douglas Furguson, a Ford Foundation Project Officer. The formal proposal was developed by Dr. Albert Solnit, Director of the Yale Child Study Center and Mr. Samuel Nash, Director of Special Projects, New Haven School System. After the Ford Foundation had accepted the proposal, during the 1967-68 academic year Yale and New Haven school officials elaborated the guiding philosophy, organization, and methods. I was completing my child psychiatry training in Washington, D.C. during that year. In 1968 I returned to direct the Child Study Center contribution to the program.

The Yale-New Haven program was one of several across the country supported by the Ford Foundation as a part of a national effort to utilize the resources of universities in support of public school programs.

The Problem

In 1968 the problems of New Haven schools typified those of most systems serving inner-city and minority populations. The most critical of these was exemplified by the results of a 1968 survey by the New Haven School System reading staff which showed that 26 percent of the fourth graders in eleven inner-city schools were two or three years below grade in reading and that from 50 to 80 percent of sixth grade students were reading below grade level. Reports from teachers, principals, and social workers indicated that a high percentage of inner-city children were not motivated, were disruptive or apathetic in class, were unable to profit from time in school, and appeared to be disinterested in school materials.

Parents and community workers complained that schools did not create the kind of self-esteem needed for adequate academic achievement and that parents felt cut off from the school. Teachers and administrators felt that social and behavioral scientists, educational and housekeeping personnel offered inadequate support. The school staff felt abandoned, left to do the best they could and then criticized for not overcoming their personal limitations, those of the schools, the problems of families, and the society as a whole.

Program Hypothesis

We developed a working hypothesis around which the program design was built: The application of social and behavioral science principles to every aspect of a school program will improve the climate of relationships among all involved and will facilitate significant academic and social growth of students.

Program Population and Facilities

The Baldwin and King elementary schools were selected as program sites. The pupils in these schools were among the lowest in academic achievement of pupils in the city's 33 elementary schools. About 70 percent of the students in the Baldwin and King school districts received AFDC (Aid for Families of Dependent Children). Both schools reported serious attendance and behavior problems. Morale among staff and parents was low In short, the Baldwin and King Schools were representative of inner-city schools everywhere. These two schools were to serve as a research and development subsystem of the New Haven School System.

Ninety-five percent of the Baldwin (320 students K-6) and King (270 students K-4) families were low or low middle income, and 98 percent or more of the pupils were black; the balance were Puerto Rican and white. Class size in both schools ranged from thirteen to twenty-nine.

In both school areas there had been gradual population changes from largely middle-class whites in the 1950's to black middle-income then black lower-middle and lower-income people. Baldwin had been characterized by severe social disruption among students, high turnover, and apathy among staff. King, as a new school, drew its student population from several older schools and had to manage the usual urban problems in addition to providing a transition for students and the community.

The Baldwin building was an old one which held classes in the basement and on the first and second floors. The physical plant was an impediment to communication among staff. The King School program had operated for the two previous years in the Congregation Mishkan Israel Synagogue, the same Congregation founded in New Haven in 1840, now in a neighboring suburban town. The modern design of the new King School—classrooms built around an open all-purpose area—lent itself to better communication.

Staff

I was the co-director of the Baldwin-King program and the head of the Child Study Center Team in the schools. Dr. Albert Solnit, Director of the Yale Child Study Center at the time, conceived the project and obtained support for it from the Ford Foundation, asked me to direct it, and provided much guidance and support during the first seven years. Mr. Samuel Nash, Director of Special Projects and Planning for the New Haven School System at the time, was the co-director of the program.

There were nine classroom teachers and one resource teacher at King. There were thirteen classroom teachers and two special education teachers at Baldwin—one of the latter was a primary special education teacher and the other was an intermediate special education teacher. The special education classes served several school districts. The original teaching staff was largely white and inexperienced. The replacement staff during the first and second year was largely black but some were white. Most of the replacement staff was more experienced. The teaching staff received their preparation from three different kinds of schools of education; state universities well known private schools, and predominantly black schools.

Our Child Study Center staff included a chief social worker, a second social worker, a curriculum specialist, a psychologist-evaluator, a special education teacher and logkeeper, a coordinator and secretary, and, in the second year, a program coordinator.

Structure

STEERING COMMITTEE

The Steering Committee membership was representative of the several groups involved in the program—administrators teachers, parents, aides, professional support staff, Yale Child Study Center Mental Health Team—and operated much as a corporate board of directors. Initially there were fourteen members, six of them parents. The committee was to give overall guidance to the project—planning, implementation, and evaluation as well as suggesting structural, content, and process changes to facilitate problem-solving. Early in the program these functions were taken over by an Administrative Team in each school.

ADMINISTRATIVE TEAM

After the first five years the Administrative Teams replaced the Steering Committee as the policy bodies for each school. The teachers, principals, and support personnel who comprised the team were responsible for the day-to-day management of the schools. Later, the School Advisory Committee replaced the Administrative Team. The size and style of the governance bodies has varied over the years but remains essentially the same as the original Steering Committee in composition and responsibility.

SCHOOL COMMITTEES

Three school committees were created by the Steering Committee. These were the Curriculum, Personnel, and Evaluation Committees. The principal and the Child Study Center Mental Health Team social worker served on all three committees. Parents and teachers elected representatives from among their respective groups to serve on each committee. The Yale Curriculum specialist served on the Curriculum Committee. The Yale evaluator served on the Evaluation Committee. The purpose of these committees was to interview and select staff and develop or oversee the development of curriculum and evaluation programs.

YALE CHILD STUDY CENTER MENTAL HEALTH TEAM

The Yale Child Study Center Team had six members (Comer, Glasgow, Snow, Carol, Janis, and Slaughter), a child psychiatrist, two social workers, an educator with early childhood training, an educator who had been involved in training teachers for many years, and a psychologist-program evaluator. This composition varied over the years but remains essentially the same. After the first year and a half, the psychiatrist, Comer, was not involved in the day-to-day work of the team. The chief social worker, Glasgow, directed the activities of the team in the schools. Comer directed the overall project, served as a consultant to all team members, met regularly with principals during the first five years of the program, provided workshops for parents and staff, and served as a conceptualizer and trouble shooter.

The key objective of the team was to help school staff understand and apply the principles of the social and behavioral sciences to the problems and opportunities of the two schools.

PUPIL PERSONNEL TEAM

Initially the psychiatrist-director and the social workers cooperated with the school principal, nurse, community relations worker, special teachers, and aides as a team, providing support services to teachers and services directly or indirectly to students. After the first three years, the work of the psychiatrist-director was taken over by psychiatrists working on a part-time basis. Other helping professionals inside and outside of the school participated in pupil personnel meetings as necessary. Thus speech and hearing teachers, city welfare caseworkers, or others participated when the problem involved a child or family on their caseload. Initially, teachers participated in pupil personnel meetings only when they presented the case of a child in their classroom for whom they were seeking help. Eventually, the Pupil Personnel Team meeting became a seminar for all teachers in the King School.

The functions of the Pupil Personnel Team changed as conditions in the school changed. As behavior problems decreased the team added educational services to its responsibilities.

PARENT PROGRAM

Small stipends supported ten to twelve parents who were teacher aides in each school. These parent-aides assist with the academic program in the classrooms. They also form the nucleus of the parent organization that plans social and educational programs with the school staff. These and other parents serve on the governance bodies and various subcommittees. In so doing they bring the attitudes, values, ways, and needs of the community to these committees and activities.

FOCUS

The Focus Program is designed to help children who are a year or more behind their grade level in reading and math.

Children are seen in groups of two to six at least three times a week to supplement the work being done in the classroom. This program is funded by Title I.

WORKSHOPS

Workshops were held for two weeks during each summer of the first five years of the program. The workshop objectives were to bring parents and teachers together so that they could know one another as personalities rather than as role-figures—teacher and parent—to permit a sharing of perspective and to facilitate the planning of academic and social programs of the schools by parents and teachers during the regular school year. Because of a reasonable level of social comfort and shared perspectives teachers and parents were eventually able to plan and work together without disruptive distrust and conflict. New ideas and ways could be considered on their merit, less charged by intergroup (parent-teacher) feelings and antagonisms.

EXTENDED DAY PROGRAM

Teachers received small stipends to participate in after school programs. Initially this was required, but after the second year of the program it was put on a voluntary basis. The change was an effort to decrease resistance. Teachers met three days a week for an hour and a half. Seminars, workshops, grade-level meetings, and other arrangements were developed to enable teachers to learn more about child development and behavior, teaching and curriculum development, the use of the arts in promoting academic skills, and so on. These programs included techniques such as teacher role playing, didactic lectures, demonstrations by experts, teacher participation with specialists in the development of academic and arts curricula, etc.

Staff meetings and parent participation programs were also held during the extended day. The parent participation program permitted parents and teachers to work together on a variety of projects. Open houses, book fairs, gospel choir programs and the like were planned by parents, with staff, to support the curriculum and social programs of the school.

Organization and Operation Rationale

The Baldwin-King program developers felt that a subunit, two small schools, rather than many schools, would permit the kind of interaction that would reduce communication and interpersonal problems. A second rationale was that starting with a program planned in detail and imposed on a school creates inflexibility and resistance. Such a program commits financial, personnel, and psychological resources to a given approach before the nature of the problem is adequately understood. Our approach permits shared identification of problems and requires a cooperative effort to develop a solution. In the process of working out goals and methods of achieving them, program participants internalize and come to "own" them and to develop a stake in their outcome.

Without internalized program goals and methods, program direction is not clear and communication breaks down. People talk past each other, or when things are bad enough, do not talk to each other at all. Without a problem-solving mechanism available to all involved, problems get out of hand. Anxiety, mutual distrust, and disrespect grow like weeds. Chaotic conditions develop, and good innovative programs or ideas bite the dust. Large size and little opportunity for constructive interaction between program participants is a major barrier to establishing trust and mutual respect.

The likelihood of anxiety during a program change is often heightened by the fact that many participants do not have an opportunity to make an input into the planning, implementation, and evaluation process. As a result, there is inadequate communication of goals and methods of achieving them, but more importantly, there is little "gut level" acceptance of these goals and methods on the part of many program participants. There is little sense of ownership of the program and less than the necessary commitment to make it work.

The above problems often lead to the frustrating but common cycle of new program ideas, rapid implementation, failure, and then more new ideas. This is a cycle which has led many to accuse schools of "innovating for innovation's sake" and has led to widespread disillusionment about all school innovations. Our organization and operation were designed to prevent such a cycle.

Major Program Goals

1. To modify the climate—social and psychological—of the school in a way that facilitates learning.
2. To improve the achievements of basic skills, particularly reading and mathematics, at a statistically significant level.
3. To raise motivation for learning, mastery, and achievement in a way which will increase academic and occupational aspiration levels of each child.
4. To develop patterns of shared responsibility and decisionmaking among parents and staff.
5. To develop an organizational relationship between child development and clinical services (Yale Child Study Center, in particular, and Yale University, in general) and the educational program at the Baldwin and King schools as well as the whole New Haven Public School System.

Major Theoretical Assumptions

Our intervention program was not based on a single theory of human, institutional, or system behavior. In fact, one of the problems in intervention research in schools is that there is no theory broad enough and specific enough to be very helpful. Our approach was to bring our knowledge of the various theories of human and institutional behavior to the school setting, learn about the school as we applied the principles of the social and behavioral sciences that appeared most helpful, and in the process, elaborate a theory of intervention specific to our program, with principles applicable to school intervention across the society.

When applied separately, human behavior or social system functioning theories focus on individuals (in this case, teachers, administrators, custodians, parents, students) or on structural factors (the curriculum, facilities, and/or socioeconomic indicators). Thus a tendency develops to look for the problem and cite the cause as individuals or specific activities. An ecological assessment model is more helpful. In human ecology the focus is not only on individuals or elements in a system but on the way people and their environment interact.

In the process of trying to understand problems and to be helpful in schools—in the framework of an ecological perspective—numerous theoretical principles are utilized: learning, re-education and rational principles as well as principles of psychoanalytic, existential, behavior-modification, psychodrama, systems, organization and management analysis, etc.

GOVERNANCE

Governance bodies—in our case, a Steering Committee and Administrative Team—representative of all the program participants, when properly functioning, can reduce the distrust, conflict, and alienation between community-home and school staff; among the various in-school groups such as teachers, support staff, and custodial staff; and between teachers and children. You do not decrease distrust and alienation by simply moving the source of total power from one group (black, white, parents, school staff) to another. This simply changes the location of power monopoly problems. It can best be done by enabling all persons and groups involved in a program to participate in decision-making; *with the important stipulation that no person or group can be allowed to paralyze the person responsible for making the final decision;* the person responsible for program outcome—usually the school principal.

It is within the governance bodies that the observations and perspective of all the groups involved in the school enterprise can be shared—where educational, social, and behavioral science expertise can be applied to program planning, implementation, problem solving, and evaluation. The governance bodies permit mutual agreement or consensus on school goals and methods. When the principal serves as an effective leader of this group, he or she receives a mandate for the responsible exercise of power. The power of the principal is then restored.

STAFF AND STUDENTS

Most students will try and are able to learn in a school where the staff is optimally secure, energized, motivated, and able to meet their psychological, social, and intellectual needs. Good people, techniques, innovations, and materials will be unsuccessful in a confusing, chaotic school climate where the staff is unhappy, isolated, and overwhelmed. Defensive responses to such a situation intensify the problem, and the quality of education goes downhill.

Many young teachers struggle with their own mixed feelings about the exercise of authority. They do not fully appreciate that judicious use of authority is a major source of order and a sense of well-being for children. Children learn to control the gamut of dysfunctional impulses and actions; they learn how to function in a personally and socially acceptable way by responding to and modeling their own behavior on that of just and important authority figures. The failure to understand this and to respond accordingly is the root of many control problems in schools. Inappropriate and unfair exercise of authority can promote rage and rebellion or withdrawal and apathy.

With an increase in a principal's ability to understand the dynamics of student, staff, and parent behavior, he or she will be able to respond to them more efficiently and effectively. This will reduce the number of crisis situations and will give the principal time and energy to serve as an educational leader more than as a disciplinarian, keeper of records, or buildings and grounds manager.

Teaching skills and curricula can be improved in several ways. The first is to provide a specialist of proven expertise to help teachers detect factors that interfere with or facilitate the child's capacity to develop and learn in school. A second is to acquire leadership of a specialist and thereby increase the range of acceptable teaching options so that experienced teachers can experiment with different ways of helping children to

learn—team teaching, open classrooms, individualized instruction, diagnostic, prescriptive teaching, pilot programs, independent study, use of the arts, and physical education in regular classroom activities to complement academic learning but
also to provide success experiences for children who have academic difficulties. Finally, teaching skills and curricula can be
improved by introducing and making available a wide range of
teaching materials—special interest books for classrooms and
the library, learning centers, individualized reading programs,
and manipulative materials.

PARENTS
Parents are more likely to support a school program in
which they are partners in decision-making and welcome at
times other than when their children are in trouble. Parent
interest and support for the school and its staff makes it easier
for youngsters to relate to and identify themselves with the
goals, values, and personnel of the school, a powerful motivation to tune in and turn on to education. At the same time,
parental involvement insures that their cultural values and
interests are respected.

Parent-staff committees that are encouraged to select staff
who believe strongly in the learning potential of inner-city
children and who have a strong commitment to finding ways
to improve inner-city education help to create staff attitudes
that make improved learning possible. In addition, parental
participation places an element in the teacher, administrator,
mental health, paraprofessional, community politics, and
school politics mix which demands that excellence and strong
decision-making skills are tapped when it would be easier to
be satisfied with easy solutions. The parent presence, then,
creates conditions that support student development and
learning.

SCHOOL/UNIVERSITY/COMMUNITY RELATIONS
Respectful interaction and visible gain through efforts such
as the Baldwin-King Program, in which a small part of the university and the public school system are engaged in efforts
which are mutually helpful, will make it possible to enlarge

the relationship between the school system and the university. Other groups in the community—business, religious, social, and other organizations—can eventually be mobilized to also support school programs.

When school children experience the tangible ties to the larger community, opportunities for future participation in the community become apparent. With parent and staff support for learning, academic, social behavior, and occupational achievement aspirations can be raised.

PROGRAM IMPLEMENTATION

The principal should be the leader of the representative governance group. A task-oriented, problem-solving, facilitating style is more effective than an autocratic, authoritarian, controlling one. Good use of professional and nonprofessional advice and the delegation of power to others to achieve specific tasks permit other members of the governance groups to grow in competence, confidence, and commitment to achieving program goals. But the principal cannot abandon his or her responsibility as leader—that is taking the position most beneficial to the program in cases of disagreement, acting on personnel problems when necessary, giving input, review, approval, and disapproval to all governance proposals and taking final responsibility for the outcome of every aspect of the program.

Timing is very important. Attention must be given to all aspects of a program at the same time. But initially more attention must be given to the creation of a climate of good intergroup and interpersonal relationships. An important part of establishing such a climate is reducing the behavior problems of children in a school. This is best achieved by enabling students to meet their developmental needs in the school setting. It is then possible to give more time and attention to teaching and curriculum development.

Process

The two-week workshops held each summer served in the long run to reduce the social distance and distrust among par-

ents, teachers, and administrators. Through the joint examination of school problems and opportunities, these groups began,
tentatively at first, to develop a common perspective about program needs. This made it possible for representatives of these
groups to work together on the governance body—Steering
Committee, Administrative Team, School Advisory Committee—to plan, implement, and evaluate school programs on an
ongoing basis. The governance body permitted change in
response to problems and opportunities as they arose—not in
response to an expert's theory, opinion, or an administrator's
power.

The tasks of the Steering Committee were to improve the
climate of relationships between parents and school staff,
among school staff (administrator-teacher-professional and
nonprofessional support staff), between staff and students and
to improve teaching, the curriculum and staff selection, and
program evaluation. Parents and staff planned and carried out
(and continue to do so) social activities that support the school
program—book fairs, fashion shows, talks on various aspects of
the curriculum and child rearing, gospel choir programs, pot
luck suppers, etc.

Eventually these programs generated an integrated
approach to curriculum; the arts, athletics (to a limited degree),
and social skills blended into the academic program. For those
parents who could not participate in the academic program,
the integration of nonacademic activities provided a meaningful role in the school. The stipend program insured a nucleus
of involved parents. The parent-staff sponsored programs were
important in helping to improve the climate of relationships
between home and school primarily, but also among staff, and
among teachers and students.

The Mental Health Team supported social activity development through participation on various planning committees,
interjecting ideas based on social science, behavior, and system
principles when and where it was appropriate in the course of
discussion. When necessary the Team helped parents and staff
to develop the skills needed to carry out planned activities.
The same approach was used by the mental health person serving on the governance body. As parents and staff became more
sensitive to how people respond to time, location, format, sea-

son, and change, the mental health representative became less involved, less visible.

The major role of the Mental Health Team was to help teachers manage children with behavior problems. This work was carried out primarily through the Pupil Personnel Team. Referrals were made by the teacher to the principal and were passed on to the social work coordinator of the Team. Programs to address the problems were worked out with the teacher, some involving the cooperation of the entire staff. Developing methods to help a particular child sometimes led to providing additional support to one or more teachers and to changing, eliminating or creating new school rules, procedures, and programs such as a Discovery Room, a Crisis Team, new methods for bringing in transfer students, etc. These efforts greatly reduced the level of staff-student conflict, and in turn, the level of conflict among staff and between staff and parents.

Teaching and curriculum improvement programs existed from the beginning but became more effective as the overall climate of relationships improved and as the severity of behavior problems of individual children decreased. Parents, teachers, and administrators then had more time and energy to address the teaching and curriculum program. At the point that King School had a reasonably good relationship climate, it was possible to begin to integrate the teaching of social skills and the arts into the academic curriculum.

For the first five years, and then for the following years when only King School had an active program, all of these developments moved both schools toward one of the best attendance records in the city, greatly reduced student behavior problems, minimized parent-staff conflict and achieved near grade-level academic performance. King School is now among the top third of all schools in the city in academic achievement.

Evaluation

Initially we had not allocated either time or money for evaluation—probably for two reasons. First, we assured con-

cerned parents and community people who were deeply suspicious of university researchers that we would write no
papers or articles about the school program until there was
ample evidence that it was beneficial to the children involved
and might be helpful to similar children in schools elsewhere.
We requested minimal evaluation funds and confined our
research to a "low profile" evaluation which would be used
internally to guide the development of the educational and
extracurricular programs.

Second, some of us were ourselves skeptical of the value of
traditional research techniques in fluid, uncontrollable community settings. Initially, we were much more interested in getting our feet wet. But it was clear early in the program that we
would need a systematic evaluation in order to transmit our
findings. What amounts to a formative evaluation was done
during the first two years of the program, 1968-70. A baseline
study was conducted during the 1970-71 year. Summative
evaluations were done during the 1971-73 years.

Some administrative issues circumscribed the evaluation
design. For example, although no comparison schools were
used as control groups, a number of comparisons were made
within schools. Ultimately a variety of evaluative methods,
including consumer evaluations (by staff, parents, and to a
lesser extent by children), reports of outside evaluators, studies
of children's academic achievements, specific studies of art
and physical education programs and of the educational and
clinical support services were made. A number of smaller studies were also undertaken.

The evaluation we did do during the first five program
years was inconclusive. But the academic and attendance
records, among other indicators at King during the past three
years show that the major program goals have been achieved.
The King School fourth grade ranked twentieth in reading and
thirty-first in mathematics among thirty-one schools on the
Metropolitan Achievement Test in 1969. Since 1975 the students at King have ranked ahead of all other inner-city schools.
The Iowa Test of Basic Skills was used for the first time in
1978-79. The King fourth grade ranked tenth in reading and
mathematics, behind only the highest socioeconomic schools
in the city and ahead of a few.

Student attendance at the school has been second and third among the thirty-one schools in the city in the last three years. Teacher attendance is the best in the system. Numerous observers report a positive social climate—minimal student conflict, high motivation, and desirable interpersonal relationships among parents and staff and among parents-staff and students.

5

Scenario for a Disaster

On the first day of school, I walked down the hall at Baldwin School and I was almost attacked by a teacher in trouble. She was anxious, wild-eyed. She grabbed my arm and said, "Help me! Help me!" and literally pulled me into her classroom. What I saw was almost unbelieveable. Children were yelling and screaming, milling around, hitting each other, calling each other names, and calling the teacher names. When the teacher called for order, she was ignored. When I called for order, I was ignored. That had never happened to me before. We headed for the hall, confused and in despair.

Her classroom was not the only one in trouble. The school was chaotic and noisy. Children were milling around in the hallways. Some were running aimlessly and laughing without apparent cause. Teachers and administrators raced back and forth trying to register late students, trying to find room for the overflow. Three hundred and ten children showed up at Baldwin

76

School where two hundred and fifty-five had been enrolled the year before; two hundred showed up at King where one hundred and seventy-five had been the year before.

Teachers could not find supplies. One parent from outside the district appeared, saying that she had been advised to bring her youngster—a child who had had serious behavioral problems in school—to Baldwin because they were going to have all kinds of psychiatrists, social workers, and people to help him there. Of course, children from outside the district were not authorized to attend the school.

The first week was a short one, Thursday, September 5 to Friday, September 6. We left for the weekend shaken, with mixed feelings of impending doom and some vague hope that all would be better next week. The log entry of September 6th tells me that my denial mechanisms were operating at top form. I suppose I just could not bear to admit the extent of the problem we had.

LOG ENTRY, SEPTEMBER 6TH:

Things went well in both schools, but there were difficulties in three classes—two difficult children, perhaps one poor teacher. We want to move in to give those teachers support quickly. We had a few angry parents, but no emergency.

Joe Leon (Principal for Instruction) has "progressive" ideas and they won't work. He regards the Yale people as invaders, wants to protect teachers from them. There is a continuing battle between two approaches. Our focus of concern is on setting limits (establishing expectations). His emphasis is, "Don't put a lot of restrictions on the children." (Adult repression is the cause of all evil).

While I was using denial, I knew at the same time we were in big trouble and would have to move fast. On Sunday, September 8, I called our chief social worker, our educational consultant, and the director of the program from the school system, Sam Nash. We all agreed that there was an urgent need for planning. We would have to let the children know our expectations and we would have to set limits. The educational consultant suggested that we could do this best by planning several school assemblies featuring student and teacher entertainment. At that time, we could introduce some discussion about the expectations and goals for the school. Sam Nash suggested this approach to both the Baldwin and King Principals for Administration and Instruction.

We had lost a planning battle just one month before, so we approached this one with some trepidation. In August, the mental health team had suggested that detailed planning for the arrival of the children would be extremely important. Leon, who had pushed for an out-of-state workshop and other activities related to open education, objected to an assembly or any other arrangement "to lecture children" as stuffy and authoritarian. I explained that the idea was to give the children a sense of belonging, direction, and security; that it could be done while introducing the staff, listening to music, and talking about what was expected in school; that this was routine school procedure. He still did not like the idea. To avoid a struggle, it was decided that rather than imposing assemblies on the staff, the idea would be discussed the next day at a joint staff meeting. His position was really a question: "Who's in charge here?" We went along. We were committed to the notion that the educators and the New Haven School System were in charge rather than the mental health people and the Yale Child Study Center.

Leon did welcome the offer of a teacher from the staff of the Child Study Center helping out in the classroom of a teacher in big trouble. The notes kept by the helping teacher convey the climate that permeated the school, although conditions were less troublesome in most other classrooms.

SEPTEMBER 25, 1968 (LOG SUMMARY OF FIRST TWO WEEKS):

The first day was shocking. The second day was even worse. There was constant disarray. It flared into wild disorder many times. There was no quietness, very little listening. There was fighting; there was thumbsucking; there was crying; there were continual cries of "teacher!" There were wails of "I want to go home." "Do we go outside now?" There was no sense of structure, or organization to the schedule of the day (even though, Nora, the classroom teacher, had a very definite one and tried to announce it).

The kids impressed me as being very slow, both emotionally and intellectually. They seemed to be like nursery school age children, difficult, most uncontrolled of the pre-kindergarten children I had known. I couldn't believe that these were supposed to be first graders, that many of them (how many I did not know) had gone to kindergarten. Later as I got to know them better, I could see that there was actually a wide range in their development.

Every transition, every change during the day, was a disaster. They screamed and yelled and pushed as they lined up at the door to go downstairs. They rushed down the halls, yelling more. The lavatory with its high ceiling, its echoing walls, its many toilets with doors seemed to incite the children to new heights of excitement and wildness. [I spent most of the time in the girls' lavatory, but, of course, these same things were going on in the boys'. We had reports that the boys were screaming and racing around, of one boy urinating on another, etc.) In the girls' lavatory, they would bunch up in one "john," screaming and laughing, standing on the toilets, locking the doors, crawling in and out, refusing to finish, refusing to come out, making me chase them if I was determined to get them out. When they did emerge from the lavatory, there was great difficulty in getting them to line up. Some would race down the hall away from the group. Others would hide behind doors and refuse to come. When finally everyone was more or less gathered, there was a mad, loud dash up the stairs and racing into the room.

It was impossible those first few days to get them quiet enough to read a story to them. Even if, by some miracle, everyone was seated, you could not be heard above the din. I went around a few times from child to child, from table to table. There was a great deal of talking to one another going on and little noises being made, banging crayon boxes against the desk, kicking their feet, etc. But the most amazing thing was to hear how many children were just making sounds on their own, humming sounds, or talking avidly to themselves. Quietly and in a free period this would have been okay, but this was at a time when the teacher was doing everything in her power to get their attention.

On occasion, several children would dash under the table or start chasing around the tables. Now and then a few made a bee-line for the door. Richard would announce he was going home and a minute later, he was gone—however, it turned out he was just standing in the hallway. Meredith was especially difficult to get out of the lavatory and back in line. At recess time, she simply would not come in; would run off. Richard and Meredith were extremes, but others were behaving in a similar way.

There were only three jump-ropes and a ball to take outside. The children would grab and fight over these few things. Pat, the other first grade teacher, told us about a lovely walk she had taken with her class. We must have been crazy. We decided it would be a good thing for us to do. Outside, our class was almost impossible to hold together. The two children who had shown tendencies to run away the day before, Richard and Meredith, really ran off this time. Richard at one point was up near the main avenue. We were afraid for his safety. We could not run after him, feeling that we would make him go into the street. Finally, with the help of the building leader, Mrs. Norwood, we were able to get them back into school.

I cannot describe the physical, mental, and emotional exhaustion we reached by the end of the first two days, with two of us working every minute at the top of our completely inadequate capacity. Nora thought it had been better than Friday of the first week—but nothing could have been worse than Friday—and I think she was so relieved to have somebody in there with her that it did appear different. I was appalled at the situation and our inability to deal with it. Like victims of a storm, we picked up the pieces and prepared for a staff meeting.

Keep the climate of this classroom and school described above in mind as you read the log of the September 9 staff meeting in which we discuss the idea of assemblies or other means to transmit expectations and establish order.

SEPTEMBER 9TH (STAFF MEETING, SUMMARY)

ADMINISTRATOR: There is a need for a school assembly. . . . What is established at the beginning becomes accepted for the year. . . . Children are testing because they have not received clear messages of expectation.

DON ECKHART: (a teacher, in a strident and demanding voice) Assemblies are not useful . . . lecturing to kids . . . stuffy . . . authoritarian, etc.

ADMINISTRATOR: The idea is not to lecture, but to introduce them to the school, to our expectations. . . .

SARA BURNS: (the teacher who yanked me into her classroom on the first day). I am struggling with custodians, not enough basic materials and a large room that's acoustically bad. I'd like my class size reduced.

TEACHER: We don't need to talk about feelings. We need things. I didn't order milk. I didn't know it could be done.

TEACHER: Can't the school be open later—after 4:30 p.m.— and not get up so early in the morning to fix up our rooms?

TEACHER: Why can't we get into school on weekends? Only janitors can—some kind of sacred rule!

ADMINISTRATOR: Custodians have a contract with the city. No one may be in the building without a custodian.

TEACHER: We need an emergency fund for needed materials, and a complete inventory listing books and materials.

ADMINISTRATOR: Nothing will be delayed because of bureaucratic hang-ups.

TEACHER: I ordered things last July, then I ordered them all again—and the order has not come.

ADMINISTRATOR: If we want to get supplies and reduce disorder, we're going to have to have some organization, rules and regulations. (Angry response from many staff members.)

TEACHER: Each teacher must make order in his own room.

ADMINISTRATOR: Some teachers can and some are having trouble. Wouldn't it help to have the leader of the school help establish order through an assembly in which he addresses all children? (General uproar, several people, said, "No.")

TEACHER: Each teacher must do it himself—no lecture!

ADMINISTRATOR: An assembly is getting together to feel you're a part of the larger group. There are 125 new children at the school. There are new teachers, new faces. There is a need for induction into routines, for a sense of belonging in the school. A songfest would promote school spirit. Let's define the range of operations for the children . . . that's what we really mean by limits and not really crushing the spark or spirit out of the children.

TEACHER: Teachers have to work out the rules between themselves first, then transmit them to children.

DON ECKHART (still strident): Is the assembly being imposed on us or do we have a choice?

ADMINISTRATOR: There is no intention of the administration to impose things on teachers.

DON: You have told us . . .

TEACHER FROM KING (cutting Eckhart off): Shouldn't we have separate meetings? This is more Baldwin business! We need to have a feeling of our own, just as children do.

ADMINISTRATOR (attempting to respond to the question Eckhart did not get to raise): There are 37 extra kids in third grade. We had to arrange for a new teacher. We couldn't wait to consult everybody. In time we can develop procedures so that teachers can participate in decision making.

TEACHER: The extra kids . . . that was a mix-up downtown. I wish we didn't have to talk about it. Can't we dump the extra kids back?

ADMINISTRATOR: There may be people around who won't be too unhappy if we have a lot of trouble. We must pull together. We have five years (period of funding) to do a job.

TEACHER: We have to think about the next three weeks—sink or swim. We need help, aides—or we'll quit.

WENDY GLASGOW (social worker): I went into a class to consult about a problem child. Four or five people had been in already. That's too many.

SARA BURNS (teacher with chaotic classroom): What's the good of people coming in and lecturing our kids—or saying, mocking the building leader, "What are we going to be?— good!" It will take away all authority from the teachers.

Leon did not say a word throughout the entire meeting. Yet, I thought I heard his voice . . . at least his position. The King staff felt that the problems of Baldwin had to be worked out separately. A Baldwin staff meeting was scheduled for the next day.

The need for leadership was abundantly clear. Neither the Steering Committee nor the Administrative Teams had been organized long enough or well enough to be effective at this early stage and with this degree of crisis. Because of the many problems most of the first year Steering Committee Meetings were characterized by angry confrontation rather than cooperative efforts. Faced with chaos, conflict, and confusion, all agreed within the first full week that the assistants to the principals, building leaders, must take full responsibility for trying to bring the schools under control. Other administrators were working to secure new teachers, supplies, etc.

Instead of starting the September 10 Baldwin Staff Meeting with the very difficult and charged issue of trying to establish order, the discussion began with the problems and inequities in the milk program. The building leader brought the staff back to the real problems. All acknowledged, as a first step, the need to bring order into the process of children entering and leaving school. After a brief discussion about whether lining children up to enter and leave school did not represent some form of repression, all of the teachers finally agreed to do so. Mr. Eckhart, the previously strident teacher, asked for help from administration with some difficult situations—such as the case of a boy who yelled at him, "Whitey, take your hands off me!" He was given some suggestions, and it was agreed that this was a matter that should be discussed in more detail in a professional development session.

Mrs. Norwood's conduct of the meeting, as well as her help in handling problems in the hallways and classrooms, was beginning to provide the first clear signs of leadership. It is significant that she was one of the two teachers from the year before, one of the most experienced teachers in the building, and one of the few black staff.

During all the early problems, the parents at Baldwin had been remarkably tolerant. Several were very angry and saying to each other, "I told you so." This feeling was due largely to parent opposition to the leadership arrangement, a principal for administration for both schools and a principal for instruction for both schools.

Parents had opposed this plan from the beginning, pointing out that some one person had to be clearly in charge. Some were unhappy that the previous principal at Baldwin had been transferred to another school. Some did not like the fact that the principal for administration of both schools had been the principal of King the year before. He was familiar with that school, but not with Baldwin School. The compromise was that if the new arrangement did not work out, the program would revert to a single principal in each school.

In addition, parents at Baldwin and King were leery of Yale. "Yale has been in this community for all these years and has never shown any interest. Why now? Doesn't Yale want to make guinea pigs of our children . . . study them, write a book and then leave?" In fact, one parent at Baldwin later told me that a teacher from the year before, who transferred to another school, told her that Yale planned to make guinea pigs of their children.

In spite of these questions, confusion, and parental disappointment, it appeared that they were going to give us a chance to pull things together. They held several emergency meetings outside of the school, but did not make a formal protest.

In the meantime, Mrs. Norwood moved to foster organization and planning. She offered help to the teachers in trouble. She organized playground time by grades, worked out schedules for the use of the water fountain and lavatory, and urged enforcement of the no gum or candy rules. She suggested that children who needed more help than could be given in the classroom be sent to the principal.

In memos, she mixed praise with suggestion and criticism. In a mid-September memo she wrote, "There seemed to be more order, more quiet, more satisfied faces everywhere today. Many children like helping to clean up classrooms." Criticism by inference: "I hope Opening Exercises include the 'Salute to the Flag.' It is encouraging to note that black parents still have faith in our country."

A later September memo urged teachers to join the PTA, to develop their own style of teaching, to modulate the voice, to cooperate, to give as well as accept help from colleagues, and to use lesson plans. "I should like to begin looking at your lesson plans to see if there are any helpful suggestions I can make to increase your effectivenss. Please prepare a folder of instructions for substitute teachers. Feel free to ask our reading specialist and myself for help with your reading program. We would love to have a chance to pass on to you our ideas and suggestions or listen to yours."

Mrs. Norwood defined the role of the teacher aides. "Teacher aides do not teach. They may assist in review activities or in giving individual help. Nor should they be assigned the housekeeping chores only. Teacher aides are not disciplinarians and should not be used in this manner. Further, it detracts from a teacher's effectivenss if students look to aides for control. Ascertain the strength of your aides and use their abilities wisely."

The memos were intended to be helpful, but some teachers felt that they were insulting and demeaning. There was little trust and cooperation at this point.

Each side felt that the other was letting it down badly. When the teachers were recruited, they were told they would have everything to work with. Yet, many materials ordered in June and again in August before the school year started, never arrived. Teacher aides were not in the classrooms very much as late as mid-October because they were undergoing a training program which they should have had prior to the start of school. The custodian at the time was a problem in every way one can imagine. It is understandable then that the teachers felt exceedingly deprived at this point. But administrators, with no control over most of the problems, felt equally handicapped and were angered by complaining teachers and resistance to the measures they (the administrators) had designed to help relieve some of the immediate problems.

King seemed to be going reasonably smoothly. The building was brand new and of modern design—windows, carpets, and all that. In fact, it was so new that it was uncertain whether it would be ready on time in September. The parents had organized themselves to urge the central administration to take steps to make certain that it was ready. It opened on time. As a result, the parents were feeling successful with some sense of power and influence. The school was named in honor of the recently slain civil rights leader, Martin Luther King, Jr. Thus King School had strong emotional and historical forces going for it, giving the school a sense of purpose and hope.

SEPTEMBER 25, KING OPEN HOUSE

Over 125 parents came to the King Open House and, for the most part, they were pleased. Their one concern was a desire to have a hot lunch program. Leon, without consulting anyone or knowing anything about administrative procedures, suggested they they get together and go downtown and demand what they wanted. At that moment the entire program was a hair's breadth from destruction. Everybody in town was watching—some gleefully waiting for us to fall. We were all working like mad just to hold on. The last thing we needed was a time-consuming, alienating confrontation full of sound and fury, signifying (and gaining) nothing . . . at least nothing that we could not get through regular channels in time.

SEPTEMBER 26, CHILD STUDY CENTER TEAM MEETING

The Child Study Center Team met. We were concerned about an attitude of "we-they" which had developed between our staff and the school staff. We discussed what could be done about a great many problems: low teacher self-esteem, too many administrators with overlapping roles, too few blacks in the program, a cross-principalship that was not working, little physical space for the building leader at Baldwin, and on and on. We disagreed about which focus was most appropriate to deal with the urgent problems—educational issues or problems of behavior in the classroom. As a result of this meeting, we tried to focus on educational issues but, as mentioned above, it did not work. We were quite concerned about the fact that we were forced to deal with administrative issues and other kinds of problems which were outside of our area of expertise.

The meetings at Child Study Center were eventually dropped to destroy the impression (and the actual possibility) that the program was being run from a "cell" at the Child Study Center. Dropping this meeting was helpful but in some ways a problem. We were in fact outsiders and felt very much so in the beginning. At some time during the first year each member of the Child Study Center Team felt terribly depressed, hopeless, and some were in tears. With a team identification, we were able to provide mutual support to each other. As members of the school staff—but not really—we often felt very much alone.

SEPTEMBER 26, BALDWIN STAFF MEETING

Wendy Glasgow warned of increasing parent dissatisfaction and encouraged us to prepare for the Open House PTA Meeting at Baldwin. It had been postponed to permit us to establish better order and was now set for October 9. She pointed out that a number of parents wanted to go to City Hall and picket as a result of the difficulties in the program. Teachers responded to her comments with statements of their own dissatisfaction, again centering on supplies, the custodian, the handling of discipline problems, and so on.

SEPTEMBER 27, (EMERGENCY MEETING, BALDWIN STAFF)

Parents were definitely going to protest, to "take our children out of school until it becomes organized." Several of the parent leaders had told the social worker that they wanted improvements in discipline most of all; second, they were unhappy with the "open classroom" approach several teachers were using, and again they expressed their desire for a single principal. They felt that no real teaching or learning was taking place, that the school was just as bad as it was the year before. One parent said, "If I wanted to take my child to a zoo, I would do that"—a reference to the large number of gerbils, rabbits, and other animals in one classroom. They felt that many teachers did not understand what the black child in this community needed.

One teacher wanted to know what they meant by "what the black child needed." This was the most sensitive of questions. It was the kind of question that should have been answered at another time and in another place, but not then. These were inexperienced, young, mainly white teachers with a high personal commitment to success and improved opportunities for black children but sensing failure, not ready to acknowledge difference, unaware of their own racial stereotypes with an aroused black community at the door, with black-white conflict just below the surface—when it was not right out in the open. We tried to back away from this comment, indicating a desire to discuss the issue in professional development meetings later on. We felt that it was important to better organize and build good staff relationships before we could handle the very sensitive issue of racial difference, stereotypical thinking—albeit liberal—and so on. But Don Eckhart kept pushing.

His questions and attitude irked me because of what was going on. I understood the frustration of those young people. They wanted to do a special job, a job unlike that of their parents and others before them. Later on, one of the teachers described what she called the hypocrisy of her own family—once joining with a community group to buy a house in their neighborhood to keep it out of the hands of a black family and now praising her for her work in a black community. These teachers wanted to do better by black people, poor people, and young people. They were being stymied by a whole host of situations. They did not know who was responsible (and neither did I). They did not know who they could trust. While most of them were soon to express disapproval of Eckhart's approach, in these early months he did reflect the feeling of many.

But he was too much. I had grown up in a community not unlike this one. I had watched three of my closest black friends from elementary school days go down—alcoholism, psychosis, criminal behavior. The social worker and curriculum specialist had been involved and concerned about issues of inner-city schools for years. My brother and sisters had been involved in teaching and administration in inner-city schools for years, and thus I had lived my adult life listening to the problems involved. In fact, all of the senior people in the program—from the Child Study Center and the New Haven School System side—had spent a lot of time thinking and trying to do something about the problems of inner-city schools. And there was Don Eckhart, in effect, asking us, "What the hell do you old bastards know about it?" Or maybe he was just playing an adolescent–young adult vs. adult establishment game. I did not know what he was doing, and I could not have controlled myself at that point if I had.

I lost my cool in the open meeting and let him have it (verbally): "You have been either missing or sabotaging meetings. . . . Your classroom is a mess and a major focus of parental concern. . . . You want to fight but not help!" After a moment of shocked silence, the meeting took a conciliatory turn. One of the new teachers called for the staff to pull together and try to hold on.

SEPTEMBER 30

The parents came. As a result of talks with the social worker and the assistant to the principal, the parents came to the school instead of making an angry march on city hall, which would have blown the program sky high—newspaper reports, radio reports, rumors, confusion, anger. They were in a no-nonsense, tense mood but thoughtful, cordial, and fair. They indicated that they wanted to speak with the black staff only.

The parent spokesman indicated that they were not sure whether the problems were racial or not, that they did not have any malice toward whites, but that they expected the blacks to make a special effort to straighten out the mess. They made two specific demands. The first was to return to the traditional, one principal for each school administrative arrangement. The second was to appoint Mrs. Norwood as the permanent principal. They pointed out that they had been promised that the schools would revert to the traditional approach if the new innovation did not work.

Evidence that parents were more concerned about improving conditions than racial take-over is seen in the fact that they did not push the burning issue of that period, which was local and parental control of the schools (blacks) as opposed to central control (largely whites).

The black staff agreed with the parental assessments and recommendations. We agreed to support these changes but pointed out that we did not have the authority or power to make them. We pointed out the procedures needed to make the changes. We spelled out all the efforts that we had made to improve conditions so far and others that were planned, indicating that it would take time. They were temporarily satisfied but it was clear we had only "five minutes" to turn the school around.

Now we were in *real* trouble. The university team had hoped only to be in the schools and to provide service for a year and then with all involved—parents, staff, children—begin to develop approaches that would better serve the needs of all. The following log entry explains the problems.

OCTOBER LOG ENTRY: "OPINION BY AN OBSERVER"

It seems to me that when things came to a head this week, Dr. Comer and Mrs. Glasgow—of the University team—were right in the middle of it, beseiged on all sides. They were carrying the ball for Baldwin School. They conceived of themselves as coaches, but they found themselves playing on the field. They were acting for Administration—both as negotiators with the parent group, and as major exhorters of teachers to get organized in the classroom and to face community realities.

As a result, in my view, it was a muddied identity that the University people now had in the school. Sometimes advisory, consultant, observing, offering services and insights—and sometimes exercising power, running the show, pushing hard for things, and possibly affecting jobs and livelihoods. I know I am oversimplifying. There were crises. There were power vacuums. The program was going down the drain. And it is true that in the day-to-day rough realities of the school, you cannot make delicate distinctions which half the time seem not to exist. But University roles were unclear—and remained unclarified—not only with respect to clinical and educational functions, but far more seriously, with respect to what were the specific powers the University sector exercised over the people in the program.

As a result, clinical and group behavior insights offered by University staff—and there were many—got mixed up with attempts to get things working and moving. Perhaps this explains, in part, why many teachers took most things pointed out to them as negative judgements. Thus did the role of the University clinical group undergo a metamorphosis or shift from the full-time consultant status, to every day, partial leadership status in the schools,

The university team was now like a quarterback forced to move out of the protective pocket and scramble, looking for someone to hand off or pass to. But the principal for administration became ill early in the year and eventually underwent major surgery. Leon was so convinced that he was valiantly defending his ideas and protecting his group from "Ice Age" enemies of progressive education that there could be no meeting of the minds—

in spite of several meetings that attempted to identify a common ground I knew we held.

But even more troublesome was his uncritical support of several teachers who were having extremely serious classroom management problems. On one occasion, a youngster was moving from one activity to another, investing no time in any, and disrupting the work of others. A teacher intern under Leon's supervision indicated that the child was a curious scholar in search of knowledge. He strongly defended the intern in spite of the viewpoint of educators with far more experience than he himself that the child could not concentrate because of the classroom disorder. Parents began to point to him, identify him as the reason the new, and in this case, unsuccessful approach—open education—was being jammed down their throats,

One problem after another kept the climate of chaos at hand or just beneath the surface at Baldwin, and eventually the disorder spilled over into King. A teacher new to the Baldwin community left her purse in view of the hall window. It was reported that a teenage youngster from outside the school walked away with it. (A number of people "just passing through" added to the confusion.) The teacher aides did not receive their first checks because of an administrative snafu. Already irritated about having to take the major responsibility for keeping order, being treated like servants, and having little representation and voice in administration, this was the last straw. They went out on strike.

Planned staff development seminars were cancelled during the first month in favor of staff meetings to help bring order to the school. They were resumed in October in the hope that they would become the focus of teacher attention. But understandably, this did not occur. There were just too many issues, frustrations, and concerns more pressing than staff development.

The response to Dr. Carol's efforts in the first re-established seminar reflects the problem. She raised such questions as: "How can the curriculum be made more relevant? What is to be the substance? How do you communicate there is order in the world to enable children to move more easily, to better cope with their environment?" Some teachers stated very directly that they were uncomfortable and that they had more immediate concerns. Most of the group wanted to talk about "behavior control, teacher-parent relations, etc." Some challenged Dr. Carol's concerns—should there be order in an unjust world? Many voted for small, grade level meetings for reasons ranging from a real belief that such an approach would be more helpful, to a desire to get rid of some provocative colleagues.

As the psychiatric consultant, I had held several seminars. Probably because behavior issues were of greater concern at the time, I had received somewhat more cooperation from the teachers. I also suspect that the fact that I was black and in charge of the Yale Child Study Center component of the program made it more difficult for young, white, liberal teachers to attack me. I found most of the teachers respectful, even when they resisted some of my notions. They were particularly uncomfortable about the notion of cultural and social difference.

In a later publication Leon criticized my notion that there was often a difference in the level of inner control between youngsters from difficult family backgrounds and those from family backgrounds more fortunate in the quality of relationships. Many of the teachers were eager to learn more about the principles of child behavior. Unfortunately, some of those with the greatest interest and acceptance had the greatest difficulty applying these principles in the classroom.

One of the very cooperative young teachers had classroom control problems. She asked me to observe and advise her. While discussing the matter with her after school, a youngster from another classroom came in and asked to play with her violin. She believed that a teacher should be friendly with children but she was busy. She hesitated and with great reluctance said no, without saying that she was busy or telling him when he could come back. In fact, her manner and facial expression conveyed the message, "If you pester me enough, I'll give in." He did. Finally she had to eject him forcefully from the room and put up with his protest outside.

The assistants to the principals were not certified administrators. In a power showdown they probably would not have had the full backing of other principals and administrators in the school system. They had authority only through the consent of program participants. The aggressive, young, predominantly white staff knew this, but on the other hand both assistants were black, experienced, known to the community, respected and supported by them—and the teachers understood the implications of this. The power standoff in the middle of real frustrations and problems for administrators and teachers fostered more conflict than cooperation.

In one way or another, all potential leadership was submerged or paralyzed. To stay alive, the university team members—not always aware of it—went back and forth across the leadership-supporting participant line. Too much was at stake to let the program go down the drain—a grant to try to improve inner-city education, both locally and nationally. And it was the opportunity for several members of our team to work in a school in a way that we had longed for. It was 1968, when many educated and middle-income blacks could not find inner peace without a commitment to the black community. This was our chance, a belief that many white staff shared as well.

The emotional factors in our various motivations did not make the situation better. It probably contributed to our seeing "enemies" outside of ourselves rather than in the mirror.

Events moved rapidly in October. Parents had complained to Mrs. Norwood about the conditions in the classroom of Don Eckhart and his teaching style. He had a generally "junky" room they said, a large old tub, many caged animals, wood and cardboard and paper scattered all over the room, and so on. They described his style as buddy-buddy at times, but he could become angry and verbally aggressive on the other. Mrs. Norwood spoke with him several times regarding such problems. Generally he ignored her suggestions. On one occasion he allegedly grabbed, shook, and slapped a youngster.

Forty-five parents came to the Baldwin Open House on October 9. A small number visited Mr. Eckhart and told him—privately and nicely—that they disapproved of the way his room looked and of his teaching style.

Eckhart indicated that he felt that the parents had been put up to confronting him. As far as I know, they had not. A parent-teacher dialogue meeting was held at Baldwin the next day. This meeting was scheduled because of strong parent discontent. Because only four parents attended, Eckhart suggested that parents were not as discontented as some of the administrators contended. While the small attendance was due to the time (late afternoon for working parents of young children) and to the meeting just the day before; it was also a mini-boycott. The program had a notorious reputation at this point. The parents were saying, "Show us before we talk any more!"

In the meantime, trouble began to brew at King. The leadership group had greatly neglected King in an effort to prevent Baldwin from going under. A "minor" issue—rules about chewing gum—caused the teacher-administration battlelines to be drawn at King. Most of the teachers wanted to go along with the rules but they did not want to impose them on others. Several were opposed to any rules about gum-chewing. At issue was more than when to chew gum.

Part of the problem was concern about the decisions being made at Baldwin. Several of the teachers at King were from the same teacher training program as several of the teachers at Baldwin who viewed themselves under attack. The confusion about leadership was also a factor. Most important, the issue of gum-chewing was really a disagreement around how much freedom and autonomy is desirable for children in school and for teachers.

By mid-October, things began to come to a head. Two letters confronted the program—one a letter to Sam Nash signed by twenty-seven concerned Baldwin parents. It requested that Mrs. Norwood be appointed immediately as principal of Baldwin. The other letter, from Don Eckhart to Dr. Solnit, detailed Eckhart's criticism of the program. The appointment of Mrs. Norwood was an expected and agreed upon first step in the process to affect an administrative change. Don Eckhart's letter, on the other hand, was unexpected and did not go through proper channels.

Eckhart's letter was turned over to me. In it he listed a number of complaints: we do not have materials; a hierarchy has been established; they do not want teacher participation in decision-making; we are being treated like children. He remorsefully added, "too bad a program like this should fail." He had shown the letter to several teachers before sending it, primarily the "open classroom" group—but not to any of the black teachers. At about the same time I learned that he had been told prior to coming into the program that he would eventually be able to run a program for teacher aides. His impatience and shrill attacks on administrators appeared to be related, in part, to his frustrated desire to become an administrator immediately.

I had a talk with him and pointed out that the Child Study Center was not in charge of running the day-to-day activities of the school, but that had he wanted to express his viewpoint he knew that it should be expressed through the Administrative

Team. If he had wanted to express concern about anybody on the Child Study Center team, he could have talked to me directly. I told him that I thought he was fighting back because parents, teachers, and myself had expressed disapproval of his performance in the program. Surprisingly, Eckhart was reasonable and expressed a willingness to work more cooperatively. I thought that the matter would end with our conversation.

But when the letter was discussed in the next Administrative Team meeting, two teacher representatives supported him strongly, "Don is the kind of teacher I *want* to be! He is doing things I want to do! When the community comes in (and criticizes) why doesn't the administration say that what Don is doing is desirable?" There was just as much anger on the administration side. Even Joe Leon, the Principal for Instruction, pointed out that teachers had not really been accountable to parents.

As the discussion continued, the teacher representatives— both of whom had read the letter before it was sent—realized that they were the channel through which the discontent should have been expressed and that they had been by-passed. With this realization, they decided to check the views of other teachers on Don's letter. They found that many teachers (perhaps half) were outraged that Don had sent it: "It was not the right thing to do," "Going through the wrong channels," and so on.

Given this response, the Baldwin teacher-representatives, with the permission of the assistant to the principal, called a teachers' meeting without administrators to discuss Don's letter. The feelings expressed reflected remarkable change. Teachers were fed up. They expressed the viewpoint that administrators should make decisions and all teachers should spend more time teaching.

Black teachers boycotted the meeting. For some time they had been concerned about the way some of the young white teachers worked with the children both socially and academically. A couple of the black teachers, even before the letter incident, had indicated that they felt the continuing challenge of administrative authority was on racial grounds. Going over the head of the black University Director to the head of the Child Study Center (who was white) did not set well with them. Several black parents and black administrators had expressed the same feeling.

Whenever the issue of race was raised, however, the young white teachers, especially the supporters of open education, insisted that they were "color blind." Several had rented apartments near the school in what was almost a totally black community. They spoke strongly against racial prejudice. I believe that most of their behavior reflected their youth, their desire to help, and their impatience with anything and anybody who appeared to stand in their way. But they failed to see the racial and class attitudes behind their efforts to immediately impose their thinking and style on the parents and children. Blacks involved picked up another attitude, "Follow us (the superior group) and we will show you the way." This perception rubbed the involved blacks the wrong way.

During the summer before the program, without the knowledge or participation of any New Haven School System or Child Study Center program participants, Leon called a meeting with some of the parents at his home in the community. One parent likened it to a "calling of the darkies to the big house." She also felt that it was a power play. Another parent watched him throw his leather jacket on the floor in the corner of the principal's office and rush—in motorcycle boots—to a staff meeting and said, "And I'm supposed to want my child to be like *that*?" Several parents expressed fear that a couple of young teachers, who usually dressed in mini skirts and lived in troubled apartments in the community, might be attacked, bringing embarrassment to the community.

The parents were not interested in symbolic gestures. A meeting held later on to discuss the need for a program coordinator provided dramatic evidence of what most parents really wanted. One parent, overcome with emotion, pounded on the table and said, "If a coordinator can make this program work, get one! I don't care how we do it. I just want Baldwin School to provide my son a good education. I want him to go to work with a shirt and a tie and some books . . . just like you!!!" She looked right at me, the only black program person at the table. As a youngster, my own unspoken ambition was to go to work in a shirt and tie. She knew that I knew the obstacles. She was charging me with the responsibility of protecting her son's interest—a tough position in a system you cannot control.

The letter, the black teacher boycott of the meeting to discuss the letter, and the discussion in the meeting itself resulted in a significant change in teachers' attitudes. At the next Administrative Team meeting, the mood was conciliatory and a desire to cooperate with the administration was expressed. Like Don Eckhart and all of us they wanted conditions to improve, but they did not like Don's method. He stood almost alone.

Out of this meeting came a suggestion of a smaller group to set up a new organizational plan. The plan included a principal for each school with full authority and primary responsibility for carrying out the program. Three major committees that were to be consultative and advisory—curriculum and community relations, evaluation, administrative and personnel—were to be established to enable parents and teachers to make an input. My role was changed from the head of the Child Study Center team in the Baldwin-King Program to co-director of the program. But I still did not have official administrative status within the school system. This was a problem in that I now had official responsibility for making the program work without the power to do so. It appeared that we had a new lease on life, but it was a heartbreaking mirage in a desert of frustration and despair.

We lurched forward. One of the young teachers from the "open education" group, who was also the teacher representative on the Administrative Team, began to act more independently of the group and more cooperatively with the administrators. Others followed. He and other young teachers found Mrs. Norwood, the building leader, to be very helpful in bringing order to their classrooms. There were two or three very successful curriculum meetings during this period. Teachers came voluntarily to several sessions to discuss child behavior. Very shortly thereafter, Mrs. Norwood gave a party at her home for the entire staff which was enormously successful. Hope, fun, and good feelings were everywhere that afternoon.

The school appeared to settle down. Parents who at first insisted vehemently that their children should have desk workbooks and a painful amount of homework, now began to listen to questions about the value of some of their demands: about the ways in which learning could be fun, the wastefulness of hiring a full-time nurse and part-time doctor, the possible dangers of being severely punitive with children, etc. They began to talk more about what they wanted for their children. We all began to smile again. The Thanksgiving vacation brought us relief and time to write up organizational plans, rules, regulations, and other organizing documents that had been discussed with teachers in a series of meetings. In early December the new organizational structure was put into effect.

But the problems did not go away. Every adjustment to solve one problem created a new one. In 1968, there were plenty of jobs for teachers. A teacher who was hired after the beginning of the semester was less likely to be a prize find than one recruited for the job. That was the situation for a couple of the teacher replacements we had to make. Mrs. Norwood was designated as acting principal for the rest of the program year and had the best chance for the permanent position once she completed the several courses she needed to meet the academic requirements for a principalship in the state. But near the end of the first year of the program it became clear that she was still too far away from the licensing requirement to be named principal—a development that was not well-received by the parents. She eventually transferred to another position in the school system.

Even the change back to the traditional principalship created a problem. This move left us with too many people at Baldwin trying to do the same or a very similar job. We had an acting principal with an interest in curriculum development, a curriculum specialist from the university team, and the Principal for Instruction. We also had a science and mathematics specialist and a language and social studies specialist. Thus, we had five people with potential leadership roles in the curriculum development area, all struggling for direction, when not struggling for power.

In an effort to clarify roles, meet the demands of parents, and best utilize all talents, Joe Leon was asked to function as Institutional Coordinator for the Use of City Resources. He was to mobilize inside and outside the schools, help teachers to develop activities around these resources, and to integrate them into their instructional program. This included the responsibility for field trips. We talked about the change of role for Leon as a lateral move. While he agreed to do it, the move was viewed by others, and probably by Leon himself, as a demotion. Perhaps it was. He had come to the program as a Principal for Instruction and had been expected to function as the educational leader. But leaders of the parent group had indicated that they wanted him and others of similar philosophy removed from the school altogether. They were willing to settle for his removal from a major leadership role.

The change in Leon's role put three teachers in the position of seeing the supervisor of their college academic program demoted in the field—a most unfortunate position for them, for the supervisor, and for all of us. Several teachers who felt that Leon alone was carrying the banner for open education were in a similar position. Some gradually came to a better understanding of the unfortunate conflicts and actions on both sides that led to the personal and program tragedies of that first year.

If only something had worked that first year, the story might have been different. Paper, pencils, rulers, crayons, and chalk remained in short supply most of the year. The custodial service was not really improved until the second year. Cliques formed among teachers, administrators, Child Study Center staff, and so on, which was troublesome because the members supported each other, justified or not, rather than search for the most beneficial problem solution. Racial issues, generation differences, teaching and discipline approach differences, the status of one's college, and finally just petty personal issues were always beneath the surface and occasionally flared into interpersonal and interclique conflicts.

The climate of conflict among staff was transmitted directly to the children, and they acted out the conflicts. As a result, during the first semester at Baldwin alone, over forty children were referred to the Mental Health Team for evaluation and treatment.

The Baldwin-King project had an "Extended Day Program" for which teachers were paid extra to participate in educational and behavioral in-service training conferences. But overwhelmed by problems, teachers were often too tired to pay attention. Some nodded. Some were irritated and disruptive. Some went through the motions. We had a few good sessions.

Tired, disappointed, and mildly to moderately depressed, teachers were vulnerable to illness. Absenteeism was high. The effort-reward ratio was low. Morale sagged. But we struggled into the Christmas vacation still trying. We scheduled an out-of-state trip for early in the next semester to visit a successful innovative program. It was to involve parents, teachers, administrators, and aides.

The program we were to visit had overcome first-year difficulties and we wanted to demonstrate that it could be done. It was also an effort to pull everybody together and to get off to a good start in the second semester. For reasons that I never fully understood, but which involved misunderstandings within the educational leadership group, the trip did not come off. That was the signal for me. If with all that time, energy, and effort, and with well-trained personnel, we could not organize a successful trip, the level of interpersonal conflict was too high to try to continue. It was going to be necessary to hang on for the balance of the year, find new staff, a full-time project director, and plan and organize properly for the second year.

Due to contract requirements, all teachers had to be notified whether they would be offered a new contract by the end of February. We knew that most of the young teachers wanted out. To avoid hurting anyone, they were given a chance to indicate if they wanted to return or not. It was our plan to try to persuade the most effective teachers to stay and to counsel those having difficulty who wanted to stay to find a setting in another program in which they had a greater chance for success. Most of the teachers who had had a difficult time did not want to remain. A few had mixed feelings. But the counselling process went haywire and the matter brewed into a painful fight with much hard feeling.

At the separate requests of three teachers who had been hurt in this and other situations, I had long conversations with each. Their hurt was painful to me. Their questions, expressed indirectly, were nevertheless clear. "Did we hurt the children? Did we destroy the program?" I assured them that the program and the children would recover and that we understood they had made a sincere effort. To their point, "It was not all our fault," I couldn't have agreed more, and I said so. But from February to late June was a long, long time—very much like riding on the post-game bus of a good team that had just been beaten . . . or worse.

Our situation deteriorated. Conflicts between teachers flared again. The behavior of many children became troublesome. By mid-May, many windows in Baldwin were boarded and the playground was strewn with glass and other debris. Several teachers resigned in a huff. Parent discontent grew. You could almost put your hand on hopelessness.

The wrath of the neighborhood was upon us. It all exploded in a fiery community meeting in the Baldwin School gymnasium early in the spring. The Administrative Team agreed that organization and planning was our greatest need. In order to do this—and to reduce other sources of tension—we had to have a full-time project coordinator, more experienced teachers, a better racial balance among teachers, several transfers of personnel, better custodial service and so on. The central administration had agreed to make these things happen and the assistant superintendent, who was about to be named superintendent, came to the meeting to assure the parents that these moves would be made.

The meeting was a knock-down, drag-out affair. He faced an angry group of parents and several community leaders. Everybody with an axe to grind laid it on the grinder—in this case, the next superintendent. Months of frustration poured out. Fortunately he understood the cause of the anguish and was tough and able to spar with the speakers—he had on an "asbestos" suit. His sincerity came through, and most parents accepted his explanations that a number of unfortunate circumstances had marred the first year and that the program could and would be better in the second. The parents agreed to support the moves we all felt were needed.

Unfortunately Baldwin School conditions continued to be troublesome. Some parents understood that we had made changes which would make things better for the next year. Some felt that they had to make their position clear and called a boycott against Baldwin School in May. Parents bought promises the first year and got burned. A boycott, before agreeing to go along, underscored their skepticism.

The facts are not clear here. But the King parents did not join them. By this time there were many problems and much tension at King but they had agreed to "wait till next year." In response to the boycott, the Child Study Center and the New Haven School System offered to cancel the program at Baldwin rather than impose something on the parents that they did not want. The parents then indicated that they wanted to keep the program. They wanted a good program. We could all drink to that and we limped . . . no, collapsed into the summer recess.

6
Up from Chaos

During the hectic first year, many people speculated that our program was an experiment to study the behavior of young teachers in a chaotic setting. That was not the case. But the rapid deterioration of high hopes and objectives did expose us in one year to the kind of school problems and possibilities that one can usually observe only over a decade or so. And as painful as it was, we all learned a great deal.

We gained significant appreciation for the problems around the three interfaces—community, home, and school; among teaching and other school staff; school staff and students—and how they interacted. The engagement with parents we needed to address these problems occurred around issue after issue throughout the first year. In discussions with parent leaders, the Child Study Center and Baldwin-King leadership groups assessed the problems and made several moves we all agreed were necessary to reduce the problems interfering with the operations of the schools.

It was obvious that we needed a "buckstopper" and coordinator, someone directly responsible to the New Haven School System but working full-time in the project schools. We were lucky to find a good administrator leaving a Yale-sponsored education program that was being phased out. His job was to coordinate activities between the central office of the New Haven School System, the Child Study Center, the parents, community, and the project schools.

The coordinator permitted me to get out of a partial administrative role. It was, and is, my belief that the proper role of a social scientist and/or psychiatric professional in the field—be it a school, factory, government, etc.—is to help institutions and people do better what they themselves determine they want to do. We do this best by providing insight as to how people and their institutions function and interact and how modifications to improve their functioning can take place—not by engaging in the day-to-day administration of a program.

A parent committee, the new coordinator, the King School principal, and teacher representatives from both schools went over the entire original proposal, line-by-line. As originally proposed, they attempted to delineate the spheres of responsibility of educators, support staff, and parents. A June 20, 1969, excerpt of their report gives some idea of the issues and responses. They wrote, "We [parents] should determine the kinds of curriculum we, as parents, feel is good for our children [consulting, not dictating]"; with regard to evaluation, "As parents we want to have explained to us and be involved in all forms of evaluation." With regard to supportive services, "Parents request that the Child Study Center provide services as determined needed by the principal and teachers and that all records be open to us."

A new principal was recruited and assigned to Baldwin. The Principal for Administration of both schools returned to a full-time principalship at King. The coordinator worked with both principals to secure supplies and take care of the management details that were irritants and distractions in the first year. He worked with the central office to improve custodial care at Baldwin School, to clarify financial arrangements, and to make central office staff more aware of what we were doing, how, and why. Schedules, lists, and plans were everywhere. A faculty guide was developed during the summer, describing everything from what the program was about to what to do when a child's knee is bruised on the playground.

We made other changes. On the first day of school, during the first year of the program, we knew that we needed a better balance between experienced and new teachers. We knew that we needed a better racial balance and that a black community with a choice would not tolerate a predominantly white staff in 1968. We had a desirable mixture of teaching styles among teachers the first year which we tried to maintain in recruiting teachers for the second year. Three of the most successful teachers at Baldwin during the first year returned for the second—with a little pleading. Five teachers from King School returned. It was difficult to recruit seasoned teachers to what was known all over town to be "a sinking ship." Again we were lucky.

Five veteran teachers joined us—after we sold stock in our future and explained the problems of our past. They were all people who felt strongly that it was important to demonstrate that black children could achieve well in a good educational environment. Four were black and one was white. We also got the cooperation of the central office personnel staff in sending us teachers we thought would be interested in looking at themselves and at better ways of working with children. Four teachers from outside the New Haven School System and three first-year teachers joined us.

It should be noted that these major changes are organizational and managerial. We recognize the existence of individual psychological and social problems, but it is our contention that much of what is called behavioral pathology will not manifest itself in a climate of relationships made adequate by good organization and management. Those which do are more serious, but more people are available to respond to them because the helping staff is not caught up and overwhelmed by problems and crises generated by a poorly operating social system.

After reviewing the use of social-work time during the first year, we decided to make a major practice change. We had been utilizing the traditional casework model. A handful of children and families were eating up almost all of the social-work time with minimal results. In addition, it was clear that many in-school problems—not entirely family and child personality and/ or social problems—were at the root of child misbehavior and underachievement in school. The new strategy suggested by Wendy Glasgow, the chief social worker, was to spend less time working with individual children and families and more time applying the principles of the social and psychological sciences to helping staff and parents carry out specific programs.

Because of the need to move rapidly, the Steering Committee gave the coordinator permission to take a number of independent actions in the summer before and during the second year. This situation reverted to normal after conditions improved. The Child Study Center team capabilities and responsibilities were spelled out and formalized during the summer planning before the second program year.

Several workshops involving school staff and parents were held during the summer before the second year of the program. Parents and staff received a small stipend for their participation in these workshops. The workshops permitted parents and staff to discuss curriculum issues, the meaning of child behavior, how to help children behave well, and the way administrative procedures affect behavior and achievement in schools. There were grade-level discussions in which parents and teachers, with the input of academic specialists, discussed philosophies and goals for their respective classrooms.

There were special sessions on reading, science, language arts, art, and music. Principals discussed the importance of holding parent conferences, sending progress reports and the purpose and function of such reports and report cards. The importance of making evaluation of a student's performance a positive rather than punitive event was given much attention.

In the child behavior session we talked about the overly aggressive child, classroom and home conditions promoting aggressive behavior; about mechanisms for reducing anxiety and acting-up behavior such as proper orientation to a new setting, the proper balance between sufficient structure and sufficient freedom for children and staff, the function of authority, rules, positive rather than negative sanctions; how goal-oriented activities and the possibility for success reduces acting-up behavior; the consequences of feeling wanted and valued; the withdrawn child, learning disabilities, etc.

In short, we tried to do three things: First, we tried to make the administrative changes necessary to establish order and permit an average level of school functioning. Second, we brought parents and staff together in a way in which they got to know each other as reasonable people with common goals and interests. Third, we supported task-centered workshops that permitted thinking and planning from a shared perspective by parents and staff. These three efforts set the stage for addressing the problems we saw clustered at the three interfaces mentioned above.

The workshops left parents and staff with the sense that they had achievable goals to work towards. A party at the end of the workshop sealed the feeling of camaraderie that had developed between parents and staff during the workshop, and we approached the second year in high spirits. On the first day of school, as a part of my withdrawal strategy, I stayed away. (I think that was the reason.) Late in the day, with great trepidation, I called the coordinator to see how things were going. His answer was "A-O.K." We were on our way.

7
The Mental Health Program

During the second year the Mental Health Team task remained what it had been the year before—to help create a climate in which a solid educational program could emerge. To move toward that goal we had to overcome community and staff resistance and help teachers develop and use new ways to manage behavior problems. But because of the problems of the first year, suspicion and doubt about the Child Study Center Mental Health consultants remained high. We still had to prove our worth. This chapter will describe the Team's approach to gaining credibility and being helpful.[1] One of the Team's most critical opportunities came early in the second year.

About six weeks into the semester Matthew Monroe, in a fit of anger, smashed the window in the door of his third-grade Baldwin School class. Nobody was injured, although everybody was emotionally shaken. The problem had been building for several weeks and was not new for Matthew. He was ten years old, older, bigger, stronger, and smarter than his classmates and was well-known as a troublemaker. He had never completed a full year in school after kindergarten because problems of aggression had forced schools to put him on "home-bound status" for a good part of each school year. The most continuity he had was a visiting teacher who usually spent an hour a day with him.

This time Matthew was suspended temporarily to allow him and his teacher to cool off and to permit the staff to map a strategy to help him make it in school. It is important to point out that if these same events occurred today he would not be suspended. (No child has been suspended from King School in over nine years.) There were no suspensions during the last two program years at Baldwin.

The principal called a meeting of the Pupil Personnel Service. Matthew's teacher presented the problem. We learned that Matthew's parents were separated; that a brother four years older was beginning to run with a problem group at the high school; that his mother was clinically depressed; that his father had a serious drinking problem. Talking about family problems made us all uneasy. One teacher on our faculty had grown up in a housing project, and she complained vigorously about professionals who "gossip about poor people." Our Team agreed that we should not focus solely on the problems of home and the community, but rather would concentrate on making the school a decent place for children like Matthew to live.

Matthew had a minor reading disability and consequently read very slowly. He was embarrassed by and defensive about being two years behind in school. He was emotionally fragile and exploded at the least suggestion that he was deficient or was behind. But the level of his anger and acting-up was due to more than what was going on in school. We had to know at least a minimum about his home life in order to understand what was troubling him and what kinds of intervention might be helpful. In this, as in other cases, we stressed that confidentiality and responsibility are critical. What was *not* relevant—like who was sleeping with whom and the like—we did not want to hear.

In the conference we discussed the impact of his parents' serious difficulties upon Matthew; how youngsters of this age often feel that they are responsible for parental conflict; how they sometimes try to distract the parents by becoming a problem themselves; how when separation takes place they feel rejected, guilty, and confused; how they fear abandonment. The sense of rejection is even greater when the parent with custody becomes depressed and the other parent appears infrequently. We discussed how difficult it is under such circumstances for a child to channel aggressive energy and develop adequate inner control. We deliberately avoided psychoanalytic interpretations, first because we did not have Matthew in analysis and could not make valid interpretations, and second, because we did not need them. An additional consideration was that if we slipped and made a psychoanalytic interpretation, it usually made the staff uneasy.

Matthew's teacher had been under verbal attack for several weeks. He had been working hard at undermining her authority in the classroom. Discussing the usual behavior of a child with Matt's history helped Matthew's teacher understand that he was not lashing out at her personally; that he was not always in control of his behavior; that he was, in fact, calling for help. With this understanding she was willing to participate in a plan to help him be more successful in school.

His teacher had pointed out that he was relatively stable in the morning but grew more restless, impulsive, and prone to explosions as the day continued. We knew that he longed for his father. With these two key considerations, we developed a plan for a gradual reentry into the school and classroom. Initially, Matthew spent an hour a day with the male principal, assisting the principal in any way that was appropriate. When Matthew could be relatively stable for one hour, he would have a two-hour day, the first hour with the principal and the second with the special education teacher who would help him with his reading disability. If this arrangement worked well, he would then spend an additional half-hour in his regular classroom. During the next phase of the plan, the special education teacher would take his teacher's classroom for one-half hour, and his regular teacher was to work with him on a one-to-one basis. In the final phase, when we hoped that he would be working and not disrupting the classroom group, he was to return to his classroom for the full day.

Two months after he had broken the window, he was in class full time. His academic performance had improved, he had gained much social acceptance, and he finished the year without another major problem. During the summer he left New Haven to live with his father. Early the next year the principal received a thank-you note from Matthew's father and news that Matthew was continuing to do well.

Before the plan was implemented, we invited Matthew's parents in to discuss it. His mother made several appointments but did not show up. Finally his father came and agreed to the approach. (We would have pursued his mother had the father not come, but we understood that she was depressed and decided not to pressure her.) The principal, social worker, Matthew's teacher, and Matthew met and discussed the plan and the reason for it. We did not discuss the family problems or suggest to him that he was responding to that situation.

We then met with Matthew and said essentially, "Matthew, we know you are unhappy and that's a big part of the reason you are having trouble in school. We want you in this school. we like you, we know you can learn and get along okay, and we want to help you do so. But we cannot tolerate your throwing books, attacking other children, showing disrespect for your teacher. We know that you don't want to do these things either. We are going to go a step at a time in helping you make it in school. When you are doing okay at a given step, you can move to the next. You let us know when you think you need more help. When you are not getting along well, we will hold you back. It's up to you. Any ideas about how we can handle this whole thing better? . . . Okay, we are all agreed. Good luck."

The plan for Matthew was based on the knowledge that impulsive children often cannot handle the stimulation of the average classroom and become more disorganized and unruly as the day goes on. The plan was designed to provide clear expectations and to give him information about how to achieve and hold the interest and approval of the important people in his school environment. Our approach reduced the uncertainty and stress of whether he was wanted or valued in school and gave him a way to earn respect and acceptance. Finally, the plan was structured and carried out in a way that put him in control of his own destiny.

We used this basic approach in conferences with many children who were acting-up more than was usual for their age group. At first we thought that the youngsters might be overwhelmed by the large number of adults present. To avoid this, the principal stressed that the staff wanted to help. It is our impression that collectively the youngsters felt "all these important adults have gathered together about me . . . in all this mass of 400 teachers, children, aides and custodians in the school!" Often the question of whether teacher, principal, and others cared about him or her was what the testing, acting-up behavior was about in the first place.

"Do you love me, even though I can't read as well as Mary? Do you think I am important even though my clothes are not as nice as John's? Am I a nice person even though my father has an embarrassing drinking problem?" Such questions are rarely asked directly. With young children, the behavior is the question. Yelling at them, punishing them, and ignoring them without addressing the underlying questions can be a statement: "I don't like you, you stupid, poor, person from a troubled family!" This does not mean that a teacher should never speak strongly or assertively or lose control—no more than it means that a parent should not. But teachers must try to read the behavior message and respond appropriately to meet the child's need for a sense of adequacy, belonging, value, and worth as well as meet the needs of other children for a classroom and school condition in which there is optimum safety, order, and comfort.

The critical variable in Matthew's case, and in most cases, was the classroom teacher. Had she been unwilling or unable to use the support and advice given by our staff, the intervention would have failed. Fortunately this teacher knew she had a critical role and remained strong and in control, even when Matthew severely tested her limits. None of us gives up behavior patterns easily, even when they are harmful in the long run, because they provide more security in the short run than an uncertain new way of relating to people and one's environment. For this reason the Pupil Personnel Service met periodically with all involved to support Matthew's teacher and to remind us of the goal we had all set. We wanted to avoid the confusion and disagreement that might permit Matthew to play one adult against the other to maintain his old ways.

The breakthrough probably came about the sixth week of our plan when Matthew and his teacher were working together. She corrected one of his papers and gave it back to him with a new assignment. He had not returned a previous assignment. On his way back to his desk he dropped the new assignment on the floor, turned, and looked at his teacher without saying anything. The action said, "I won't . . . I can't . . . I'm scared . . . do I really have to change? . . . How much of my stuff will you tolerate?" (And other things.)

His teacher responded calmly, slightly disappointed, "Matthew, it looks like we are just not going to make it, doesn't it?" The loss of approval and interest of this important person was just too high a price to pay. He continued to look at her for a few seconds, then picked up his assignment and went to work at his desk. The next day he brought in the overdue assignment, crumpled but completed. Their relationship and his performance went uphill from that point. Other teachers observed Matthew's change and began to refer children to the Pupil Personnel Service.

I do not want to imply that this or any other intervention was a smooth, mechanical process carried out by near-perfect human beings. We stumbled along, doing what appeared reasonable given the situation and what we understood about human behavior. We often disagreed about the best approaches. In fact, Matthew's teacher finally cut short the last step of his reentry program because he wanted to return to class full time and she felt he was ready, although the helping teacher did not. Jealousy? Possessiveness? Overinvestment in the assistance effort? I do not know. Probably some or each and more. There were hard feelings. Working cooperatively to handle difficult human problems is not easy.

One assumption made by the entire Child Study Center Mental Health Team was that we would, whenever possible, apply the principles of the social and behavioral sciences to problems of, and opportunities for improving, relationships in the schools. As director of the Team I met regularly with our members, formally and informally. As co-director of the Baldwin-King Program I transmitted Team findings and suggestions to Arthur Smith, the co-director responsible for project operations. The two of us met regularly with the principals to discuss school operations and to share mental health perspectives. We hoped that mental health perspectives would benefit their program planning, implementation, and evaluation. In direct and indirect ways we discussed the benefits of sharing or delegating some of their power and authority to promote greater parent and staff participation and commitment to program goals and, in turn, increase their own power to do their jobs through the support and cooperation they would receive from parents and staff.

The Mental Health Team members made their major contribution as a part of the Pupil Personnel Service. We were uncertain about who would be the most effective Pupil Personnel Service manager—social worker, principal, teacher—and we experimented. But regardless of the titular head, the social worker was responsible for handling referrals from teachers, developing the agenda, mobilizing and organizing helping resources, and following through on or supervising the management plan for a student or assistance for a teacher. The social workers emerged as the persons best able to coordinate and manage the Service.

The Pupil Personnel Service met once a week. It was conducted in the format of a hospital medical case conference. Present were Mental Health Team members, principal, the referring teacher, and where indicated representatives of outside agencies. All information was treated as confidential. The referring teacher presented the problem with description of events and symptoms. The dynamics of the case were then described by the mental health professionals, after which others could ask questions and offer additional information and suggestions. A case management plan such as the one devised for Matthew was worked out. Pupil Personnel Service members observed often in the classrooms, and each case was followed up in subsequent Pupil Personnel meetings until the problem was resolved.

In order to learn what categories of problem are addressed most often, we kept track of some numbers. During the first and second year of the program, approximately 60 percent of the referrals to the Pupil Personnel Team were for aggressive physical and verbal behavior. About one in ten students were referred at King and one in eight at Baldwin. Three times as many boys were referred as girls. Children who were apathetic or withdrawn represented the second largest percentage of referrals; learning problems were referred least often. During the fourth program year the referral level remained the same, but the frequency of problems was reversed—learning problems first, withdrawal and apathy second, and excessively aggressive behavior least.

Our Pupil Personnel Service approach to problems was "no-fault"—not the fault of parent, teacher, or child. We fully appreciated what a nuisance a child's behavior was to the presenting teacher. But in discussing the dynamics of the case—developmental, home, and school conditions affecting the child's behavior—teachers often began to appreciate that they, too, can contribute to a problem. Once during the second year, a teacher dragged a surly youngster into the principal's office. Midway in a Pupil Personnel meeting about the problem, she blurted out, "Oh my God, that poor boy. And I'm handling him exactly the wrong way!" She took him back and eventually worked out a good relationship with him. Teacher appreciation of how they might contribute to a problem was usually not this dramatic. But in a climate in which they are not blamed and they are not expected to have flawless problem management skills, they are more willing to examine themselves than generally claimed.

"Wrong" was her word, not ours. We were all aware that teachers typically are not trained to understand and help children manage developmental crises or difficult behavior problems. Yet as we encountered and controlled problems, it became clear that many children were not available to learn until someone could alleviate obstacles to development.

Another task of the Child Study Center Mental Health Team members was to address social and behavior problems outside the framework of the Pupil Personnel Service. The Team worked to help teachers acquire the skills necessary to manage the average behavior problem so they did not feel they had to automatically refer children for services. To this end we held workshops, and we talked spontaneously while in classrooms, in the hallway, and whenever the opportunity arose.

The logical first step in handling such problems is to ignore minor nuisance acts and encourage activities that will bring the child positive feedback and success. But when such efforts do not work and a child increases his or her determination to challenge classroom expectations, or begins to lose inner control, he stands a good chance of hurting someone, achieving more disapproval, embarrassing himself, and thereby finally experiences a great sense of failure. Before this point is reached, he should be helped to leave the room gracefully. Teachers need the skill to make this possible, because if the child is removed from a classroom in inappropriate ways, a new, more difficult problem is added to the original one, compounding and extending it.

We suggested an approach something like this: "John, I can see that you are having a tough time today. Before we have a big problem, I want you to go and sit in the principal's office for a while until you can pull yourself together. Let's see, it's one o'clock now, you ought to be able to do that by 1:30." The routine proved effective, and a formal crisis program was developed. The teacher would usually give the child something to work on while sitting in the principal's office. This is a fairly traditional approach. The difference is that the teacher verbalizes the confidence that the child can, with help, develop self-control, handle his or her problems, and perform adequately in the classroom.

A staff person—social worker, aide, principal—was assigned and available for crisis duty. Their task was to permit the child to "cool down," talk about the problem or continue classwork until he or she could talk about the problem. The staff person was to help the child think about better ways to handle a problem and to help them gracefully return to the classroom. The children usually returned right on the dot, ready to behave appropriately. This approach works best once a school is functioning in a reasonably stable fashion.

Teachers found many ways to improve on the system once the idea of punishing bad behavior was dropped and the idea of helping the children avoid embarrassment, loss of control, and thereby achieve psychological growth was established. Many teachers, using the same concept, worked out ways of helping the children recover without ever leaving the classroom. Giving the child in trouble the responsibility for pulling himself or herself back together enabled them to snatch success (self-control) from almost certain failure (loss of control and punishment).

During an in-service child development meeting, a teacher at Baldwin asked what children get out of being disruptive. So the social worker conducted several role-playing sessions that enabled them to appreciate what it was all about. One teacher played the disruptive child. Another played the teacher. The others played the children in the classroom. They were *excellent* mimics of the children. The "disruptive child" reported that she really enjoyed *controling things*. Her "classmates" reported that they paid attention to her because "that's where the action was." They agreed that to decrease disruption it is important to involve everyone in the classroom "learning action." They talked about how assignments that children could not understand, feelings of rejection, and many other factors might cause a child to drop out of the learning action and eventually disrupt the classroom.

I watched this happen on one classroom visit. The teacher was working with the reading group. Another group had a work assignment and the third group was working with a board game designed to teach and reinforce a mathematics concept. It was a new game, and the children could not understand the printed instructions. They became frustrated and slightly irritable but tried to keep quiet because they knew they were supposed to do so while the other group was reading. As they began to make more noise, the teacher called two or three times from the reading group, "Let's hold it down back there!" Finally one boy could not hold back. Frustration, irritation, and boredom led to provocation and a punch. One child started crying. The teacher scolded the puncher. All of the classroom activities were disrupted. The children did not start out to disrupt the classroom. It happened first, because they could not understand the game and, second, because they had not been taught how to obtain help when they did not understand how to handle a situation.

My presence there was part of a routine Team practice. The purpose of the classroom visit by the Mental Health Team members was to identify the kind of classroom organization, practices, and situations that lead to disruptive behavior. We discussed our observations with teachers and often worked out changes together. This was the third year of the program, and by and large the teachers accepted and encouraged these visits and suggestions. But this had not been the case in the beginning.

Initially, in these schools—as in most schools—teachers did not want other teachers or anybody else to see their problems. To have a serious problem was considered by the teachers themselves to be a sign of incompetence. One colleague calls it the "perfection syndrome" and points out that such teachers also demand it of children. Classroom doors are usually closed. Visiting and exchanging information or ideas was most rare and seen as threatening. Yet the Mental Health Team members were strongly encouraging teachers to share, to be open about problems, and to ignore their own apprehensions about doing so.

This style among teachers is due largely to training programs that stress the teacher as a teacher rather than the teacher as teacher and learner. It is reinforced and compounded by school administrators who are under pressure and do not want to see or hear about classroom problems. Too many schools do not have the staff or the climate of relationships to provide teachers with adequate support. Without the necessary training or support, teachers close the door and try to survive.

Each Mental Health Team assist gave its members and mental health principles credibility with teachers, administrators, and parents. Teacher, administrator, and parent power was being enhanced, and, in turn, the power of the Mental Health Team members was being enhanced. As individual teachers using Team suggestions succeeded with a difficult behavior problem, others were willing to try the methods being suggested. With new skills and confidence, eventually the staff began to aggressively explore the possibility and problems involved in sharing information and insights with each other and learning from others.

In one mental health workshop in the third year, the teachers strayed from the topic under discussion and spent most of the session talking about the fear of "exposing" themselves and their teaching problems to others. They agreed that they were probably limiting their own growth by being so isolated but that it could only be done if they could trust each other to be constructive and respectful in their observations and critiques. This acknowledgement contributed to a climate of searching, growing, and learning.

It was a short step from that consensus to the obvious problem of children—far less accomplished than their teachers—and their anxiety, fear of failure, and the way they withdraw or disrupt in response. This was the kind of point that the Mental Health Team member present in such a meeting would make if no one else made it. But it became less and less necessary. Once the teachers began to routinely examine their own behavior, they were very quickly able to think from a child's perspective. At one mental health workshop, one teacher asked about the kind of adult behavior a child had a right to expect. Another posed a hypothetical question, "What would you do if you scolded a child for misbehavior and then discovered that that particular child was not at fault?" At first there was strong disagreement among the staff, then discussion, and finally agreement that the teacher ought to apologize, that children have rights.

There are many adults who perceive some loss of stature, authority, and behavior management effectiveness if they apologize to a child, particularly in front of other children. Yet one of the great sources of anger and hostility among the troubled children

I have encountered is that adults who are not fair, honest, and trustworthy (FHT) say they expect children to be all of those. Children often have teachers and other adults classified according to how they measure up on the "FHT" scale and many other personality and performance characteristics. Teachers who score at the top of the scale are best able to positively influence behavior and most likely to shape the character of a child.

Another way the Mental Health Team served in the school was through serving on various committees and participating in school activities. For example, in formal and informal situations our resource teacher, later called the Discovery Room teacher, talked with teachers about children's anxieties that result from their misconceptions about illness and death, about how "bad" language is sometimes related to their developing sexuality, about how the tattletale phenomenon is related to the strict superego of seven and eight year olds.

The social workers often helped teachers learn to respond to questions related to such matters while holding demonstration classroom meetings or sitting in on teacher-led classroom meetings. One third-grade classroom meeting was particularly instructive. Eight and nine year olds—except in extreme situations—have higher behavior standards for themselves and their peers than adults. "He fights too much. . . . She talks back to her momma. . . . He talks while I'm trying to read." The children wanted the teacher to severely punish the "bad eggs."

The teachers had to help the children be more tolerant and understanding of children who act-up and to find a nonpunitive way to help them live up to the classroom expectations. Teachers better appreciated the intensity of the feelings when we discussed the fact that children are very actively internalizing the rules and regulations of their environment at eight or nine years of age and are threatened and angry with violators. Rule-breakers weaken their own commitment to live up to rules. Understanding this developmental phase made it easier for teachers to tolerate their anger, better tolerate and help the tattle-tale and the rule-breaker, and able to help all students learn to live by just rules. The psychologist, working with teachers in grade level meetings, addressed similar issues.

Before very long, one effect of sharing mental health principles and approaches was that most people were beginning to focus on behavior dynamics. "What's going on with this child? . . .

with me? . . . between me and this child? . . . between me and my coworker? . . . between our staff and the parents and community?" At the same time we did not want to wallow in relationship issues. We resisted the suggestion of several teachers that we develop sensitivity groups. It was our feeling that the staff could best examine their own behavior around work problems or issues—whether their behavior facilitated or interfered with solving a problem or achieving a goal.

One incident pointed up the benefit of thinking about causation before taking action. In December of the third year of the program, a fight erupted while I was standing in the hallway at Baldwin talking with two teachers. One youngster, a big fifth grader with a history of violent behavior, began to attack a smaller child with a thick belt. The fifth grader was very angry and completely out of control. We separated the youngsters. But instead of the very common comment, "that *bad* John Jones is at it again," one teacher said, "I wonder what's going on with him? He was bothering the younger children in my classroom yesterday." His teacher agreed that something out of the ordinary was operating to affect John's behavior. By that time John had walked into his classroom, still upset, and angrily knocked over his desk.

His teacher walked in, but instead of scolding him or sending him for punishment, asked him what was going on, what was he upset about. After some resistance and delay, he began to cry. He explained that his father's pass from jail to come home for Christmas had been cancelled. Both father and son had been counting on it. The teacher said she understood how that must upset him and his father as well. She suggested that he write his father and express his disappointment. She promised to help him write the letter. She also told him gently but firmly that he could not fight with others when he was upset and that there were more acceptable ways to handle his feelings. He calmed down and a very serious problem was solved in a way that accommodated John's needs and was in the best interests of the school. John learned something about the way one can handle feelings of disappointment and powerlessness—a lesson as important, perhaps more important, than academic ones.

Because teachers had begun to think dynamically and respond to student feelings and needs, many potentially serious problems were averted over the first years of the program. With fewer energy-draining problems, it was easier to respond routinely in supportive and adaptive rather than punitive ways. It was more possible to help children learn to live by the expectations and rules of the school game. In turn, the children helped each other. One day during the fourth year of the program, a new King fourth grader started a fight in his classroom. Another youngster jumped up and said, "Hey, man, we don't do that in this school!" The would-be fighter looked around uneasily. Nobody else said anything. But the faces of his teacher and the other students confirmed what he had heard. He slowly "dropped his dukes" and went back to his previous activity. Even though he was new, an outsider, he did not have to fight his way to acceptance.

In many inner-city schools, turnover of student population is as high as 50 percent in a school year. Such turnover and the attendant discontinuity, anxiety, and reaction are a major source of classroom and school disruption. Helping children make a smooth transition is most important if such schools are to have a sense of continuity and stability. The overall reduction in student behavior problems and the increase in supportive and adaptive staff responses had a positive affect on students and their parents. This situation facilitated a good climate of relationships and the development of the parent and teaching and curriculum development programs.

The operation and impact of the Mental Health program was not always smooth and positive. Occasionally the various Mental Health Team members forgot to clear meetings with the principals. Occasionally the principals did not make arrangements for Mental Health Team activities. These incidents can be the result of busy people paying more attention to the task than to the administrative detail, but they can, and often do, represent resistance. These problems had to be brought to the surface for discussion, and all had to make a conscious effort to avoid communication breakdowns. Otherwise the trust, fair play, and cooperation among the various groups of adults required for changes in the climate of the schools could not develop and be sustained. When these and similar issues are not discussed they often lead to troublesome acting-up behavior among the adults, which eventually permits and promotes such behavior among the students.

Also, the very changes in the operation of the Pupil Personnel Service that freed mental health consultants to be in classrooms and to have greater schoolwide presence and impact had some negative effects. This change took place in the third year when we began to make more services available to teachers faster and to more fully utilize the skills of the nonprofessional and student professional members of the team. With this expanded effort, each Pupil Personnel Team member responded to requests for service prior to a team meeting and case work-up. It was the first year a student social worker and a student psychologist had significant autonomy in the program. During this year, Child Study Center staff members began to build on their experiences by undertaking graduate program work and by making professional appearances outside of the schools. In addition, one of our social workers became ill and eventually had to be replaced.

Teachers reported that they felt abandoned; that they liked the students but felt that the students were not getting enough support from the professional staff; that the Mental Health Team services were fragmented; that they did not see me, the Mental Health Team director, enough.

When unhappiness exists in a complex social system, the cause is often elusive. In my judgment the student social worker and psychologist actually performed and got along quite well with the staff. Social work time in schools was actually slightly more than during prior years. I was taking my turn in the rotation in response to service requests. In retrospect, we probably made too many changes and expanded activities too soon. The teaching staff was not involved in making Mental Health Team personnel and operation changes. Thus, understanding and digesting what we were trying to do was difficult. Also, at Baldwin, clear signs of significant disagreement began to develop between the Mental Health Team, some staff and some parents on the one hand, and the administration and some teachers on the other.

For the fourth program year, the more experienced social worker agreed to transfer to a potentially more difficult situation at Baldwin and the new social worker was assigned to King. We phased out the social work and psychology student participation except as they could assist in conducting psychological tests. We went back to a Pupil Personnel Service arrangement similar to the previous one but enlarged the scope and operation.

During the first three program years, resource teachers, learning disabilities teachers, community relations workers, teacher aides, and others provided a variety of teacher support services. They often worked in conjunction with the Mental Health Team members serving with the Pupil Personnel Service, but all were independent and responsible only to the principal. Cooperation between these individuals improved as the severe acting-up problems among students and staff were reduced, but their work was not well coordinated and services were duplicated and fragmented. As the Pupil Personnel referrals shifted toward withdrawal, apathy, and learning problems among students, the opportunities and needs to combine mental health and special education services became apparent. For the fourth program year, the Pupil Personnel Service was enlarged to accommodate a combined effort and the service was renamed the Education and Pupil Personnel Service Team. The social workers, who reported to the principals, served as coordinators of these teams.

At this point, largely because of educational consultant problems that will be discussed later, we hoped that the teams could assist the staff with the teaching and curriculum development programs. But our expertise proved to be more limited in this area than we had thought. But the emergence of an Education and Pupil Personnel Service Team did allow the mental health and educational resource people to begin to relate better and to integrate mental health and child development issues to academic learning issues. The social worker in each school coordinated mental health planning, implementation, and evaluation, and coordinated those activities with planning, implementation, and evaluation in the parent and teaching curriculum development programs.

During the fourth year, the Pupil Personnel Team meetings became so successful that teachers other than the presenter began to drop in. The social workers then invited all the teachers and almost all came. These meetings became informal seminars. Teachers shared observations about common classroom management problems. They made suggestions to the presenting teacher based on how they had handled similar situations. Occasionally a brother or sister of the child under discussion was in another teacher's classroom. Reports of similar or radically different behavior among siblings helped us understand the troubled child.

During the fourth year, the Baldwin team pieced together comments made by several teachers, pupil personnel service, and community persons employed in the school and uncovered a traumatic event related to a fire that was responsible for the mute condition of a kindergarten child. Each person working alone had a piece of information but was not aware of its significance. With mental health experts there to assist, the teachers were able to understand the problem. We then provided treatment that eventually permitted the child to begin to recover and to participate in class and school activities.

Thus far I have discussed a number of ways in which our Child Study Center Mental Health Team members worked to assist teachers and other staff and, in turn, assist the students. But consistent with our notion that most student behavior problems are due to the complexity of systems beyond the school, we addressed operations or systems matters in the ways they contributed to parent, teacher, administrator, and student interactional problems. An incident during the third program year best reflects how this took place.

One Monday morning an eight-year-old youngster was brought to the school as a transfer student. The Friday before he had been part of a tight-knit family and social network in rural North Carolina. He had been well supported in the warm familiar climate of his family, school, church, and neighborhood. An aunt had brought him to New Haven to get a "better" education up north. He was now in a strange town, with a relative he did not know well. He was taken to a new school and dropped off as his aunt went on to work and was introduced to a stranger—the principal. He was taken directly to his new classroom.

His new teacher had had three transfers the week before and unintentionally and nonverbally managed to convey, "All I need is another one." The youngster took one look at the teacher and students, kicked her in the leg, and ran out. The Mental Health consultant thought this was a relatively healthy response, but as you can imagine, the teacher did not think so. This was a youngster who could have been labelled "bad" and punished. Such children often react to the punishment in ways that will get them into more difficulty with classmates and staff and are often eventually labelled as disturbed and are referred to a mental health worker.

Instead, the staff discussed the problem as a classic case of fight or flight. Once the teachers had considered the social and psychological dynamics—what happens to an eight year old in a stressful situation without his support system—they were able to come up with a number of ideas to support the youngster in his new environment. His teacher had her students make "Welcome Johnny" signs and display them on the door. The new youngster was introduced to all his new classmates, allowed to describe his family and his North Carolina home, and in general was shown respect. A successful student in the class was assigned as his helper. The tone of help and support was set.

The decisions about Johnny and the success of the "help and support" approach provided impetus to review and change the admissions procedures. Now no student is admitted directly to a classroom on the first day of school. All are given an orientation to the school, its opportunities and expectations. Where appropriate the student takes placement tests, thereby avoiding anxiety that comes from improper placement and consequential acting out. Testing is delayed if a child appears too apprehensive. New students return to a classroom welcome and to orientation the next day. These and many other procedural and system changes worked to reduce student and staff anxiety and behavior problems.

The Child Study Center Mental Health Team members did very little direct child treatment work. Our belief is that most children can function at an acceptable level in a positive school climate. In fact, even in very chaotic communities most students are not psychologically ill. Thus our highest priority was to help in establishing a good school climate. Once established, those children truly in need of counseling and treatment were visible and we had staff and energy available to assist them. Children in need of service in a good school climate are not in competition for services from students responding to problems generated by a chaotic school setting. The most severe problems were referred for mental health services outside the school.

Thus the Child Study Center Mental Health Team members established credibility and gained power by helping the educational staff deal with student behavior problems. In turn, we learned about problems of education from the staff and were able to apply some mental health and child development principles to the educational process. We believe that developing a positive open climate of sharing, honesty, and trust contributed to a reduction in the number of behavior problems. With less disruption, we were free to develop a parent participation program and the teaching and curriculum development program.

The parent participation program, particularly parent participation in school governance and management, was the major factor responsible for improving the quality of living and the level of learning in the Baldwin-King Schools. This program is the subject of the next chapter.

8

The Parent Program

During the fourth program year we had a Christmas program at King in which over 400 parents, relatives, and friends turned out—in an inner-city school that only had an enrollment of approximately 360 students. During that year we consistently had parent attendance of 250 to 300 at King and around 200 at Baldwin. This was far from the 15 to 30 persons who turned out for similar events in the first program year. During the fourth year parents were working effectively in their own parent groups and on governance bodies and committees. But this occurred only after a slow, uneven, often uphill climb.

In retrospect, the fact that our program got off to a bad start is understandable. An effort to involve parents directly in the life of schools is a major change in educational practice and is as recent as the 1960's. Change in long-standing practice without a powerful mandate and a promise of immediate benefits is difficult.

Proponents of parent involvement made at least three strong arguments. First, parents have a knowledge of their children and a relationship on which school personnel can build. Second, the presence of parents could improve accountability and help tie school programs to community needs. Third, if parents themselves are involved in a school program, they will develop a greater interest in program outcomes and will be supportive of budgetary and other school-related economic and political considerations.

The need for parental participation is greatest in low-income and minority communities or wherever parents feel a sense of exclusion, low self-esteem and/or hopelessness.[1] Parents are the first and most important models and teachers of their children.[2] If parents feel excluded, of little value and hopeless, they will be likely to transmit these attitudes to their children. Such attitudes have behavioral consequences that are the opposite of what is necessary for good school learning or the achievement of long-range goals.

The need for parent participation is not quite as critical in middle-class districts where parents are often cut from the same social fabric as that of teachers and administrators. In such settings parents and teachers are often friends, colleagues, or members of the same church or club; they may be former schoolmates. They transmit the same range of values, hopes, desires, and wishes to chidren. When parents are of similar or higher social status than the teachers, there is less potential for conflict and alienation. Middle- and upper-income parents often feel excluded from school, but for the most part their social roles and status protect them against feelings of impotence and ineptitude. Yet all parents are important to the education process.

Recall again that early learning occurs best when the teaching comes from significant others. If the school teacher stands in opposition to parents and others to whom the child is attached and draws sustenance and security, the child may rebel against the school teacher and reject the learning situation. Thus the home, parents, and neighborhood and the teacher, school, and school program must not be at odds. This was our major motive for trying to bring low-income parents together with the largely middle-income public school faculty.

Though children in schools would benefit from high parental involvement, school personnel often resist such involvement. One study of minority administrators in the state of Indiana shows strong opposition to parental involvement in school governance.[3] Is this a matter of class, prejudice, or a need for social distance on the part of the black middle-class administrators? I believe the resistance is more complicated than class or race-related issues.

Many teachers and administrators, regardless of racial or ethnic origin, attribute school problems to a willful failure of youngsters to work hard enough and behave well. Some are in an ambivalent position; they care a great deal about the youngsters but often are frustrated by and angry about behavior and academic performance which they know will limit a student's chances for success. Many of the administrators who are members of minority groups went to school with parents of some of the most troublesome youngsters, yet themselves worked hard to overcome personal hardship and obstructions. They remember that some of the parents of today's troublesome children were yesterday's troublesome children. Many see the parents as the problem and not part of the solution.

If parents become involved in school policy and practice, school personnel are sharing power. Most of us do not share power well under any circumstances. Often an unspoken fear is that if power is shared, power is or will eventually be lost. Administrators perceive their difficult job as impossible without the little power they have. Too few appreciate the way in which parent participation can enhance their power rather then diminish it.

Ironically, the other major area of resistance to parental involvement is the parents themselves. Our experience was that many low-income parents accept invitations to participate in school programs against their better judgment. We heard a lot of, "aw, they ain't gonna do nothing" in the neighborhood. Those who do reach out and dare to hope once more risk being told, "I told you so," by others if a new program fails. Many parents are concerned that they are only being brought in to be told about the failure of their children, and parents perceive this to be a statement that they themselves have failed. Many schools call parents only with bad news. And many parents are embarrassed by their own limited academic skills. They feel that once in a working relationship with college-educated school staff, they will appear inferior to the staff. Professionals often underestimate the degree to which this concern exists.

After the second year of our program we had a feedback session involving parents and staff. The purpose was to hear from parents about what had been helpful and what could be improved or discontinued. One parent stood up and thanked the staff for being the kind of people who made parents feel comfortable in the school. She pointed out that when she first got involved in the program she did not think that she had anything to say that could be of benefit to the professional staff. By the end of the year she was a major contributor to the program. Her perception of herself was quite different from the perception of the staff. From the beginning staff members had thought of her as one of the brightest, most articulate, poised and dedicated people in the entire program. Her feelings and comments indicate the way professional status intimidates low-income, undereducated parents—even the brightest and most able—and makes them reluctant to participate in school programs.

Sometimes, inadvertently and with the best of intentions, parents are placed on important committees to discuss matters about which they, the parents, do not have experience or expertise. In this situation, parents usually withdraw, attend sporadically, or may even become defensive, obstructive, and difficult. Too often administrators observe these responses, and claim, "we tried, but the parents just aren't interested" or "parents are just too difficult to work with." This sequence of events is often cited as evidence that parents cannot be involved in school program governance. The outcome is that parents conclude, "they didn't want us in the first place," and the next time around the parents are pretty sure "ain't nothing gonna happen anyway." That is a vicious cycle that can be avoided, and should be, with careful planning at the outset.

The major objective of our parent program was to break the cycle and bring the vitality of the community as it had existed naturally in the past into the school. We wanted to establish trust and mutual respect so the school would not seem a place different and more alien to the children or their parents than home, neighborhood, and the church. But there were few precedents and few models for sharing power. We had to chart our own course. Thus we made mistakes and progress was slow.

Our initial engagement with the parents during the first year of operation was heated and potentially destructive to the program—but it produced a source of energy that eventually helped the program work. Those parents who fought most heatedly against the "intruders" from Yale and downtown eventually developed a great investment in the program outcome. More systematic parent involvement took place in the parent-staff workshop held in the summer before the second year of operation. Through these activities parents developed a close, though sometimes difficult, relationship with the program leadership and teaching staff. As they achieved small goals—hosting a "Welcome Back to School" party, sponsoring a Halloween party for their children, helping to select a teacher replacement—the fighting among parents, school, and university staff declined, and the focus was more on the solution to problems and the achievement of goals. The governance boards facilitated the change.

The structure and function of various governance bodies have been described. Several incidents and attitudes related to parental participation in governance are important to relate here.

Participation on the Personnel Committee, which selected new staff, was one of the most important parental activities and a very real departure from the traditional operating of system schools. Generally, two or more parents served on the Personnel Committee with two or more teachers and the principal. This was a very delicate arrangement in that it gave parents their greatest sense of influence and investment in the program. But only the cooperation of our principals made this possible. There was no legal requirement that they discuss personnel selection with the parents. On a couple of occasions the parents sensed that they were not being heard and this led to a drop in attendance at Personnel and other committee meetings. Fortunately the principals were open to discussion about this and other matters and these situations were resolved.

From time to time principals, teachers, and prospective staff members all commented on the fairness and wisdom of having the parents on the Personnel Selection Committee. These parents were selected by their respective parent organizations, but we confess to tampering with democracy just a wee bit here in the early years of the program. We (the two program co-directors, principals, and the social worker) discussed the sensitivity of the work of this committee with key parent leaders, and they made certain that very thoughtful, strong but fair people were selected to serve. One incident in particular demonstrates the need to do this.

During the third program year, we had to select a new social worker. Among the candidates we identified, two were outstanding. One was black and one was white. The black candidate elected to take a job out of the area before we had made our decision, and we had to decide whether to hire the white person. The social work position is more sensitive in a low-income black community than that of teacher or principal. The image of a social worker is too often tied up with that of the public welfare worker who has great control and power over lives of poor people. This power is sometimes abused consciously and misused at other times simply because the welfare worker is overwhelmed by the quantity of work or is in a no-win position between the client and government.

The Personnel Committee interviewed several additional candidates but agreed that the white social worker best met the program needs. But there was much uncertainty and ambivalence expressed by the parent members on the committee. The social worker candidate finally responded, "You like my training, expertise, and style. The only question now is whether you are willing to give a white person the same chance as a black." The parents looked at each other, smiled, and shortly thereafter agreed on her selection. The parents felt that her ability to stand up for herself was the quality needed to be effective and helpful to others.

The participation of parents gave a good balance to the Personnel Committee. The professional staff tended to focus on technical competence. Parents tended to focus on attitudes and beliefs. As the program direction took shape, committee members developed a set of criteria for staff selection that incorporated both interests. The committee rarely makes a personnel selection error.

One of our initial objectives was to create a good climate for parents, staff, and students. We felt that the extracurricular activities of the school provided a good vehicle to do this. This was also a good place to involve parents because participation in these activities did not require that they have academic skills; in this way we could involve a significant number. Initially, the planning for these activities was carried out by subcommittees of the Steering and Administrative Team with only the parents on these teams having a major role. The Parent-Teacher Association did not have much responsibility here.

During the second year, the major projects sponsored were a "Winter Snowball Festival" and a "Spring Festival." Parents, teachers and administrators, Child Study staff, and their spouses attended. These affairs were catered by the custodian from the King School. This was a deliberate decision to involve "all in the family" wherever possible. Custodians, secretaries, aides, central administration, school board members, and everybody related to the school in any way were invited to major programs, staff parties, and celebrations.

There were other school functions. A Baptist Church choir sang at several affairs. Pot-Luck suppers and fashion shows like the kind put on by some of the same parents at church were built into the school extracurricular program schedules. The arts, music, and physical education teachers worked with parents and curriculum specialists to decorate and provide entertainment at these various affairs, and parents who had special skills or talent were invited to give demonstrations.

These activities went a very long way toward eradicating stereotypes and reducing mistrust among the community, school, and Child Study Center staff. Several parents were amazed to learn that I danced—and well. Professors are not supposed to dance, they thought, not even black ones!

Parents in the school sent clear messages to children that school was friendly turf. Children saw their parents respected and contributing to the school program. They saw their parents on friendly terms with the teachers. Even the children whose parents did not participate actively benefitted. Several of the parents who were in the school pointed out that children from their neighborhood, or some who just took a liking to them, often came up to them to show them a good paper, talk about their good performance in school, or to ask for help or guidance of one kind or another. Most importantly, parents talked and word got back to the community that this school and these people were okay.

Despite improved parent-community and school relations in the second and third years of the program, the parent participation program was not what it could be. Too few new parents took leadership roles. The staff, particularly the arts teachers, social workers, community relations worker, and administrators, had

to play too active a role to help bring off parent sponsored programs. Interest in committee work fluctuated and still tended to
be crisis oriented. Parent participation in curriculum committee
work will be described in the next chapter. But, in short, it was
uneven.

Also, changes in the operation of the Mental Health Team in
the third year adversely affected parent participation programs
in both schools. At the same time children of some of the experienced parent leadership at both schools graduated and the skills
of these parents were no longer available. The potential replacement parents had not been in positions in which they could prepare for leadership roles. At Baldwin, there was still some skepticism about the Yale connection and the degree to which parents
were welcome in schools. In short, the parent program was in
place but not thriving.

The social workers and community relations workers at both
schools met with parents to try to identify and respond to factors
limiting parent participation. Two problems appeared to be responsible. Extracurricular activities put on by the subcommittees of the Steering Committee, with input by a few parents,
were not "owned" by the parents. In addition, parents pointed
out that they wanted to participate in program policy issues but
that they could not do so unless they had some way to learn about
and understand school operations. Sitting on committees was not
experience with the system as a whole. Under the supervision of
the principal, parents were given primary responsibility for
sponsoring extracurricular activities and coordinating those
with the school and consulting staffs. This change in operation
gave parents a major mission, responsibility, and their own turf.
Social workers and staff arranged to share their expertise with
parents through participation in the planning and implementation of parent-sponsored programs rather than in didactic teaching sessions.

Out of the Baldwin meeting grew a Parent Interest Group, a
revitalized PTA, and a string of very successful curricular and
extracurricular activities sponsored or participated in by parents, staff, and children. The former was to enable them to learn
about children and schools, and the latter was to plan and implement programs. The King parents and staff dropped their PTA
affiliation and renamed themselves the Parent-Teacher Power
Team to signify greater participation and responsibility. Two

new programs, "Coffee and Conversation Hour" and "Parent Advisory Board Meetings," reinforced learning and planning skills.

At both schools, teachers belonged to the parent organization, and one teacher usually served as an officer but never the president. Parents took the leadership. In this way, parents and not middle-income professional staff were providing programs to help themselves and other parents learn about child development and child rearing, teaching and learning, and about general school operations.

In unobtrusive ways, social workers and teachers shared their skills and expertise with parents. The social worker met at least once a week with the president of the Parent-Teacher Power Team to plan for public presentations, meetings, correspondence, a weekly article for a small local newspaper entitled, "From One Parent to Another." The social worker discussed good recordkeeping methods with the secretary and treasurer. Teachers shared their skills with parents as members of the Parent-Teacher Power Team through service on other committees and in the subject area workshops they presented.

The parents in leadership positions began to actively recruit new parents. They arranged to utilize as many of the new people as possible. Room-mother volunteers were not hard to find; they assisted teachers and served as a liaison between school and other parents. In that way other parents were encouraged to participate in the school program. At King they addressed the loss of leadership problem by enlarging the body of officers. They created an assistant at each officer position. In this way, someone was there assuring continuity.

The Parent Interest Group at Baldwin sponsored five Saturday workshops in a series called "The Mini-School Day." Parents assumed the role of children in the classroom during one of these sessions and re-experienced school life. Teachers in the school volunteered and led math and reading workshops, the two academic areas of highest priority. The purpose was to help parents understand teaching methodology and the problems and joys of learning as children. With this exposure they would be more likely to be sympathetic, more likely to talk with their children about school, and better able to help them with it. A summary workshop refocused the current status of the Baldwin-King Program and the projected goals.

The PTA took a role in the parent participation process by planning a series of activities. These helped to recreate the good climate of relationships which had slipped a bit and to encourage more parents to participate actively in the program. The PTA established a lending library for parents. A bake sale, a pre-school play group, a school newspaper, an all-school cookout, and class visits by parents helped to achieve many of our goals by the end of the fourth program year. The parents took much more leadership in putting on the annual spring festival in the fourth program year than they had in previous years. These activities cooperatively sponsored by parents, staff, and sometimes students and coordinated by the social worker put the Baldwin Parent Participation Program back on track.

The parents at King developed guidelines for operating the Team. The precedings of each meeting were recorded, mimeographed, and sent to all parents by the secretary and the social worker. The Team sponsored the "Parent Advisory Board Meetings." The officers of the Team and room mothers were always at these meetings, and all other parents were invited to attend. But the existence of a group of parents in the school guaranteed a core group in attendance. Usually the only school staff present were the social worker and the community relations worker, although the principal attended at times and members of the teaching and paraprofessional staff attended when they were directly involved in program planning. The Parent-Teacher Power Team sponsored a number of projects in support of the school program. Some were to raise money for student activities not available from school system or special project funds. Another was simply to create a good relationship climate in the school.

At the start of the fourth program year, the Parent-Teacher Power Team held a September open house and general business meeting. In early November they sponsored a family supper and talent show. A family togetherness night with gospel music was held just before Christmas; everyone met for a business meeting in late January. Parents were involved in a State Department of Education workshop in mid-March. They put on a fashion show in early April and had a business meeting and election of new officers in late May. The final event was a Spring Fling Dinner-Dance in early June. The first parent activities were largely planned by the school-community relations worker and the social worker. The Spring Fling Dinner-Dance was planned and carried out almost entirely by the parents. This transfer of leadership and responsibility was planned at the beginning of the fourth year.

Parents gained the knowledge and skills to implement these programs through alternate week workshops. One week the presenters focused on child development and academic subjects and the following week on parent program planning. The former took place during the workshop designated the "Coffee and Conversation Hour." The latter took place during the "Parent Advisory Board Meetings." Because we discontinued our Baldwin School program after the first five years, I will discuss only the King parent program here.

Over the course of the fourth program year twenty Coffee Hours were held at King. The social worker, the community relations worker and several core group parents organized these sessions. All parents were notified through mimeographed notes sent home a few days before each session.

Videotapes of classroom visits were shown twice. Twice parents made actual observations in classrooms with follow-up discussions. There were twelve sessions devoted to the academic subject matter—reading, math, language arts, and creative arts. The King teachers volunteered to conduct these workshops. The workshops were designed to give parents a simulation of the child's experience. I conducted the two sessions on child development and child rearing. At two sessions parents studied a guide developed by the social worker, the assistant to the principal, and to a lesser extent the parents, themselves, entitled, "A Parent's Guide to Children's Learning." This guide directly addressed the most frequent request of the parents: help us become informed observers of school operations so that we may better serve in governance capacities.

This is the Table of Contents of the guide.

WHAT TO LOOK FOR AND CONSIDER WHEN OBSERVING IN A CLASSROOM

    I. TEACHING
        (a) What is being taught (what subject) while you are there?
        (b) Does it appear to be meaningful?
        (c) Are the children attentive and interested?

(d) Put yourself in the position of a child—are you interested in the lesson?

(e) Are the directions clear?

(f) Are the children carrying out the tasks assigned?

(g) Does the activity of the children appear purposeful?

(h) Are the children able to work independently when the teacher is working with another group?

(i) Transition periods—do the children move smoothly from one activity to another?

II. CHILDREN'S ATTITUDES TOWARD ONE ANOTHER

(a) How much are children able to initiate activity on their own?

(b) How much independent activity is there in the classroom?

(c) Do the children appear to like and respect one another?

(d) Do they appear interested in what is going on?

(e) Do they disrupt the teacher?

III. DISCIPLINE

(a) Does the teacher assume his or her role as a leader?

(b) How does the teacher handle disruptive incidents?

(c) Are the rules for the class clear?

(d) Are they expressed in positive terms?—It is better to tell children what they should do, rather than what they should not do. Example: "Write the paper neatly" is a better approach than "Don't do sloppy work."

(e) How does the teacher handle incidental learning—that is, answering questions asked by the children?

IV. GENERAL APPEARANCE OF THE ROOM

(a) The classroom should be set up in terms of convenience for the children in order to create the most efficient learning environment. Check lighting, seating arrangement, condition of equipment.

(b) Are there materials for creative use as well as materials for intellectual development?

(c) Are supplies being well used?

(d) Bulletin boards—are they attractive? What do they display? Are they varied—children's work, teacher made etc.?

(e) Chalkboards—does the handwriting display good standards of penmanship and manuscript?

(f) Is there a reading area with a good supply of books? Are there other interest centers such as social studies and science?

IF YOU QUESTION SOMETHING, ASK THE TEACHER ABOUT IT BEFORE MAKING A JUDGMENT. ALWAYS ASK FOR THE REASON WHY SOMETHING IS DONE A GIVEN WAY.

A rating scale using the "yes, somewhat, no" continuum, enabled parents to evaluate a classroom and teacher. Other parts of the guide instructed parents on how to understand and make the most of conferences with teachers and how to help the children at home. The teaching staff gave its full support as the guide was written and many of the questions and suggestions in it were supplied by them. These parts of the guide reflect the values and methods of the King teaching staff and are as follows:

WHAT TO ASK AT A CONFERENCE WITH YOUR
CHILD'S TEACHER

Every parent should make a point of seeing each of his children's teachers for a conference at least once during the school year. Parents should call and ask for a conference *at any time* they have a question about how their child is learning when they suspect problems, etc. If the teacher sees a problem first, he will call you; if you see a problem first, it is your responsibility to call the teacher.

I. Academic progress

(a) Reading—ask to see your child's reading book, workbook and other reading materials. Ask what grade level your child is currently reading on, as well as what grade level he was reading on at the beginning of the year. For example, a child may be in second grade and reading at first grade level. If he could not read at all when he came into second grade, this may be good progress; if he was able to read at first grade level in September and has not progressed, the child is having difficulty which should be looked into. You may ask to have your child evaluated by the reading teacher if you and the teacher feel he is not progressing. What areas of reading are most difficult for your child—i.e., sounding out new words, comprehension, oral reading, etc.

(b) Math—ask what is currently being taught in math and HOW it is being taught. There are many methods of teaching math; you must be aware of what method is being used with your child so that you can help him at home. Ask to see math books, worksheets, etc. that are being used. Ask what kinds of concepts your child grasps easily and what kinds of concepts he has trouble with.

(c) Social studies and science—ask what is currently being taught; are there enrichment activities your child could do at home. For example, if your child is having a social studies unit on "Families Around the World," you might help him clip pictures from magazines, etc. Ask the teacher about this.

(d) Spelling—ask how spelling is being taught—is spelling tested regularly—ask for a rundown of your child's scores. Should your child be reviewing words at home?

(e) Testing—ask what testing has been done on your child —both teacher made and standardized. Ask what the grade level scores were, and also what areas showed deficiencies. Ask if Metropolitan Testing has ever been done on your child and if so, what scores he achieved. Ask the teacher to explain what these scores mean.

II. Child Emotional and Social Adjustment

(a) What is my child's feeling about himself? Does he appear to view himself as a learner in the class? How does he get along with the other children in the class?

(b) Is my child responsible—does he follow directions— what social areas are most difficult for my child?

(c) What do you do when my child misbehaves? What measures are most effective? What methods are least effective with my child?

(d) What could I do at home to help my child?

Remember: To say that a child is "doing fine" does not tell you anything. What does doing fine mean? In order to help your child you must get a complete *objective* picture, and not vague generalities.

WHAT YOU CAN DO TO HELP YOUR CHILD AT HOME

In order to help your child get the most from his school experience, it is important that he know from you each and every day that education is important and highly valued by you. You must demonstrate to your child your concern about his school career by:

(a) Each day when your child comes home from school ask him about what he did that day. Did a special teacher come to your class (i.e., music, language, etc.). Ask your child to tell you about it. Your child may at first answer "nothing special" but will begin to give more information as he notes your consistent concern.

(b) Each day ask to see your child's papers and any no- ·tices from school. Go thru the papers with your child. Your child's papers are an extension of himself— something that he made. If you throw them aside, your child hears, "my parent isn't interested in what I do." Look at each paper—have your child do over papers where he has made many mistakes—hang the good papers on a bulletin board, on the back of the door, on the refrigerator—pick a place for school papers to be displayed. Put a star or a sticker on good papers.

(c) Have a quiet time each day when the children sit down to do their homework. This can be between ten and thirty minutes, depending on the age of the child. During this time TV is OFF.

(d) A child must get proper rest in order to function in school. Even if your child does not fall asleep right away, it is better for him to rest in bed than to be up and about late at night. Suggested bedtimes are as follows:

> Kindergarten and grade 1—7:00
> Grades 2 and 3—7:30
> Grade 4—8:00

Before your child goes to bed, try to take a minute or two to talk to him. Tell him a story or ask him to read to you. This is reassuring to him.

(e) You take charge of the TV and decide what your children will watch. Children should not be allowed to watch adult movies, programs about murder and violence, and programs where good standards are not presented. Watch TV with your child—think—"Is this something I really want my child to see."

(f) Use the newspaper and magazines with your child. When he is in the primary grades, let him cut out pictures—for example, ask him to cut out pictures that begin with "A," "B," etc. Look thru the magazines with him—ask him to count how many cars, babies, houses, etc. he can find. Use the large print to help your child learn letters. Ask him to draw a circle around all the letter "A's" etc. on a given page. Later, ask him to cut out the words he knows—let him put them together to make sentences, his own studies, etc.

(g) Each child needs a place that he can call his own and where he can keep his things. This can be a carton, a drawer, etc. It is important that it be a place where younger brothers and sisters cannot reach to tear up a child's possessions.

(h) All things for school should be assembled the night before—this includes homework, notes, etc. This will avoid confusion in the morning.

(i) It is important that your child leave for school in a good frame of mind. Each child should have a routine to follow in the morning that is the same every day. For example, get dressed, get washed, make bed, eat breakfast. Children must eat in the morning before leaving for school. Breakfast need not be an elaborate affair—peanut butter on toast and milk, or cereal and juice, or a glass of "Instant Breakfast" and toast is fine. If children come to school hungry and irritable, they will not be able to function. *We all have bad mornings!* If things have not gone well—if there has been a crisis at home—if you ran late and couldn't get breakfast—*call the school or write.* Note: Let the school know so that we can help your child BEFORE he gets into difficulty. In an emergency, we will get your child breakfast, talk to him about a fight at home, etc. We will need to know from you when your child needs help.

(j) Come to school as often as you can. Wednesday is parent day at King School. Coffee hours, which are parent-interest educational seminars, are held on the first and third Wednesday of every month. Parent Advisory Sessions are held the second and fourth Wednesdays. The door is always open. Feel free to call the school or drop by at any time. Voice your questions and concerns. When your child sees you at school, he knows you care about his education and about him.

Attendance at the coffee hours averaged thirty parents per meeting with as many as fifty-five at one and as few as fifteen at one session. Attendance was lower after school vacations when the routine was broken. It was the highest for direct classroom observations and when videotapes of classroom activities were shown. Attendance varied with weather conditions. (Incidentally, we contracted for videotaping because we used tapes only occasionally and therefore did not need to buy expensive equipment.)

During the fourth year, an external evaluation team questioned levels of parent participation even though parents were increasing leadership activities. The consultants felt that too few parents were involved. At first we were concerned and defensive. Then we realized that our parent participation pattern was consistent with what one sees in all institutions, participation at several levels of involvement and responsibility. The social workers studied our parent participation program and began to identify a three-level pattern. It had already occurred but was easier to facilitate once there was a conscious appreciation of the reasons and the process.

At the first level approximately 1 to 5 percent of the parents worked with the staff in making curriculum and operation policy determinations. The second level is where parents participated in the day-to-day life of the school. About 10 to 25 percent are involved here. The third was the broad-based activities of the school which involved 50 to 100 percent of the parents.

At level three, parent participation was in activities such as general business meetings, fund raising, attending special events such as dinner dances and suppers, attending report-card conferences, and other conferences with staff. Parents who did not have the time or inclination, or were not comfortable working elsewhere, participated at this level because they felt good about the school staff and because they had some real sense that their children were benefiting from the school program. Many started their school involvement here and eventually became more involved at this or another level.

The parent-staff workshops and room-mother activities were some of the ways parents were involved in the level two day-to-day life of the school. Parents have also done volunteer work in classrooms, the lunchroom, library, and playground. Some have worked as tutors, made talent or interest presentations in classrooms, worked on special classroom projects, accompanied classrooms on field trips, and worked with the Mental Health Team on projects for children in need of special experiences. This group of parents form the core of parent strength. Again, at Baldwin, the Parent Interest Group and the Parent-Teacher Association, and at King, the Parent Advisory Board and the Parent-Teacher Power Team were the organizations sponsoring participation at this level. Leaders emerge from this middle level to serve at level one in governance capacities.

The governance committees planned, implemented, and evaluated total school activities although particular programs were delegated to and carried out by other groups. Parents elected from their own organization served on these committees with staff. This is the most influential level of parent participation. The parents working on governance matters with staff still work directly or very closely with the parent organization.

Through these arrangements parents are able to participate where they are capable and comfortable, and change as their needs and desires dictate. By the fourth year it was no longer necessary to tamper with democracy. There was a positive enough relationship with the staff and enough of an investment in program outcome so that parents selected their representatives for governance committees on the basis of ability and program needs rather than a need to play power games with the staff. They were interested in selecting parents who would represent their interests without confrontation.

Because of uncertainty about our future, the parent participation program floundered again about the middle of the fifth
program year. It was again revitalized when program direction
was established in the seventh year. The greater integration of
the program into the life of the school will be described after I
have described teaching and curriculum programs and related
innovations. But some questions remain regarding parent participation and will be addressed here.

Does a school staff have time to work with parents in this way
and teach children as well?

First, it does not take long. The King social worker recently
pointed out that the now traditional Spring Fling took one hour to
plan last year. Several years ago it took one hour to decide what
kind of plates they should use for this program. Second, the organization and planning skills parents acquire are as important,
possibly more important, to the future education and achievement of their children as the academic skills teachers are so concerned about.

Children who are able to maintain their interest in school, future training programs, and work are more often those from families where people are able to plan and organize their lives to
solve problems and bring off one successful endeavor or project
after another—hold a job, spend wisely, pay bills—and thereby
prevent disruptive and harmful social consequences in their
lives. Parents who have such skills are able to pass them on to
their children.

Often, low-income parents give their children every other
thing they need for successful participation in school and the
world of work except the planning and organizing skills and habit patterns needed to operate in complex settings. Many intelligent and able college students from low-income backgrounds
confront these deficits when faced with a heavy assignment load.
In fact they often fail in disproportionate numbers because such
skills and patterns have not been acquired. These patterns are
best acquired at an early age and need to be quite well developed
by late elementary school or twelve or thirteen years of age.

It is not unusual to find young people from low-income backgrounds trying to plan programs in one month which in fact take
six months to a year to plan. Such programs are doomed to failure or minimal success. They lead to frustration and a sense of

inadequacy. Jealousy and anger develop toward persons able to pull off a similar affair with apparent ease although they do not appear any more intelligent. Such feelings and frustrations often lead to dropping out of school and work programs and the loss of talented people who are able but who lack the necessary discipline, planning, organizing, or social skills and habit patterns.

Rather than considering work with parents an extra burden, schools should think of it as an opportunity to educate students and parents at the same time. A school has an opportunity to help children learn in the classroom when it helps parents develop skills. A frequent lament is that "we have them only a few hours." Helping parents help their children holds the potential of being a better mechanism for adult education than the current approaches being used in which adults must admit to deficits in seeking to improve their basic educational skills. In current adult education programs, the motivation is low unless a job is at stake. This is not the case when they are working to help their children.

Several parents in the Baldwin-King program began to help their children and were motivated to return to school themselves. One parent became involved because another encouraged her to do so. Prior to that time she had been depressed and had felt that her life was without direction. Within a year's time she became a leader in the school program, a leader in her church, and, most recently, she received a B.S. in social work. Others became mobilized, acquired confidence, and secured jobs they never before dreamed they could obtain and hold.

It is true that as low-income parents learn more about the goals and operation of schools, they begin to ask more pointed questions about school problems. Some do so from the beginning, but as two or three raising questions they are often "crying in the wilderness." As an organized nucleus of parents, they can effectively confront a school administrator. This is one of the reasons that so many school administrators would rather not have parents deeply involved in governance and school management issues.[4]

But as we know, we are in a new era. Even the poor are better educated, less intimidated by persons of prestige and authority, better represented by community change groups when necessary. It is far better that parents and school administrators identify and address problems together than for school officials to resist and be forced into embarrassing and educationally unsound positions and programs by adversary groups—where too often the interest is more in victory and advancement of the group leaders than in the best interests of children.

9
Teachers, Teaching, and Curriculum

The key goal of our teaching and curriculum development program was to significantly raise the reading and mathematics achievement levels of students in Baldwin and King Schools. Also we wanted to develop a curriculum that would motivate students to learn for the satisfaction of learning, mastery, and achievement and not just to raise their achievement test scores. At the same time, we wanted a curriculum that would motivate students to aspire toward demanding occupations and give them the basic academic skills to have a realistic chance of achieving the occupations to which they aspired. Toward this end, we held a corollary objective, which was to motivate teachers so they would assist in meeting these academic objectives.

We believed that such programs take place in social climates in which school staff, parents, and students believe in and have hope for themselves and each other. Such a climate usually does not exist *a priori* in low-income, minority communities.[1] There are too few economic and constructive social opportunities to create such conditions naturally. They must be *created*, and the teaching and curriculum development program was one part of the mix. The teaching and curriculum development program, including the arts and athletics, had to be integrated with parent participation, mental health, and the constructive social climate development programs.

Given the depressed attitude and skills of school staff in settings with little hope, it was necessary to stimulate hope before they could move efficiently and effectively toward self- and curriculum development. We believed that teachers so stimulated could then move—or be assisted—toward levels of competence they did not believe they had; toward levels of student social and academic behavior that teachers, parents, and students alike did not believe possible. Our program leadership's task was to facilitate such movement.

Change of this nature is difficult. It requires an academic leader with good understanding of the principles of teaching and learning, a fine appreciation of human strengths and weaknesses, and good management skills.[2] It also requires a good sense of timing and a bit of luck. But most of all it requires perseverence and a process development on which the next step can be firmly based. The ultimate goal of this process was to develop a skill-sequenced program in which basic skills were obtained without crushing creative and learning excitement.

There are ready-made skill-sequenced programs. But we believe that it is important for a staff to go through the process of identifying teaching and learning needs and resources, developing and implementing programs. If the staff does not participate in such a process, it is possible to teach to a mythical norm, judge too many to be inadequate, and miss the potential for moving each student along from wherever he or she is to whatever level he or she is capable of achieving at appropriate rates.

Our teaching and curriculum development program moved more slowly and with more ups and downs than did our Parent Participation Program. In the fourth program year, outside evaluators found that the academic program did not measure up to the excellent social and psychological climate that had been established in the school. There were many reasons for this. One

was that the presence of a Mental Health Team focusing on relationships and social climate in the absence of a similar education
group focusing on teaching and curriculum development distorted program emphasis. But this was not by design.

In the initial proposal Dr. Solnit spelled out the role which he
felt was appropriate for the Mental Health Team from the Child
Study Center to play in the teaching and curriculum development
areas:

> The Child Study Center is prepared to contribute in a sustained
> and systematic manner to the establishment of a new model in
> which the knowledge and experience of clinical specialists in child
> development, especially in child psychiatry and social work, are in-
> tegrated into the educational programs of schools . . . Clinical
> theory and child development can be translated and applied as
> part of sound pedagogy when it is integrated into an in-service
> training program in which the questions, discussions, and solutions
> are related to every-day teaching problems and to principles of
> education.[3]

As I described in an earlier chapter, our plans for educational leadership did not materialize during the first year. In the second program year, the project coordinator took responsibility for
organizing the teaching and curriculum development program.
Dr. Carol, the curriculum specialist from the first year, was to
work as an educational generalist under the direction of the coordinator and lead subject area specialists and teachers. Dr.
Carol's efforts began with summer workshops between the first
and second year in which resource persons presented parents
and staff with educational objectives and methods. The hope was
that parents and staff could then help select appropriate text-
books and prepare to work together to improve the curriculum
and teaching program.

Because of heavy teacher turnover after the first year, many
in the workshops were new to the schools. The parents had had
confrontation experience but little collaborative experience. One
principal was new to the school system, and the other was just
recovering from a long illness. Learning how to make educational
choices and to implement educational objectives is a very complex task. We simply had not reached the stage of program operation or parent and staff development to manage such a complex
problem. Thus the workshops served to improve relationships between parents and staff but did not help to improve the curri-

culum or teaching program. In addition, the notion of "teacher autonomy" had grown very strong during the first year of the program and had been presented as an important feature of our program in the recruitment of new teachers.

The notion of teacher autonomy was a shorthand prescription to remedy the fact that the classroom teacher is on the front line dealing with problems and opportunities on a day-to-day basis; nobody seems to pay too much attention to what he or she has to say about curriculum, school organization and procedures. Yet teachers are often blamed when students fail. In fact, when teachers participate in curriculum planning they are too often expected to rubber stamp the viewpoints of superiors.

It appeared to me that this situation must stifle teacher interest in analyzing learning difficulties of particular children and developing creative ways to present material. I felt that this was part of the reason that some teachers become bored, lose their imagination and excitement, and become listless especially when the children, parents, and administrators all appear to be in a conspiracy, in one way or another, to promote teacher failure. I concluded that teacher powerlessness was more the problem than ineffective teaching methods or negative attitudes.

I shared my opinions with many Baldwin-King teachers, and they seemed to be attracted to this notion. But what I either did not communicate clearly to teachers or they did not hear clearly was that there should be an initial period during which teachers learn and share impressions about student needs, try various kinds of programs devised by teachers and educational specialists, and then adopt a flexible but relatively uniform consensus approach to curriculum and teaching. I envisioned that every teacher would be required to show how his or her curriculum and teaching approach was consistent with the assessed student needs and goals of the Baldwin-King Program and the New Haven School System at large. Commitment to teacher autonomy made many teachers less receptive to ideas presented by the curriculum specialist and the subject area supervisors.

Nonetheless, in the summer workshops before the second year, the new program coordinator worked with most of the teachers, many parents, the principals and Child Study Center staff members (one being the curriculum specialist) to write a combined faculty, curriculum, and parent guide for the Baldwin-King project professional staff.

The major curriculum concerns listed were to be as follows:

1. To teach basic skills through a curriculum that is reality-centered and relevant
2. To teach pride in belonging
3. To teach pride in contributing
4. To affirm difference
5. To enrich through diversity

But once the second year started, I sensed that most teachers were going their own way without going through a process of learning about and identifying student needs, without developing programs based on their knowledge. The curriculum was fragmented and inconsistent. For example, classroom texts were being used in the Baldwin-King schools that were not being used in other New Haven schools. When children from our program transferred to another school they were sometimes at a disadvantage. At one point we had a departmental rather than self-contained classroom arrangement at the fifth and sixth-grade level. This required movement between classes and was a source of much disruptive student behavior. At the same time, we were developing a program that would allow children to remain with the same teacher for two years; our objective was to increase continuity. The departmental program arrangement—with a different teacher for each subject—broke continuity.

The curriculum specialist whom we had hoped would give leadership to the Teacher and Curriculum Development Program favored a discovery approach to learning. The coordinator and I agreed with her assumptions, although I tried to stay out of the teacher and curriculum development side of the program except to provide Mental Health Team support to whatever was developed by those responsible. Unfortunately, discovery education sounds nebulous and unrealistic to those who have never been involved in the challenging process of designing it. For teachers— with parents, supervisors and administrators looking for results —these notions are nice, "but how about teaching children how to read and count—with no delay!"

To be comfortable with the discovery approach, teachers needed specific demonstrations of how to teach basic academic skills while at the same time using the local environment to stimulate inquiry—to turn children on to learning. Although the educational generalist articulated her philosophy and gave demonstrations, the faculty did not hear or see the specific methods. It was all too new as an idea to put into practice that quickly. Of the consultant one teacher said, "She never put out a clear philosophy. Math was her main thing. I think her plan was to start with math and go from there. We had several math workshops which were very helpful and after that she would just come in the room and kind of sit and listen, which did nothing for anybody. Theresa [a teacher] told her that if she was going to come in, she should do something with the children. After that we had some more workshops, but there was never any clear-cut math philosophy. We [teachers] couldn't figure out where she was going or wanted us to go—putting a yardstick over a waste basket, a ball on top of blocks. I didn't know what she was doing."

The curriculum specialist was in fact a very experienced and competent person, but the climate of trust, cooperation, and sharing had not been adequately established. There were still too many questions in the air. Was she from Yale? The New Haven School System? The Baldwin-King subunit of the school system? And her authority was not clearly identifiable. She was a college professor. What did she think about public school teachers? She was in the program the previous year. Was she part of the open-classroom and "progressive" thinkers of the first year?

The teachers who were confused by the specialist were the teachers who had to give the children the basic academic skills they missed during the first year. One reported, "I called a reading group up and you'd never believe it. They couldn't even hold a book, not to mention holding a place in it. You had to teach the most basic skills!" An educational specialist (and all of our area specialists) were suspect, even though in my judgment the problem was not their fault at all.

A necessary but troublesome trade-off probably contributed to the doubts, fears, and resistance. As previously mentioned, in order to overcome some of the first year problems as quickly as possible, the coordinator was granted permission to make a number of personnel and program changes without Steering Committee approval. Although this initial arrangement was agreeable, an underlying concern among the staff about who should be and who really was making the final decisions was always present.

Although teachers made contributions to the development of the "Program and Curriculum Guide," some did not think of it as their document because the coordinator had written it.

During the first and second years the various academic specialists attempted to develop programs in their respective areas. It was hoped that the classroom teachers would increase their own skills in these areas through collaborative work with the specialists. But the overall educational leadership role in the school was confused and, as a result, good teacher-specialist collaboration never developed. The in-service meetings for these purposes conducted by different specialists often turned into gripe sessions, more in the first year than in the second. The specialists often felt they were not receiving enough guidance and support from the educational generalist, the coordinator, and principals. They were trying. But even in the second year they still had to attend to many problems related to maintaining the stability of the schools, and thus of higher priority.

To clarify and resolve the educational leadership confusion and conflict, the coordinator assumed full educational leadership responsibility. This was a temporary arrangement and could not substantially help the various educational specialists and teachers because he was not an elementary school curriculum or teaching specialist. He developed a number of programs to permit independent individual teacher development. I will describe these later. With this approach, some teachers flourished and some floundered. Some felt empowered and some felt powerless. This uneven response was one reason the academic program became fragmented and without clear direction.

It became clear that the academic program needed coordination and integration more than in-depth concentration in specific area—mathematics, reading, social sciences, and music. Through transfer and resignation, the curriculum specialist (educational generalist) and most of the academic area specialists left the program after the second year. We were unable to find another experienced educational generalist until the fifth and final year.

A psychologist new to the program in the third year had had experience helping teachers identify their objectives in working out curriculum and teaching approaches, and she provided some assistance. In an effort to promote coordination and integration she worked with teachers in curriculum development meetings at grade levels K-2, 3-4, and 5-6. Again we faced the problem of several new people trying to adjust to and work with persons from a previous year. But this time the teachers were more established, and the support and helping staff were new. Not knowing each other well and being from different disciplines, the classroom teachers, reading disability teachers, and psychologist sometimes talked past each other. This situation is not unusual when persons of different disciplines try to work together. Again the problem was that trust had not been firmly established. For example, the psychologist singled out one teacher's open style and attitude as the essential ingredient of an open classroom, although her room did not have all the physical signs of an open classroom. The teacher initially heard it as a criticism for not having an open classroom.

Other school problems: a weak teacher anxiously taking over grade level in-service sessions with her problems; different needs between Baldwin and King; a specialist in the arts who did not work out. Such situations precluded the possibility that the in-service grade level curriculum and teacher development meetings could achieve as much as they might have. Yet progress *was* being made.

Later in the year, the same teacher who had felt criticized by the psychologist said, "I'm less of a frontal teacher [directing activities from the front of the room] now than I was when I first came to the program." The teacher went on to point out that until the psychologist had commented on her teaching, it had not occurred to her that she was changing her style. She also gave the probable source of her misunderstanding when she added, "When you are insecure, you don't like people criticizing." This was an excellent, veteran teacher. But teachers, experienced and inexperienced, talented or just hard working, all feel vulnerable in a change process.

In the third year the coordinator, now a co-director, met with me and the two principals on a weekly basis, discussing the curriculum and teacher development program. He was also meeting with each grade level group. The psychologist also met with the grade level groups. Teachers were being encouraged to visit neighboring schools, private schools, and each other. The purpose of these visits was to permit teachers to develop a wider perspective and to see other teachers doing some things well and other things not so well.

We believed that observing in other classrooms would stimulate the teachers to think about their own objectives and achievement strategies and to discuss them during in-service meetings in our schools. But as one teacher said, "When they suggested that I visit somebody in particular, I couldn't help but feel criticized." Another teacher pointed out a problem. "The whole thing of visiting different people with different philosophies, open vs. traditional . . . you began to wonder who is right and who is wrong and how should I teach—it's like not having anything to stand on!"

Looking at the options, making choices, and then actually changing often results in disequilibrium. Unless the whole process is skillfully managed by a master teacher with broad-based training, a good understanding of human weaknesses, and an ability to identify and promote strengths, the process can be painful for those being asked to change. Nobody in the leadership group considered herself or himself to be the kind of curriculum and teacher development specialist that we all agreed was needed.

We began to think about another possibility. We had hoped that we might become a kind of research and development unit for the entire school system. We held several meetings with the school superintendent (the same one who had, as an assistant superintendent, helped us to solve some serious problems during the first year), central office pupil personnel staff, and other central office administrators regarding our interests. As a first step, during our fourth year the system-wide academic specialty supervisors were invited to provide workshops for the Baldwin-King staff members. We hoped that this would improve relationships between our subsystem and the central administration, provide leadership to teachers as they worked on curriculum changes and self-development, lead to better coordination of the academic program at Baldwin-King, and the incorporation of useful ideas and approaches into the larger system program.

The initial workshops by the several supervisors were exciting and successful. But the realities of an urban school system began to create problems. Due to emergency and general logistical problems, workshops were often late or missed, and teachers were disappointed. Some of the same problems we had had when we had our own area specialists within the program came up with area specialist supervisors from the central office. Going beyond introductory workshops would have required an interaction between teachers and the supervisors that was more than anyone had anticipated. At that time, which was our fourth program year, the central administration was experiencing a number of problems and personnel changes which claimed higher priority than trying to relate to, integrate, or incorporate the Baldwin-King program.

It was clear that the arrangement with the supervisors was not going to move the Baldwin-King curriculum and teaching efforts toward the goal of a skill-sequenced program with integration of the arts, mental health, and parent programs, although I think it did establish better communication among the members of program staff and school system personnel. During this period the issue of the selection of texts was resolved. The staff and the reading supervisor discussed this problem and felt that in general it was not fair to the children to have a reading textbook—or any basic text—that was different from the ones being used in the rest of the system if the difference was sufficiently great to create discontinuity, frustration, and failure on transfer to another school. The arrangement with the supervisors was discontinued, and we continued to look for an educational leader who could aid curriculum and staff development.

In the meantime, change did take place, side by side with efforts to be more in step with the larger system's academic program. We were trying to strike a balance—adequate attention to the teaching of basic academic skills, use of texts and materials which would help children acquire these skills in step with other children in the system, and, at the same time, permit teachers to use new materials and styles wherever it appeared possible and appropriate. Again the idea was to find ways to help children acquire basic skills as they became active learners.

Innovation was encouraged in a number of ways. As mentioned, the co-director developed an arrangement in which teachers could write up a proposal and, if approved, obtain money for special classroom-based projects. They had to demonstrate how the project would achieve their objectives and that the project activities were in keeping with their teaching strategies. Other teachers, who served on the project review committee, sometimes helped to modify or improve a proposal. One of the drawbacks, of course, was that a lot of time was allocated to too many committees! As one teacher said, "Sometimes we were so saturated with meetings you would say yes to most anything."

Some teachers developed innovative approaches on their own. When initiating major changes, they worked with the principals and consultants. In the fourth year, two teachers at King—a man who worked more with the boys and a woman who worked more with the girls—established a team teaching approach. At regularly scheduled times they worked together. They devised this approach because they believed that educational, social, and sexual development were interdependent and interrelated. They discussed the possible benefits and drawbacks with the principal, with me, and with other mental health consultants. Their arrangement appeared to reduce "showing off" among the boys and excessive antagonism among girls. Everyone could work in a less disruptive environment and have a more open classroom in both a physical and a psychological sense.

Two of our teachers worked with a Yale University instructor in developing what they called "Whole Earth," a social science curriculum. The objective was to enable children to see themselves in the context of the solar system, earth, other primates, human beings, and their local environment. The teachers planned related field trips and experiments. Projects, such as the construction and painting of models of the solar system, earth, and local neighborhoods, lent themselves nicely to the effort to integrate the arts into the academic subjects. Teachers participated in a related Yale seminar, and the thinking, planning, and evaluation required proved to be a good preparation for effective total staff involvement in the development of a curriculum.

In both schools, teachers were trying exciting projects. Children in one classroom built model African villages for social science assignments. With the assistance of their teacher and parents, they brought the black experience up to the present by preparing and serving a soul-food supper. All of the teachers emphasized Afro-American competence by supplying books, magazines, posters, and other materials about black achievers. One teacher taught language skills through drama. These efforts promoted self-esteem in the children as individuals, as members of the Afro-American community, and as citizens in a larger society. These efforts, like the "Whole Earth" curriculum, allowed some integration of the arts into the academic program.

While the academic area specialists had difficulty finding a niche, the arts specialists fared better, largely because the value and success of a specialist in this area is less threatening to the classroom teacher—and because our art teacher, Mary Boyle, was a very skilled consultant. Her way of working made the integration of the arts possible. During the first year our supplies were scarce, and those which were available were unequally distributed. Because in the past no strategies or objectives had been identified specifically for the arts program, the materials were being used randomly. As a first step, the art teacher/consultant collected all the available supplies and pooled them for distribution. In this way she could find out what teachers were interested in doing.

In addition, she began to visit classrooms and talk informally to teachers about the possible application of art to their various lessons. It was customary for many teachers to take a break when the art or music teacher took over. But she began to give demonstration lessons with the teacher present to help the classroom teachers see what was possible without specialized training or skill in art.

Her approach was first to discuss with the classroom teacher the strategies and goals of a demonstration art lesson. She would then discuss ways to structure and delineate the project in order to meet specific objectives.

With the students she would talk a little about art concepts like shape, color, and texture, using anything in the room to illustrate the points she needed to make. After most of the students were involved in a lesson—asking and responding to questions— she would give two or three sets of instructions and then leave them on their own, helping when asked or when students needed help in order to avoid embarrassing themselves or experiencing extreme and destructive failure.

As classroom teachers watched the demonstration, they began to think of ways they could use art to enhance their academic lessons. They learned new skills and gained confidence in their ability to handle art lessons alone. The art specialist assisted the teachers as they tried new approaches.

In the second program year, art, music, and dance operated as separate programs and were viewed largely as pleasant, relaxing, and entertaining experiences for the children, but not vital to the academic program. The colorful decorations and displays gave life and excitement to the school. The singing and dance programs gave pleasure to the children, parents, and

teachers. These programs enabled children to feel good about
what they were doing and to release pent-up energies in constructive activities. These activities and outcomes all helped to
improve the climate of the schools. But the systematic integration
of the arts into the academic program did not begin to take place
until the workshop before the third program year.

A committee of parents, teachers, and administrators planned
this workshop. They created a model open classroom where parents, teachers, and administrators participated as students.
They began to learn about a variety of available materials by using them. The mix of professional and nonprofessional people involved in common tasks in which there was not a great disparity
in knowledge or skill helped to break down barriers between
them. Parents made things they were proud of and came to appreciate what such learning and achievement did for their children. Some were delighted to see some of their own work on display or used in the classrooms the next year. Teachers learned to
make decisions about materials and ways of carrying out a project that reduced the chance of its failing in the classroom.

The workshop had five aspects—music, movement, creative
arts, reading and language arts, and math. Each participant attended two sessions each day. This was a hands-on experience in
which teachers, parents, and administrators learned by working
directly with materials and by implementing ideas. Each session
was built on activities and understandings of the previous day so
that the cumulative result was that participants acquired an in-
depth knowledge of a subject area and ways to apply that knowledge in curriculum planning.

The music program was further developed and meshed with
the academic programs during the summer. Participants learned
several music concepts first and then moved from making up simple rhythms to listening critically. The participants made and
played musical games and instruments; they used flash cards
and other materials that they were later able to use and enjoy
with their children in the classroom. As music and movement lessons merged, those not in good physical shape were surprised
and pleased to rediscover or discover for the first time the pleasure of exercise. The participants learned about the development of body and muscle control, poise, coordination, and
rhythm essential for good physical and mental development.

Our reading and language arts teachers, Willa Conquest and
Maye Edmonds, demonstrated many activities and teaching aids

that combined music, dance, and art with language and reading. A math consultant pointed out the possible blend of the arts with math—for example the potential application of mathematics concepts to carpentry, sewing, and ceramics.

A verse written by one of the parents reflects the value and tone of these sessions:

> Music, movement, art—math, reading.
> Everyone doing his part . . .
>
> Language arts, believe it or not,
> Is what brought on this silly what me not . . .
>
> Math—new math, 66 then 149,
> Counting base 7 will blow your mind . . .
>
> Afternoon session, who needs this?
> Hot, drowsy, cram again.
> Learning, hoping to achieve a better goal,
> For our children to get a firmer hold.
>
> *Thelma Thorpe*

The arts boomed after this workshop. Not all teachers participated in the workshop, nor did all of them highly value the arts. But as large and colorful papier mache solar systems, model African villages, and scale models of the neighborhood began to go on display, or were seen in use in various classrooms, more teachers became interested in what could be done with the arts. Several skeptics asked if the art teacher was not giving some teachers more time than others. She pointed out that, in fact, she was actually giving less time to those using the arts the most, simply helping them to think through what they wanted to accomplish and helping them to plan and organize the activity. More teachers began to integrate the arts into their teaching program. The art teacher was satisfied when most were planning their own programs and calling on her when they needed "just a little bit of help."

In programs since Baldwin-King, she has done even less demonstration. She stresses that she had to be "real honest" with teachers from the very beginning, to talk about what was right and what was wrong, what was their responsibility, what was her responsibility and how they felt about what they were doing. Obviously such openness, observation, and criticism has the best chance to survive in a climate of trust and mutual respect.

As a result of the arts and child development workshops, the teachers became very interested in developmental readiness; that is, the activities children are able to do or can be prepared to do at certain ages and stages. The art teacher said, "It wasn't until I was involved with people talking about child development that I saw the arts as a natural extension or critical bridge between their physical equipment and their ability to learn." The importance of the arts as an essential component of learning, and not just an add-on or frill, was beginning to become apparent.

Teachers who avoided areas such as science were less reluctant to tackle these subjects when they could anchor the abstract concepts in art projects. The application of other art forms to curriculum areas became apparent. Eventually students and teachers were writing their own classroom plays and performing them for other classes or the entire school. Some parents participated in these and other plays. One aide, the parent of a child in the school, played the lead role in *Hello Dolly* at Baldwin School. Handwriting, spelling, grammar, speech, and many other academic areas were taught in connection with these productions and other art activities.

The frenetic running and fighting of the early years gave way to relaxed hallways and bubbly children walking and talking. The arts played an important role in creating this climate.

The art teacher was named coordinator of the entire arts program after the second summer workshop. She brought in professional artists to teach dance, movement, and drama. The new adults widened the children's contact with people and activities outside their daily world. Because of the good atmosphere, adults and children were able to connect and grow.

Many adults in arts or enrichment programs designed to aid the social, psychological, or intellectual development of poor children are unable to do so because the environment is chaotic. In this case, we had prepared an environment in which the children could receive and benefit from the experience.

Teachers were sometime surprised to see children with short attention spans, who were usually apathetic or volatile in the classroom, concentrating and carrying out intricate dance movement routines or designing and carrying out complex art projects. These were the "oh, my God, how can you stand so and so?" children. Some teachers feel that such children willfully act up during an academic lesson but do not do so in the arts classes because arts lessons are fun and easy. Usually such children have not had the developmental experiences that permit interest, control, and concentration in academic areas. Participation in the arts can facilitate inner mental control and eventually permit concentration and interest in academic subject areas.

The arts can be useful in other ways. Children take in the world with all their senses—including touch. Some need to cut out a letter of the alphabet, make the letter with their bodies, see it big and see it small, feel the letter cut out of sandpaper, sing it, rhyme it, dance it, weigh it, taste it. Only then do they "own" the concept. Only then is it no longer abstract, something foreign that the teacher told them was an "A", something to be forgotten soon for too many children who are not able to handle abstract symbols and concepts.

We adults march right along in learning new material, filing it away in well-developed learning, storage, and retrieval machinery. But for many children, some more than others, the machinery is incomplete or seriously underdeveloped. For example, kindergarten teachers are often upset when children come to school and can only scribble. In one kindergarten classroom children were given crayons and asked to color a clown. About half scribbled with one color. As it turned out, the scribblers had used ballpoint pens or pencils before, but not crayons. They needed much work with colors, as well as hand and eye control, before taking on this task. But we press them to move along so that we can cover the five points and twenty-five pages in the manual which is required "before the twelfth of never."

Even after introductory work, many will need to color a clown or repeat a dance step or a phrase over and over until they master whatever the particular skill. A good teacher will move them along in the areas where they are ready and give them time to integrate new ideas where necessary. He or she will offer students support and assure them that they can move along, be a little neater, and perform a little better when they are frightened, stuck, excessively sloppy, or ambivalent.

Teachers were encouraged to present some exercises based in the arts to assist children with limited confidence. In the arts, pupils are not faced with absolute standards against which their work must be judged. Four minus two has an answer that can be marked right or wrong. But an original design can at most be judged pleasing or not. Children with moderately severe developmental lags can make up ground in the early years quickly and painlessly in a rich arts program—if the teacher knows how to use materials and projects for more than recreation. In addition, a child can take the arts in small doses, at his or her own pace, more readily than if the typical curriculum is the basis for skill development.

A very interesting and important occurrence was that teachers reported improved reading and math performance at the same time that an art problem was solved.

Art problems? You bet. The arts require many of the thinking, analytical, and problem solving skills required in academic subject areas. Painting, dancing, and writing start with feelings, involvement, and often kernels of ideas. Watch a child stand back from his or her painting, examine it and redo it, changing its color and shape. The change expresses more closely what the artist wanted it to say. Watch a child wipe a paint brush to have just the amount of paint needed, painstakingly mold clay, or perfect a dance step. Each of these activities requires problem solving. This involvement in problem solving is the bridge children travel to achieve manipulation of more abstract symbols and more complex problems.

The arts teacher often helped the classroom teachers learn to observe developmental lags and difficult tasks, and they worked with classroom teachers to design exercises that were intended to remediate problems. It is easier and more fun to learn left and right or the difference between a rectangle and a square in a game rather than in a book or on the blackboard. And the book and blackboard seem less abstract when the body has been through the motion of the concept in a game. When teachers can identify developmental lags and needs, they can find many casual opportunities to use the arts to help children gain various concepts—the curve of puffy clouds suggests a partial circle; rectangular sides of a house can be pointed out. At this point the arts and academics are one.

In giving attention to developmental issues, one must guard against overanalyzing or overinterpreting. On one occasion the art and classroom teachers observed one child painting with black paint only, going over and over the original painting. They immediately thought that the child was depressed or upset. But she did not look upset. They decided to observe. Finally they had to ask her what she was doing. As it turned out, because of the direction of the light that day, black was the color that she could best use to see the reflection of her face in the painting.

One of the most important benefits of the arts program was the opportunity for parents to have a role other than that of "disciplinarian" or academic tutor in a school program. Parents helped with the planning and organizing of arts programs both in the classroom and as part of the extracurricular activity program and participated in arts programs themselves. Often parents who had artistic hobbies and skills—knitting or painting for example—gave demonstrations in the classrooms. As mentioned, the opportunity to participate and contribute outside of the academic area is particularly important in communities where many parents are uneasy about the level of their own skills.

The art specialist has a theory about community decay that is subjective and therefore difficult to evaluate, but it is certainly worth thinking about. She believes that where aesthetic concerns or interests do not exist, people are more willing to tolerate decay. While hopelessness, apathy, and depression—most often in response to poverty or near-poverty—are factors, I suspect her notion is meritorious. She pointed out that a work-study program was recently developed in New Haven in which children participated in the arts rather than make-work activity. The youngsters were paid to create an all-city marching band, an all-city choir, and to paint murals around the city. They took great pride in their achievements, a pride which, if reinforced, can bolster their concern about the appearance of their home and neighborhoods.

Because of the fine results achieved when we introduced an arts program to which our staff was truly committed, I am troubled by the continuous cutbacks in art and athletics, both in middle-class and low-income school systems. Few jobs are totally exhausting. Few jobs allow one to produce a complete and beneficial product in a short period of time. The arts and athletics represent areas where people can still receive a sense of accomplishment once received from work. The arts are humanizing and helpful, if not necessary, in an age where so many of the effects of technology are dehumanizing. We believe, in fact, that the arts (and probably athletics) are the lifelines to higher levels of academic, social, and psychological development for children of low-income families, and one of the ways to build bridges out of the devastating cycle of poverty and undereducation.

In the latter half of our fourth year, an impressive educational generalist, Rex Harris, who was directing a teacher support program in town, was asked to work with us. We invited him to participate in the summer workshops between the fourth and fifth program year. The workshops were structured as open classrooms, and again parents and teachers participated as students. Rex helped the principals and coordinators structure this program and led the math workshops.

Teachers commented on that summer program:

> They were the best workshops we ever had. They really were excellent . . . tri-wall construction, building bookcases, math sessions. . . . I don't think he was trying to push any particular philosophy. . . . I think he was just trying to upgrade the way we did everything. We had gotten to the point that the building was contained, and good things were happening, children weren't at loose ends and we liked each other. I remember thinking, "This is our year, we're going to go!" I think Rex's [the educational generalist] job was to get us to reach higher, develop a higher sense of what was possible.
>
> "He was low key . . . not a brow-beater . . . not threatening. He made you feel comfortable, even if you were poor in a subject area. He worked in a way to help you see that you had competency; that you just needed to elevate yourself a little more. I remember the workshop in math, base eight and two, base seven, things that I had never heard of. If you sat next to someone bright, they would want to do your work. He'd say, "She can do it herself." He was just good . . . low-keyed . . . gave you confidence.

I do not want to minimize the ability of the educational leader, yet I should point out that by this time conditions in the school were very stable. This permitted greater teacher receptivity and creativity.

During the year following this exciting summer, Rex arranged to work with the Baldwin-King program on a half-time basis. He worked with several members of our faculty to develop a model for a competency-based accreditation procedure being discussed at the state level. The objective was to determine what children should learn at every grade level in every subject area, develop a related teaching program, and a pre- and post-test program based on what was taught. This was the kind of rigorous analysis, goal-setting, teaching strategy within an open, innovative environment we had hoped to establish from the beginning of our program.

In a memorandum to the staff, Rex wrote:

> In all my years of working in elementary schools, I have never observed greater concern for children . . . and more energies directed toward the solution of social/emotional problems than at Baldwin-King. . . . The staff's clarity and understanding of the social and psychological expectations and needs of each child did not come about quickly or by chance. It required great effort, much time, competent people and a very clear plan for development and implementation. The achievement of the same degree of clarity and understanding of the instructional objectives will also require time, committed people and a well-thought-out plan for communication, development and implementation.

He pointed to several programs elsewhere in the country that had competently implemented instructional objectives for elementary school children. The common components of all these programs were to (1) state instructional objectives clearly; (2) utilize diagnostic instruments to assess student progress, the area and kind of learning difficulty a child has, and for program evaluation; (3) develop or utilize existing learning activities and curriculum materials related to the stated instructional objectives; and (4) record-keeping and feedback to children. In addition, careful organization and matching of teachers, children, and program were cited as important, as well as careful scheduling of the instructional content of a school day based on a rationale developed and shared by the staff. Rex reminded the staff: "The degree of success (of any instructional program) has often been more related to the process utilized, the degree of staff involvement and the level of 'gut' commitment than to a particular model."

Awareness that process is equal to or more important than content and method marked a turning point for many of our teachers. The process we began was, as most important processes are, actually built on all previous efforts. We appointed a language development committee and a motor (movement) development committee for each school. The principal from Baldwin was to head one committee and the principal from King the other. Each committee was composed of teachers and parents from both schools.

At this point, our fifth programmatic year, the educational program took a most promising turn. Unfortunately the Teacher and Curriculum Development program did not take the quantum leap we had all hoped for because the educational leader got caught trying to resolve growing differences in philosophy and style between two groups of staff and parents at Baldwin.

The delay eventually led to some teacher disappointment. This manifested itself in some unhappiness with Rex's rough outline of an approach to academic skill development. The outline was to be a guide for more discussion in which teachers would make a significant input. It was perceived by some as "the last word." Nonetheless, considerable progress in teacher and curriculum development was made. His work with the staff went into high gear in some very exciting summer sessions after the fifth program year. It stopped abruptly. Because of problems outside our program, he took an attractive job out of the area. Our inability to secure and hold an educational leader points up the perilous nature of school change projects. "The best laid plans. . . ."

Nevertheless, significant gains were made over the five years, although we were a long way from meeting our teaching and curriculum goals. The staff was energetic, hopeful, and reasonably respectful of one another. A teacher strike the next year brought bitterness to the city and divided our staff. Three or four years earlier it would have destroyed the program completely. But because of the level of hope and respect, the staff worked through painful issues and feelings to pull things back together as quickly as possible.

We created a number of make-shift educational leadership arrangements to maintain momentum in the teaching and curriculum development areas until program direction was reestablished in the seventh year. The integration of the arts, academics, parent participation, and mental health programs and progress toward a skill-sequenced curriculum will be described in a following chapter.

10
Innovations

Several innovative education programs, strongly influenced in design by mental health principles were introduced at Baldwin and King Schools. Two of the most important were the Discovery Room and Two-Years-with-the-Same-Teacher programs. Both are still in operation.

The Discovery Room program grew out of our psychologist's concern about students who were not retarded but were not learning or performing at their ability levels. Most of these children were not severe behavior problems, though some were angry and became difficult when they were frustrated by their school work. During the 1970–71 school year, Dr. Joan Costello, the psychologist and program evaluator, and her staff observed often in the classrooms. Dr. Costello concluded that a discovery approach to learning could benefit these children; and in the spring of 1971 she helped establish Discovery Rooms in both schools. The program was developed by the Discovery Room teachers with the aid of a consulting psychiatrist.

This program, like every program idea introduced, had to be "sold" to parents and staff. Because the Discovery Room program required relatively little change in parent or staff behavior, and promised some benefit, parents and staff approved. But initially it ranked relatively low on their priority list and finding physical space for the Discovery Room was a problem. This was the kind of issue that could have caused conflict between the Mental Health Team and the principals. Gentle but persistent negotiations and mutual respect prevented such conflict.

While there was a Discovery Room in both schools, there was only time to study the educational processes and practices of one of the Discovery Rooms. Since Marjorie Janis, the resource teacher at King, was also a research assistant at the Yale Child Study Center and an experienced observer of children, we chose to study King's Discovery Room. Ms. Janis was best able and most willing to devote her non-teaching time to examining the operations of her classroom.

The Discovery Room was designed to be an attractive setting that would draw children out of their defensive postures or negative ways of handling fears and anxieties. The equipment and the teaching methods were all organized to help children establish more positive ways of thinking about themselves as learners and behaving in school and to counteract the negative feelings that made them "turn off" to school in the first place.

The reasons children "turn off" in school are numerous, and we can cite a few of those we identified regularly.[1] Children who are criticized severely and punished often by caretakers—sometimes arbitrarily and inconsistently—come to feel that they are inept, clumsy, and destructive. They feel inadequate. Such children are often withdrawn and afraid of failure. They survive by avoiding academic work—by turning off school learning. The major assumption of the Discovery Room was that such children need "successful" failure experiences. They need to expect, and not be thrown by, failure which is an inevitable, frequent, and useful marker on the road to success.

Another reason children turn off at school grows out of unresolved home problems. A child who fights fiercely in school is often continuing sibling rivalry struggles. Fear of making a mess is often related to early efforts to control or punish the parents and can be carried over to teacher-child relationships in school. Some of the children want to remain overly dependent on their parents and, at the same time, want a more mature relationship. These and other factors sometimes lead to angry fantasies and feelings about adults. Some handle the control and dependency issue by acting up physically or by attempting to undermine the teacher and more successful students. But others fear retaliation by the powerful adults in their lives and avoid many school tasks that might draw them into conflict with their teachers. They are often confused and fearful that they will act on impulses that could get them into trouble. Such behavior can evoke more adult disapproval, punishment, and rejection.

For these and other reasons, many children are afraid to establish close relationships with an adult. Instead, they withdraw and act helpless and apathetic or lose themselves in a fantasy world. A good fantasy life is helpful. An excessive fantasy life coupled with little classroom participation can interfere with school learning and behavior.

In other cases the children have simply never learned how to "connect" to the school world—to live by the rules of the school game, to achieve a positive feedback from important others about their performance and thereby experience a sense of competence and adequacy. These children often continue to have real learning and behavior problems even after the climate of relationships and the general school operation are greatly improved.

The materials in the Discovery Room were designed for hands-on experience. There were concave and convex lenses, viewers, a microscope, a phonograph, and stethoscopes for looking and listening. An easel, carpentry bench, a work table, typewriter, and car models were available. A cash register, jewelry and hats, dolls and furniture, masks and magic were available to facilitate make-believe play. Play dough, sand, and water encouraged messy and creative play. Plants and turtles brought out the issues around caring, injury, illness, growing, and dying. Games, books, and other materials that stimulate thinking were in the Discovery Room. There was material for every elementary-school age and level.

The room was an open classroom. It was smaller than we would have liked but adequate. Activities were not structured by the Discovery Room teacher. The teacher's description of several children in the Discovery Room setting gives some idea of how it operated.[2]

Kate went right to the mask. She had done this during the last several sessions. She kept warning everybody not to look. And then, out went the lights and on went the flashlight as the witch tried to scare everybody and everybody tried to act scared. Ellis, who was there for the first time, managed in between times in the dark to try out the scramble cycle, Action Jackson, horses and cowboys, the play dough machine, and the skill ball game.

One day Mel just sawed. A few weeks before he had made a marvelous airplane-like contraption which he called "Superhawk." But this time he threw himself into sawing—fast and furiously, cutting back and forth into the wood until one piece after another fell off onto the floor.

Perry hadn't done very much with the great variety of toys and equipment in the Discovery Room until the day he discovered the nesting Japanese dolls. He was entranced by them. As he opened up each one he said, "Now *she* has a baby . . . and now *she* has a baby." Of the fifth and tiniest he said, "And she's too little to have a baby." He spent most of the session with them—putting them together, taking them apart, and arranging them in careful patterns. From that meaningful session he was able to get involved in the work of the Discovery Room.

The Discovery Room teacher was a warm, friendly, accepting person, but she did not let things get out of hand. She would not permit children to hurt one another, themselves, or herself. But she did not turn off feelings of anger, nor were there any forbidden subjects. She was attentive and supportive. Whatever the child did received a positive comment, descriptively and with appreciation and wonder by the teacher. In every action by the child she tried to say something genuinely praiseworthy.

For Karen, working with play dough and the play dough machine were all absorbing during her first weeks in the Discovery Room. The DR teacher would say, "Oh, look at what you are pushing out. That's terrific. Look how long it's getting to be. That star shape makes a marvelous rough surface. You are making it longer! I love the way the pink shades into the blue. . . ."

Allen played a lot with the rubbery, finger-sized monsters. He really wanted that monster for his own. The DR teacher said it could be his present at the next present-giving time just before the winter vacation. Allen talked about it, waited the several weeks, and then eagerly took it home with him.

By listening, giving, being supportive without making academic demands or behavior demands that go beyond safety and respect for self, others, and property, the teacher was gradually able to establish a positive and strong relationship with even the most withdrawn or antagonistic child. Once the relationship had been established, the teacher was able to begin to help the child with problems that could potentially interfere with classroom work and behavior. Talk about personal experiences from home as well as school was accepted as important but was not probed. Such topics as friends, enemies, anger, fighting, bad language, teeth, birthdays, brothers and sisters, birth, death, race, illness, happy times, and sad times were open for discussion. The Discovery Room teacher talked about her own experiences as well.

Once, after the Discovery Room teacher had said she would be out of school for two days to visit her father in California, one of the children, Malcolm, did not come to the next session. In discussing why, he was able to talk about his own father in California whom he missed very much and who the child felt had rejected him. Children often feel rejected, and even that they are bad, after divorce and separation of their parents, and these feelings can interfere with their school performance. A sympathetic and trusted adult who is less emotionally involved can help them begin to understand that their feelings of worth and value ultimately grow from inner strength.

Issues of control often present themselves spontaneously in the Discovery Room. Self-control, the self-control of others, and the role of adults in establishing control still has to be established for many children in elementary school. Mature adults set expectations and help the children understand why they have been established, how they can control themselves and help each other maintain control:

> When Ben burst into a fight with Evelyn, Thomas held Ben back with his arms around him saying, "Don't fight, talk about it." And when Ben started to leave the room, threatening to tell the principal—Thomas said, "You don't have to go to the principal, we can take care of it here." (These were recommendations that had been made many times by the Discovery Room teacher). A few sessions later, it was Thomas who was ready to storm out in anger to go tell his teacher. Then it was Ben who reminded him, "We can take care of it in the Discovery Room."

Helping the children develop self-control, negotiation, and conflict management skills is as important to future life success as learning to read, write, and do arithmetic—if not more important. What appears to be effective in the case of fights is listening sympathetically to detailed accounts of what happened and then, in the context of acceptance of the child's story and feelings, examining "how the other fellow may feel" and what the alternatives to physical fighting might be. With children who are a little less emotionally fragile and seem to have more confidence, often it is not necessary to listen to the story in so much detail. Several of the regular classroom teachers would not listen to the stories of what happened at all. They point out that there is a disagreement between the two combatants and that they want them to "talk out" a solution and return to them in a few minutes with their plan for settling the problem. We have observed kindergarten children go off to a corner, "talk it out," and return with a solution. That strategy worked well for most of our children.

All natural occurrences become vehicles for applying the Discovery Room philosophy. We tried to communicate to the children that no one is perfect—including the teacher who makes mistakes, does not know everything, cannot do some things, forgets, or gets upset sometimes. The message is "all things about you—the angry feelings, the loving feelings, some good and some bad actions—are acceptable and possibilities for growth." We encouraged the children to work toward being helpful, cooperative, fair, and responsible for their own behavior without permitting others to take advantage.

> Introducing a book of science experiments to the Discovery Room group, the teacher kept trying to get a needle to stay on the surface of a bowl of water. When she couldn't, she called for assistance, "Can somebody help me? I can't do this experiment."

Everyone rushed over to try. No one succeeded. Without conscious awareness, they perceived the teacher as less than all-powerful; they perceived themselves as able; they tried and failed and it was okay. It is significant that the science book from which the experiment was taken became extremely popular after that.

> Nora was upset and called herself stupid when she spilled the fruit drink she was pouring into the cups for everyone. The teacher handed her a sponge saying that it didn't matter. It was easy to wipe up. At one time or another, every member of the group poured and spilled, including the teacher. Eventually Nora and the others not only became more adept at pouring, but they reacted matter-of-factly to spilling.

Without lecturing, interpreting, or teaching in the traditional sense, the teacher was helping the children develop appropriate responses to day-to-day incidents and greater appreciation of their own competence. She was communicating the notion that a mess can be cleaned up; that broken things can be fixed or replaced; what is spilled can be wiped up; that the outcome of their every move does not make them good or bad, competent or incompetent.

"But aren't the children just playing, wasting time, instead of doing their school work?" This is a question a few of the parents and teachers asked in the beginning. Play is the most important work a child can do. Toys that require control, for instance, help children develop self-control. An electric motorcycle directed by remote control, tiny cars that are moved down streets and under bridges by a magnet, an etch-a-sketch board on which they can create things and wipe them away, all facilitate the development of a sense of personal control. Such toys help children sense that the control mechanism is within themselves and not operated by adults who appear to be all-powerful.

Playing games with agreed upon rules helps children learn to live by rules, establish the delicate balance between competition and cooperation, between fair play and justice and exploitation and abuse of others for personal gain. It helps them learn to manage the warmth of winning and the hurt of losing; it helps them to believe that there will be another chance to win the next time. Woodworking is an ideal Discovery Room activity. It permits the children to saw, hammer, drill, and generally manipulate materials. The manipulation of objects and materials prepares children to manipulate abstract symbols, words, and ideas. For younger children the same is true of natural substances such as sand, water, and clay. As they manipulate these substances they use words and concepts that help to develop language. Language and conversation are helpful in problem-solving, task mastery, and general control of one's environment. When feelings and actions can be put into words, fear and anxiety can be reduced and the world seems to come under greater personal control. This outcome is apparent in the work of the Discovery Room teacher with Carl, a seven-year-old second grader:

> Carl was the fifth of eight children. Attractive and of average height and weight, he had a muscular build and medium brown skin. He was the youngest child for six years before the birth of a baby, who arrived in October of Carl's first year in first grade.

Carl's parents were black and poor. They came north as adults, having grown up in the south. They separated when Carl was two years old, but he continued to have sporadic contact with his father, who remained very important to him. Carl's mother said that she expected trouble of boys and cited as evidence her older son, who was in difficulty with the law. Fighting and violence were frequent in Carl's home. . . . Carl's attachment to his mother, from the way he talked about her to the special teacher, seemed strong, and he tried to follow her admonitions. . . . He worked with the DR teacher twice a week initially, for half hours each time. After the first month the number of weekly sessions was increased to four. Carl and another boy in his class, Bernard, who also came twice a week, asked for joint sessions to increase the number of times they could visit the DR teacher. . . . Because the special teacher thought it would benefit both boys to work together, she agreed to their request.

Carl's first six weeks of sessions were marked by diligent drawing, unprovoked angry outbursts, and dramatizations of a ghost-monster who attacked in the dark. Initiated by Carl after he was joined by his partner, this game was played by the boys with much excitement at almost every session for almost two weeks. Then Carl brought his "bad" language to a session. He wrote DICKE and CARLMILLIEPUSSY on a piece of paper. He read DICKE out loud as "Dickhead." CARLMILLIEPUSSY was made up of three words—his name, his girlfriend's name and pussy, written with no spaces between them. He told about being beaten by a teacher for saying these words in this very same room a year earlier.

The special teacher defined her relationship to Carl and to the words as "different" from the former teacher's. She said she didn't beat children for "bad words"; she tried to help them understand what these words mean and how to decide when to use them. When she wrote DICK and HEAD separately on the blackboard, explaining that they were perfectly fine words, Carl cried out, "Don't write it! Don't write it!" as if something catastrophic would happen if the teacher inscribed these malevolent symbols. But the teacher continued despite Carl's anxiety. She pointed out that DICK was a boy's name and HEAD, the top of the body. These were quite ordinary words that did not get you into trouble.

Two weeks after the session on dickhead and pussy the teacher brought pussywillows to the little room. When she said their name, Carl again started on pussy. Carl was by himself at this session (his partner was absent), and the day before he had had his first good day in class: all work done and no fights.

The special teacher tried to make a distinction between the good word pussywillow, the name of a flower, and pussy, his bad word. But Carl got increasingly upset and angry. He insisted, "Don't talk about that!" Then he said something about "getting a baby." The special teacher followed this lead educationally, saying that "sexual intercourse is the scientific term and if a man's sperm joins a woman's egg. . . ." Carl burst out. He shouted that she must stop talking about that and not use the word pussy. His mother wouldn't let him say it, his mother wanted him to be nice. She was a bad, bad teacher. The special teacher said that she liked Carl very much, that she was trying to help him know about bad words and good words so that he could use them at the right time. She added that she talked this way only in the little room.

At one point Carl said that he was never coming back here, and he would be very bad. He turned out the lights and clapped his hands over his ears as the special teacher was saying that she agreed with his mother and didn't want him to get into trouble using bad words. (The DR teacher felt that it was important for Carl to see that his mother and his teacher had the same goals for him, even though each of them might use different means.)

Why did Carl threaten the DR teacher with never coming back because she was a bad teacher and then predict, "And I will be very bad?" It seemed to the DR teacher that in the midst of the tornado of feelings unleashed by her persistent "out loud" exploration of his terrible and terrifying words, Carl was doing two things: First, he was asking whether she was really a bad person when she used bad words, just as he was. He was also acknowledging that their struggle together to tame the power of bad words through informed use of them was somehow linked to the possibility of his becoming master of those words, not their slave. Once he mastered them he would become "good" in school. . . .

Some of Carl's "bad" words in school were not the usual sex words—they were words like *kill*. Only after he had done some sorting out of his origins—only after he had clarified, named, learned about his relationship to each of his parents, their relationship to each other, and the place of violence and affection in marital, parental, and peer relationships—did he engage in constructive peer friendships. Only then did the frequency and the intensity of his fighting and his use of bad or violent words decrease. Learning became a distancing, observing, understanding, liberating process—one of sublimation.

Near the end of the first year of his sessions, Carl listened sympathetically as his partner, Bernard, told how his father had left his mother. The two boys and the special teacher talked about how children and parents might feel in such a situation. Carl used his insights about relationships, saying, "You were mad and sad at yourself, and you were mad and sad at your mother. . . ."

Soon after the session on young children's feelings about parents separating, Carl and his partner turned to a subject that neither had raised before—the subject of race. . . . The boys thought they recalled crying when Martin Luther King was killed, and the special teacher said that she had cried too, that many white people were very sad, just as black people were. A few days later Carl deliberately provoked the DR teacher. He threw across the room a clay animal made by another boy, breaking it. The DR teacher grabbed Carl by the shoulders and spoke angrily to him, "I will not let you destroy something made by another child in this room just as I will not let anyone destroy your things!" Carl yelled at her, "Whitey, take your hands off me! I hate you!" And he threatened to leave. The special teacher removed her hands from his shoulders. For a moment they glared at each other, eyeball to eyeball. Then she said, "I won't touch you if you tell me not to. It's o.k. for you to hate me, and you can go if you want to as soon as you've cooled off. But I will stop you from doing wrong here. Sure, I was born white and you were born black. And I like you very much anyway." The special teacher felt that this was a momentous occasion between them. Carl was reacting to her now as a teacher and as a white person. (He had moved from the realm of familial relations to the less intimate world beyond, where teachers and pupils and black people and white people relate to the implications of one another's social positions and reference groups.)[3] Moreover, his anger—furious as it was—was not the volatile volcanic rage that it had been but, as she experienced it, much more contained, appropriate to the situation and controllable. In fact, Carl calmed down quickly after her response and stayed to the end of the session. . . .

For Carl, and for other children, optimal school learning requires strengths in at least three areas of psychological development: the ability to use words as symbols, the ability to ask and find answers to basic questions, and the ability to establish a teacher-child relationship different from a parent-child relationship. Even without full development in these areas, some school learning can and often does occur. But major difficulties with any of them will seriously interfere with learning in school. . . .

Children need to distinguish clearly between thoughts and actions, between fantasy and reality. Children need to know that thinking about something (or saying it) is not the same as doing it. Children need to understand that actions lead to consequences in the social world but thoughts do not, unless they are the foundation for action. Children need to know that it is possible to explore with thoughts in fantasy to thereby clarify feelings and weigh alternative courses of action. Children need to develop the capacity to be alone in the presence of others—to think private thoughts but to attend at the same time to events going on around them. Children need to differentiate by person, place, and time the acceptability of various words and actions and the consequences of violating these conditions. . . .

The next year when Carl was eight and in second grade, his sessions continued twice a week. A storekeeper game became the favorite. In this game, Carl seemed to be working out new ways of relating to the special teacher—ways that he could use to build effective relationships with classroom teachers. He would set up shop and then debate about "opening up" as opposed to "closing up" just as his teacher-customer arrived. He could be nice or gruff; typically he was gruff and unpredictable. Sometimes he would sell things, other times he would give them away. He changed the prices often. Sometimes he wouldn't sell at any price. He seemed to be negotiating a new level of giving and taking, of closeness and distance, of psychic investments and costs. The special teacher obliged by becoming the dependent customer, grateful for the chance to buy from the powerful Mr. Carl. . . .

Through the close relationship with his special teacher, in a setting designed to facilitate imaginative play, confusions about words and their potency were clarified. Gradually language and thought lost some of their magical connotations. Carl stopped treating language and thought as if they were real action with its inevitable consequences, and in time language and thought became available for symbolic representations of experience or trial actions. This transformation enabled Carl to deal with school more on its own terms and less as an extension of his memories and immediate conflicts at home. In this way, he developed more effective and more economical capacities for dealing with ordinary daily events. The special teacher's working relationship with Carl was also a bridge back to the classroom teacher; as the special relationship developed . . . his ways of relating in the classroom could improve. . . . As he was becoming a real student—a good reader and an excellent writer, fair in arithmetic—he had a much more friendly, businesslike relationship to his classroom teacher than he had ever had before.[4]

We did our best to establish a belief among the school community that going to the Discovery Room is not a stigma but rather an honor. Some of the children gained status by making it possible for some of their classmates to come with them to the Discovery Room. So many children expressed an interest in the

Discovery Room that the teacher scheduled afterschool visiting
for the curious who were not part of the program.

Progress records were kept, and the Discovery Room teacher
maintained continuous communication with the classroom teachers and other helping professionals in the school—social worker,
reading teacher, psychiatrist, and music teacher. As would be
expected, the special reading teacher was working with over
half of the children who attend the Discovery Room. Reading difficulty or failure is a major cause of turning-off and acting-up. By
staying in communication with the Discovery Room teacher, she
was quickly able to identify significant social and emotional
growth in a child, renewed confidence and a willingness to try
again, and to then tap this development during reading sessions.

One of the constraints we faced is that most adults, like children, never learned to manage temporary failure in order to use
it for growth. Our teachers and parents, then, were necessarily
possessive about their children and did not easily turn a child
over to somebody else for intensive work. In a school climate
where cooperation and constructive interaction between professionals has not been well established, teachers can feel that they
are not good professionals if someone else succeeds where they
failed in calming down or motivating a child. In addition if teachers do not fully understand or accept the method being used by
the Discovery Room teacher or a helping person of any kind, they
may avoid referring children or may undermine the work of the
helping person.

Problems of resistance diminished as the Discovery Room
program went along, but at least two other difficult problems remained. Occasionally, emotionally needy children in the Discovery Room were given gifts and food. Some staff felt that giving to
the very children who were not behaving well or performing well
academically was unfair to the majority of children who were
trying hard and doing much better in academic performance.
They felt that this giving could reinforce dependency and encourage poor performance—shades of the concern about public welfare. Black staff were most apprehensive about the possibility of
promoting dependency. Not all the Mental Health Team members
were initially comfortable with the degree of giving and concern
the Discovery Room children received.

To address these concerns, with the support of the Mental
Health staff, the Discovery Room teacher made a presentation to

the entire school staff to explain the rationale for the approach. Even after the presentation, views ranged widely from the belief that giving was detrimental to the belief that the needy required more tangible evidence of value and worth and caring. Even those who disagreed with the reinforcement approach agreed to wait and see. The giving did not promote excessive dependency or decrease the performance of either the children who attended the Discovery Room or those who did not.

The approach worked and the discomfort receded because the Discovery Room teacher had the ability to find the psychologically appropriate moment—after a trusting relationship had been established and the children were emotionally less fragile— to call on her students to live in a cooperative, achieving, and responsible way in return for acceptance and respect in the school community.

The second problem was that the teachers would sometimes withhold the Discovery Room sessions as a punishment for children who did not behave well in the classroom. This is an understandably tempting method of control in that some children appear to care more about their Discovery Room time than anything else. But denial does not work among the children who act up most. These children have pervasive social, emotional, and academic problems and cannot organize themselves to understand socially accepted conventions and sustain obedience under threat, no matter how much they enjoy and value their time in the Discovery Room. On the other hand, making it necessary for them to earn the second Discovery Room session through a week of desirable behavior could sometimes help the child to practice self-control in order to achieve a goal. In this way, inner or personal discipline is being developed rather than imposed. The adult target for resistance has been removed.

One goal of the Discovery Room was to keep the children in their regular classes and school as they received special services. In addition, the Discovery Room teacher worked hard to help the children continue to feel a part of the total school as they faced individual problems. One youngster's story, "My Father's Cast," was published in the school newspaper, the King's Voice. Excerpts are as follows:

My father came home one day and he told my mother and then my mother told all of us. He was going into the hospital to get an operation done on his leg! I felt sad because I didn't want my father to go. . . . He had an operation seven years ago. But it didn't help him.

. . . A week after he told us, he went into the hospital. My mother didn't want him to go. She started crying because she didn't want him to go. . . .

We couldn't go visit my father in the hospital right after the operation because he was sick. And then we didn't go visit him because they wouldn't let children in. But my mom visited him every day.

My father stayed one or two weeks in the hospital and then he came home. When he came home he fell because he couldn't walk with the metal crutches. He fell down last night. He tripped over my brother's dog.

My dad didn't like being home so long with the cast on and not being able to work, but he is going out more now. When he gets the brace off maybe he can drive. He wants to drive so bad! His leg is going to be all right now. The second operation came through.

It is a story of trauma, loss, and recovery. These are issues with which every child can identify and about which each person must learn to manage feelings. By expressing his feelings he reduced his anxieties about the situation. The DR teacher or others then had the springboard from which they could work to correct misunderstandings or distortions. At the same time the student gained social skills and status by telling his story and having it published.

Many of the children in the Discovery Room went through periods of difficult negative behavior. They sometimes blurted out things that were on their minds. Sometimes fights erupted with volcanic violence. Every limit set by the teacher was tested. The most minute fairness was demanded. But as they received evidence that they were respected and valued, that things could be achieved by cooperation and fair play on their parts, most of the children moved gradually toward greater self-control and increased confidence. They were able to engage successfully in a wider range of activities and achieve greater pleasure.

Obviously many of the DR tasks would be best done before children attend school. But many parents, regardless of income group and racial or religious background, are not prepared to help their children in this way. For just this reason, the parent leaders in the King School sponsored workshops to have the Discovery Room teacher demonstrate ways of playing with children and rearing them that would better prepare them for school. A recent article by the DR teacher in the *King's Voice* was about Discovery Room methods and included some suggestions which parents might find useful in helping children do well in school.

1. *Give positive attention to your child every day.* Even just a few minutes worth can strengthen your child's self image and self confidence.
2. *Make sure that your child has a safe place at home for keeping his or her own things.* Your child's valued possessions, work and products need protection so that they are not lost or destroyed.
3. *Support your child's own interests.* From play, from hobbies, from independent investigation come the exploration and learning that can lead to school success and worthwhile careers.
4. *Help your child learn how to overcome setbacks by providing a pattern of "setting things right."* Whenever possible, show your child that spills can be wiped up, broken things repaired and mistakes rectified. Give lots of extra chances. Skills, knowledge and responsibility are acquired gradually.

The methods used by the Discovery Room teacher are very close to the traditional mental health therapy approaches. Many feel that such methods do not belong in a school at all. On the other hand, none will deny that the task of the school is to promote the social, psychological, and intellectual development of children. I do not see any way that the school task can be achieved without helping children struggling with feelings and anxieties that make it difficult for them to focus on the learning task. Failure to do so often results in school failure, problems with day-to-day living, mental anguish; it aggravates, and, in some cases is the cause of mental illness. The school is the first and most appropriate place outside the family for the society to help prevent these undesirable outcomes.

The Discovery Room teacher did not do traditional psychotherapy. She used her knowledge of child development and behavior to help children feel better about themselves, develop a blueprint and a strategy for succeeding in the school world. Succeeding in primary school is a giant step toward later school success and success in the adult world of work, family, citizenship and recreation. *The observations that caused us the greatest sadness was that winners and losers were easily identifiable in kindergarten. Our mission—in the Discovery Room in particular—was to turn as many losers into winners as possible.*

The Discovery Room approach is an effective approach to helping children who are turned off and at high risk of developing serious psychological problems. In a well-managed school setting, few children will need traditional individual psychotherapy or psychotropic drugs for behavior control. No children in the Baldwin-King Program were on psychotropic medication. With the behavior problems greatly reduced, there were adequate resources for the several children who did need traditional psychiatric treatment.

The second major innovation developed within the Baldwin-King effort was the "Two-Years-with-the-Same Teacher" program. A high rate of student and staff turnover is the norm in most inner-city communities. As a mental health professional, I knew that rapid staff and patient turnover in in-patient mental health treatment centers created confusion and anxiety. Not until the new personnel had become comfortable with experienced staff did the patients feel comfortable. This phenomenon manifested itself in schools and was very troublesome. A possible resolution occurred to me when a teacher despaired that a frightened, underachieving, withdrawn child smiled at her for the first time only one month before the end of the school year. The child was just then becoming comfortable enough to relate to and be motivated by the teacher. The teacher commented, "oh, if I could only have her longer." It occurred to me that such children might be helped by remaining with the same teacher a second year.

I discussed this idea with the program coordinator and the mental health team. We knew that modifying our program would require significant change in other aspects of school operations, and we anticipated significant staff and parent anxiety about it. The coordinator presented it to the principals and staff of each school. We discussed the ways children use trusted and important people in their environment as models for developing their own skills and to build strategies for learning and living. We pointed out how low-income children more often lose familiar people and places than middle-income children; the need they have for continuity with trusted and caring adults. The staff was already all too familiar with the disruptive effect of almost weekly transfers in and out of their classrooms.

Since the teacher is a parent surrogate who stimulates, mediates experiences, modulates reactions, and helps children organize themselves in a way to acquire new knowledge and skills, we hypothesized that if a bond of trust and mutual respect could develop between them, the ability of the teacher to motivate and help a child learn strange, new things and withstand the anxiety of possible failure is greatly increased. We reasoned in developing this continuity program that children in these two low-income schools would benefit enormously from time to cement a relationship bond.

It was near the end of the second year of the program and the teachers had visible evidence of some success. They were beginning to sense a spirit of exploration and discovery. But again, change requires that one give up existing security, even if existing conditions are troublesome and better circumstances appear possible. The faculty expressed concern, but decided to give it a try. With the informed consent of the Steering Committee in both schools, the teachers stayed with their students for a second year. This practice continues in the King School whenever it is possible.

Perhaps the best way to describe the staff's and parent's concerns about the program as well as what happened in the classrooms is to report on the observations of students, parents, and staff after four years of experience with this program.

Four teachers, representing grades 1 to 4, were interviewed individually about their experiences, responding to a common set of questions. These teachers and three others representing grades 1 to 6 were interviewed in a group meeting. A small group of fourth-grade children were interviewed away from their teachers; two classes of fourth graders and one class of third graders were interviewed in group discussions with their teachers.

Several teachers pointed out that the usual difficult adjustment period at the beginning of the year did not take place at the beginning of the second year. Teachers noticed a lessening of spring fever during the first spring. In the classrooms where children were with their teachers for the second year, relationships and academic concerns seemed to flow smoothly and naturally from the first to the second year. The troublesome withdrawal symptoms, generated by fears about separation and readjustment were absent. There was no cause for anxiety. The students and teachers were actively planning together for the following year. They discussed specific projects, classroom organization, and classroom goals that represented continuity and growth.

Most educators agree it is desirable to individualize academic and social teaching and learning experiences for children. But too often teachers are not with the children long enough to know them very well. Three teachers said that they knew children much better in the second year. Greater familiarity allowed them to apply pressures that might have made children anxious the year before; to increase pressures on some and ease pressures on others. One teacher felt that he was more compassionate with children he had had for a longer time because he had gotten to know, understand, and appreciate them more. The pressure to have children measure up at the end of a year is so great that sometimes a teacher feels that he or she cannot go slowly with a particular child who may need a gentle hand. Some teachers said that the two-year span allowed them to be more patient, relaxed, and made it easier to experiment with teaching methods in order to find methods appropriate to the individual learning style of the more troubled children.

Several teachers said that as a result of this program they thought about retention differently. It appeared wise, in most cases, to keep a youngster with his teacher—rather than hold him at the same level—when he was progressing more slowly than most of the class. Several teachers reported significant gains by children who were retained but remained with the same teacher. The teachers said they believed that time and comfort seemed to be factors responsible for these spurts in achievement. If these children had to adjust to a new teacher at the end of one year, they might well have lost two years of growth instead of compensating in the second year as they did for some of the growth they had lost in the first.

The improved second-year classroom relationship gave teachers time to try variable scheduling. For example, two teachers discovered that their children learned arithmetic and reading more efficiently in the morning than in the afternoon, and therefore these important subjects were scheduled before lunch—the best training time for these pupils. They also found that their children, who were familiar with the objectives of the classroom, could make useful suggestions for rearranging programs and classroom structure.

One teacher mentioned that her improved knowledge of the children helped her to plan a more interest-oriented curriculum. One youngster in her classroom had a particular interest in trains. His enthusiasm and leadership made this an exciting project for the entire class the next year. Another boy was the nephew of a professional football player. A project about professional sports, with a letter and souvenirs from the uncle, made this a highly successful project. Another teacher felt that she could give greater individual attention to children who needed it, because by the second year more children were able to handle independent activities.

Teachers from all grade levels remarked about how much the children's increased independence, emotional security, and inner or self-control developed over the two years. Teachers attributed this to maturation, but the fact that it occurred at all grade levels suggests that it might also be a product of the two-year program. At the time she was with her children for the second year, a second-grade teacher told me that the students appeared to be less provocative of one another, less anxious about receiving attention, less likely to "tattle-tale" and better able to concentrate on work. Most teachers believed that in the second year the atmosphere was more congenial and relaxed than it had been during the first year. After the program had been in place for two years, those who taught children who had already experienced the two-year program said the children seemed to adjust earlier in the year than other pupils, and that the children contributed to a positive climate.

Teachers felt that classroom discipline was easier to achieve when teachers and children knew each other well. The children knew the teachers' behavioral expectation. Two teachers mentioned that the longer period of involvement between a teacher and his class made serious misbehaving a greater risk for the children and minor infractions less of a threat to the teacher because they both knew "how much was enough." In fact, both teachers and students worked to maintain the expected level of stability when a new child was assigned to the classroom. Recall the student who stood up and told the transfer student who was ready to fight, "Hey man, we don't do that in this school."

Because a comfortable relationship existed over a longer time, discipline could be maintained using less stringent methods—banter, teasing, or polite requests, rather than frequent and harsh yelling, scolding, and punishment.

Several teachers felt that by knowing the children well and feeling comfortable with their parents, use of social work or other resource personnel in the school was efficient. Teachers also had a base for managing student-related problems independently, and felt free to inquire about possible home-related problems. Inquiries from school often result in spankings or other punishment. But because parents had gotten to know the teachers and were accustomed to working with them, some made regular visits to the school; parents were not threatened by such inquiries and could be helpful to the children and the teachers. Parents were less reluctant to mention marital, neighborhood, or other problems that might be a source of a school problem.

All the teachers felt that they had more rapport with parents because of the two-year association. They described their relationship with parents as more trusting, less anxious, more communicative, and more involved. Parents increased their participation in class activities and their contacts with the teacher at PTA meetings and in informal ways. It was rare for a parent to come to school to "get the teacher" although in many low-income communities that is not an uncommon practice. Our parents felt the teachers cared and would not mistreat their children. Parents have come with concerns and in search of explanations. Not all the parents have had, or will ever have, contact with the staff. But word gets around.

From one teacher, a two-year teaching span seemed qualitatively different than a one-year period. The increased time demanded a much greater sense of involvement in her students' personal and home lives. The investment provided this teacher with a great sense of achievement and satisfaction in the progress of the children. One teacher pointed out that parents could more easily measure their children's progress over a two-year span than one, and consequently developed more confidence in the teachers.

Teachers felt that shy, immature, and less able children benefited most from the program. One teacher stated our hypothesis directly: For children who need stability and a sustained adult relationship, a teacher could function as a mother or father figure.

Parents felt very much as the staff the Two-Years-with-the-Same-Teacher program. Twenty-four of the thirty-six parents interviewed said they believed that spending two years with the same teacher was a fairly good to a good idea. No parents were strongly opposed. They approved for largely the same reasons given by the teachers.

The children also appeared to like the program. Some comments: "You get to know her. You have fewer tests because she knows what you can do." "*If* he [the teacher] is nice, you can learn more things." "You can keep working on a project that you started in the spring." "You know what he is like, what he is going to do."

One child mentioned his previous confusion about being promoted while keeping the same teacher. Other chldren wondered about whether or not third-grade would seem different from fourth grade. Another child said that she liked having the same teacher, but she did not like being with all the same children for two years!

One disadvantage mentioned by teachers was having to live with the most difficult children for twice as long. Another difficulty was detaching oneself emotionally from a class after two years. Teachers also said they believed that it was harder for a new class and teacher to adjust to one another after the children had had another teacher for the previous two years. They pointed out that the children had longer to incorporate the style of their previous teacher. With a new teacher, they first expected him or her to do things the way the previous teacher had. Several teachers felt that staying with the teacher for two years could be harmful to children who had serious conflicts with the teacher. We had three cases of personality clashes that could not be resolved over four program years. These children were simply transferred to another teacher at the same grade level where they made satisfactory adjustments.

One teacher felt that by the middle of the second year the best students had benefited all they could from the extended period. They were concerned that these children missed the advantage of exposure to another adult personality and style. This limitation was overcome to some degree by the presence of student teachers, volunteers, and team teaching. In a few cases, more challenging, individualized activities were made available for the best students.

One teacher remained with the class for three years. While the youngsters made satisfactory progress, she advised against this arrangement in the future for several of the reasons suggested above—familiarity of expections to the point of boredom, the possibility that another teacher might have more success with a particular child, teacher, and student attachment beyond an easily manageable point.

I mentioned that these and other programs had to be considered by parents and staff before they were initiated. This process protects against the discontinuity and chaos that well-meaning but disorderly change can bring. Our process of change allows maximum opportunity for administrators, teachers, mental health and other support staff, and parents to think together and to examine objectives and methods. The process also prevents the school from being overwhelmed by every idea, person, and research project designed to "save the children." Through the process of proposing and discussing planned change with responsible governance bodies, we adjust to changed needs in the society and school through innovation without decreasing our interest or emphasis on teaching basic academic skills.

We believe that you can maintain emphasis on the basic academic skills, develop innovation to significantly improve the behavior and academic performance of most children not doing well, and maintain order with relative freedom for school staff, parents, and children.

11
Update

During the fourth and fifth year of the Baldwin-King Program, an integration of the mental health, teaching, and curriculum development and arts program was beginning to take place, although we were not fully aware of it. We were not free to concentrate on program development enough to be aware of it because we were facing financial problems at that time. In order to obtain continued financial support for our work, we needed to show that our model could be disseminated and that the New Haven School System was receptive. Unfortunately, a new superintendent, the third in five years, was being selected and installed during the fourth and fifth year of our program. Thus the system had operational issues of much higher priority than the future of the Baldwin-King Program.

In addition, while there was documented evidence that relationships and social conditions had improved, evidence of academic achievement was subjective and inconclusive. Student achievement on the Metropolitan Achievement Test was up in both schools, but not at a statistically significant level or in all categories. A number of people throughout the school system still doubted the value of addressing school-home relationships. Thus, while there was significant support for continuation and dissemination of our program, the level of enthusiasm and the number who were supportive did not justify continuation.

Because we were hopeful that we would continue, we had not prepared adequately for termination. Differences in philosophy among staff at Baldwin existed to the point that a significant number of teachers were transferring, and the potential for continued and greater conflict existed. New Haven School System and Yale Child Study Center program leaders decided to terminate the program at Baldwin, use the sixth year to carry out a termination process at King, and write a program report that would aid transition back to a traditional school program.

At this point both King and Baldwin students were at approximately the same achievement level in reading and mathematics, had similar attendance records, and until the final few months had a similar climate of relationships in school and between home and school.

Parents and staff at King were immediately unhappy with a return to the traditional ways of operating the school. Parents, staff, and the mental health groups all felt that we had come too far to stop; that statistically significant evidence of academic improvement was right around the corner. The unspoken message I received was "now that you have material for a book, you can leave." But the Yale Child Study Center, with school system approval, made a decision to remain at King. We decided to concentrate on finding the approach that would further develop the program rather than trying to disseminate a still evolving model. The write-up was delayed. Throughout the sixth year we worked to restore the climate of relationships and ways of operating that had slipped and changed as a result of our uncertain status. We also planned for the future.

As we reviewed our program activities and the results, time and again a single factor emerged: social skill development was directly correlated with improved behavior and academic achievement. We eventually recognized the informal way in which academic subject matter, the arts, and social skills teaching were being integrated. In the seventh year we proposed and received support for a formal program of this nature entitled "A Social Skills Curriculum for Inner-City Children," which would begin in our eighth year of involvement.

In restrospect, some of our curriculum development difficulties were probably due in part to the absence of a social skills development program as well defined as our academic program. The effect of massive technological change and exclusion from economic and social development opportunities weigh heavily on families and children from low income, minority group communities. The slightly improved academic and greatly improved social performance of the first five years suggested that students were able. It was reasonable to imagine that they could achieve at an even higher level with the specific social skills and opportunities more often available to children from higher income families. Systematically teaching social skills helped make the academic curriculum more relevant, made it more exciting, and gave the staff clear direction and an urgent sense of purpose.

While planning the new program, we asked ourselves "what is a social skill?"

Social scientists do not readily agree.[1] To begin to find a definition, we reasoned that we all exist in some kind of social setting. We eventually agreed that *aside from psychological, emotional, and physical development, the capacities a child needs to function adequately in an average social setting are social skills.*

Babbling, which starts at about age six weeks, is a biologically based social skill that reinforces two-way communication and is satisfying to both parties. Words such as dada, mama, hello, and bye-bye, waves and hugs, then trigger language, speech, and social learning in its earliest form. The social learning and skill development process continues through proper bowel and bladder management, social greetings, ability to negotiate to have one's needs met without compromising those of another, caring for one's body, managing clothing, asking questions about the environment, relating to peers, planning, organizing, studying, relaxing, applying for a job, working, functioning within a family, retiring, and dying gracefully.

Opportunities to acquire social skills are thwarted or enhanced to varying degrees by the quality of a child's relationships with caretakers, teachers, other children, adults, and institutions in his or her subculture and the larger society. The kind of social skills a child acquires is influenced by the parent or caretaker's personal opportunities, experiences, and social, psychological, and intellectual functioning; by the network of social operations; and by attitudes toward his or her income, racial, ethnic, religious class or group held by the larger society and how the caretaker interprets these attitudes and instructs the child to do so.

Children whose parents feel that they can and should be a part of the social mainstream have the best chance to acquire the social skills that will lead to school and life success. Children whose parents are not a part of the social mainstream can acquire such skills if they are taught in school and there is parental support for their acquisition and use. Regardless of the background of the parents, the climate and operation of a school must be reasonably good to constructively enhance children's social skills.

Our move toward teaching social skills to low-income children grew in part from our personal background and program experiences. For me, one incident more than all others suggested the potential and format of a social skills program. King School is the precinct polling place. One of the teachers who loves to hug and kiss her students near the front door was objecting to the intrusion of voters one morning. Intrusion! I remembered that one of my fondest childhood memories was the time I went to the polls with my mother, entered the booth (probably against regulations), and actually pulled the lever myself (certainly against regulations). It was an experience that brought me into a mainstream social process. It gave purpose to school learning. I knew—because I was being told—that I needed an education to participate in the world of grown-ups—obviously an exciting world as demonstrated by this experience.

When the teacher raised objection to having election polls in the school, we were asking ourselves questions like, "Why do so many low-income children not acquire mainstream social skills?" "Where do middle-income children learn to say good morning, thank you, and please?" "Where do they learn to obtain information, learn to be on time, learn to prepare for a task, learn to carry through on a task, learn to send invitations, confirm appointments with memoranda, send thank you notes, learn to interact with and influence decision makers and important institutions, and the host of other skills necessary to function in our complex technological society?"

A quick informal survey revealed that a majority of our students did not know how to use telephone books. We hypothesized that too many low-income children are not brought into the mainstream social processes through incidental experiences at an early age. It seemed to us that by teaching social skills through real and simulated adult-world experiences we could make our curriculum relevant and thereby prepare the students better for the complexities of the modern adult world. Also the time was right.[2]

Each year school-community relationships and the quality of parent, staff, and student interaction had become smoother. As a result each group was doing its job more efficiently and effectively. The energy of the school staff was not being drained as it had been in the past. We had the freedom to consider carefully the relationship between social, psychological, and intellectual development in child and adult social functioning. Such consideration made it possible for the staff to begin an ever-changing program of integrating social skills, the arts, and academic subject matter. By 1975, two New Haven School System administrators who had been on sabbatical had returned and gave vigorous support for the work of the Child Study Center Mental Health Team.

Our experiences in the first five years of the program, together with the backslide in the school social climate during the sixth year, had taught us that parental involvement would be a key factor if this program were to be successful. The program was therefore designed to employ parents as classroom assistants for three hours per day for the 180-day school year, or a total of 540 hours. By having a representative group of parents working in the school and being directly involved in the development of the curriculum, there was no way that anyone could impose values that were objectionable to the parents. Again, the participation of a core of parents highly invested in the parent program of the school was guaranteed by this part-time work in the school. The jobs could be held only by parents of children in the school. Parents leave when their children graduate or leave.

Initially ten parents were hired. Their salary was $2.50 per hour. Ten teachers were involved in developing the social skills curriculum and were paid a stipend of $200.00 each for forty extra hours of work. Eventually, all twelve teachers wanted to be involved, and the program was amended to include them. During 1975–77, parents were paid for an average of thirty-five hours of work each month. On their own accord, they actually worked an average of fifty-six hours each month. This amounts to twenty-one hours per month of volunteer work by these largely low-income parents.

Parents and teachers reviewed the academic task at each grade level. In grade-level meetings, interviews, surveys, and through direct observation, parents and teachers studied the level of social skills among the children and discussed the desired levels. They agreed that a teaching unit or project approach would be the best vehicle for social skills education. They incorporated the arts and other school resources wherever possible.

Teachers were free to develop any project that would promote both social and academic skill teaching and learning. Each teacher developed a written proposal that stated his or her objectives, plans for achieving them and project costs. A School Advisory Committee composed of parents and teachers reviewed it, made suggestions, and determined a level of funding. Funds could be used for materials, for student travel, or whatever was necessary and reasonable to implement a project. Curriculum consultants advised teachers when necessary. Eventually, five major teaching units or projects were developed: elections or government; whole person; banking; gospel choir; kindergarten language.

As an example, the following is the Whole Person Curriculum issues outline.

1. *The body*—the outside of your body (body parts and variation in eyes, hair, skin, height, weight . . .) and the inside of your body (eating and the digestive system, breathing and the circulatory system, and so forth); what does your body need in order to grow well and feel good?

2. *Families and homes*—different family groupings—relatives who live with you and relatives who live elsewhere (parents, grandparents, sisters and brothers, aunts, uncles and cousins . . .); your home, your room, your neighborhood (mapping where you live, play, shop, visit, go to school).

3. *Emotions and behavior*—your feelings often change; sometimes you are happy, calm, sad, mad . . . ; your feelings affect your behavior and sometimes you are good, sometimes

you are bad; sometimes you make mistakes, sometimes you do things just right; that's the way everyone is.

4. *Child development*—you were a small baby once (everybody was); you couldn't walk or talk or do very much; you drank milk, slept, cried and moved your legs, arms and head; you used diapers; you learned to know and need your mother and become attached to her and others in the family; your hair came in and your teeth came in; you began to play; after a while you sat, crawled, ate different foods, and recognized people (that was all in your first year of life). And then you started to walk and you spoke your first real words! You got toilet trained; you were able to remember more. From two to four, you learned to do so many things. Your language, your physical skills, your thinking, your ways of relating to people all developed tremendously. And now you are a school child. You've come a long way!

5. *Life cycles and the generations*—you keep growing, learning and developing through the school years and you'll become a teenager and then a grown-up; there is a cycle of life: everything that is alive grows and dies; in the most complete form of the human life cycle, a baby is born, grows (through babyhood, childhood and youth) to adulthood, can reproduce itself, gets old and dies. Your parents were babies once and grew up and so were your grandparents and your great grandparents (you can diagram your family tree with whatever information you can find); generation after generation keeps going further and further back in time . . . all the way—more than a million years—to the period when human life started on earth (every one of us is descended from a small number of earliest humans). If you have a child when you are grown up you will be your child's parent; if your child has a child, you will be that child's grandparent; a child of your grandchild would be your great grandchild . . . and so on for generations into the future.

The curriculum was based on the young school-age child's pressing need to determine what is real and what is not. It was designed to permit children to learn about themselves, the ways in which they are like everybody else and the ways in which they are different. It permitted a search for one's place in time—babyhood, the present, the future. It permitted discussion about feelings and helped children to learn healthy ways to manage their feelings. It permitted an affirmation of likeness and an affirmation of difference, a prelude to helping children understand and appreciate their own ethnic, racial, and religious group and that of others.

The staff developed several projects called "Human Body Units." Three first and two second-grade teachers developed a unit designed to explain how the body functions. A pediatrician who was a post-graduate fellow in child development at the Child Study Center assisted. The purpose of the unit was to address concerns raised by the children about their own bodies and feelings, such as bowel and bladder function and losing teeth. They raised questions such as, "If I swallow a button will I die?" and "If I eat rabbit food will I get sick?" The specific and personal questions were the basis and motivation for learning more general information about the body.

The teachers met with the pediatrician once a week to plan the program. The pediatrician made initial presentations to each class once a week. He introduced body parts and functions, answered student questions and showed model organs and medical equipment. The teachers each did follow-up lessons, going over the doctor's presentation *many times* in order to simplify the material and clear up student confusion and misunderstandings. They focused on building a vocabulary of body parts and functions—esophagus, stomach, intestines, diarrhea, bowel, urine, and other words. The children built a life-size model, utlizing skills they had acquired in our arts program. They sketched body outlines from their own bodies and drew in the organs.

Of the 116 questionnaires sent out to parents about this project, 98 percent were returned. All parents knew about the unit and all but five rated it "very important." Four rated it "important" and one rated it "not important at all." Most of the parents indicated that they had learned a lot about the body from their children. Interestingly, parents did not comment on either elimination or reproduction, although in a letter sent home with report cards they were informed about all of the topics to be studied. These were the two areas about which the children asked the most questions.

The first unit on elections and government was one of the most exciting. A mayoralty election in New Haven was held in the fall of 1975. The parents and teachers in the fourth grade decided to do an election unit. The three candidates were invited to talk to students about the election. The students all wrote letters of invitation—a language arts lesson. The best letter was selected by the teachers and sent to each candidate. The same procedure was used for the thank you note which was sent as a follow-up.

Money raised by parents from a fashion show and other activities they sponsored in the school was used to rent a bus. Parents, teachers, and third and fourth-grade children toured the city looking at various social and economic conditions. In discussion, the children raised questions and learned about the responsibility of government for addressing various problems and providing opportunities. During these discussions they learned how to raise questions, to keep to the point, be respectful but direct, and how to handle disagreement.

When the candidates arrived, the students served as hosts. They asked excellent questions regarding problems and conditions in the city. Some of the questions were about their own school—the playground, lights, vandalism. The candidate who was eventually elected mayor was particularly good at acknowledging the responsibility of government, but he also called on the children to examine their role. He asked them questions and called on them to protect and care for *their* playground, *their* hallways, *their* books and materials. He called on the children to work in school so that they might become good contributing citizens as adults.

This project had an enormously positive impact on parents, teachers, and children—and the candidates. It was an unqualified success in every way.

In 1976, all classes above the kindergarten level participated in planning activities related to the 1976 presidential election. This, of course, was a follow-up to the 1975 New Haven mayoralty election unit. The goal of the unit was to enable children, parents, and staff to view themselves as able to influence the political process. In addition, the goal was to improve language arts, mathematics, and social science skills. Activities included trips to government institutions, use of media and newspapers, classroom discussions, a mini-political convention, writing speeches, letters, reports, making campaign posters, and then actually participating in a mock election.

By chance, the site visitors from the National Institute of Mental Health were in the school on the day of the mini-convention. The children could not have been more impressive. They assembled in the large all-purpose room in the center of King School. Three candidates made speeches in their own behalf. One spoke extemporaneously, clearly, and with much charm and poise. Another read his speech in a faltering fashion. A third read in a very effective manner. There was not a single snicker or put-down of the youngster who read with difficulty. There were enthusiastic demonstrations of support after each speech. Yet one request by the teacher, "Now let's hear from our next speaker," brought demonstrators back to rapt attention.

The visitors and I were fascinated. One of the great challenges of our time and to our efforts to establish a more free and democratic society is to help all children develop the capacity to be enthusiastic, spontaneous, and creative at the proper time and to be able to be controlled, disciplined, and attentive at the proper time. Here in an inner-city school, with a disproportionate number of children who have had some difficult developmental experiences, it was being achieved.

A mock election was held in the classroom after the convention. The principal later announced over the public address speaker that there was a three-way tie. Was it rigged to reduce the stress of losing? I was told that it happened by chance. Had there been a winner and two losers, I trust that the staff would have seized this opportunity to discuss desirable winning and losing behavior and how one best handles the feelings involved. No lesson in preparation for adulthood is more important.

At the end of the school year, a voter registration session was held for parents and staff at the school. We did not tabulate the number of new registrations among all parents. But fourteen new registrants were counted among parents working in the school and the school staff. Initially, few parents answered the questionnaire evaluating the election unit. With small rewards to children by the teachers, 142 of 147 of the families returned the questionnaire.

Ninety-two percent of the parents knew about the election unit from their child and/or teacher. The same percentage felt that it was very important to teach about politics, while 7 percent thought is was somewhat important, and only 1 percent thought it was not important at all. In terms of political behavior, 64 percent of all the parents said they were registered to vote, 47 percent said they voted in the 1975 mayoral election, and 61 percent said they voted in the 1976 presidential election.

The impact of the unit on students was assessed by interviews with stratified random samples of five children from each of the nine participating classes three months after the unit was completed. Each child was asked to identify Ford and Carter from newspaper clippings, explain what voting was, and to describe the role of the president. All children interviewed could identify Ford and Carter's pictures. Forty of the forty-five children saw the role of the president as heading, running, helping and/or working for the entire country. Only four children mistakenly thought the president ran the city and one child thought he ran the state. All children understood voting as the way people made a choice and/or elected their leaders. Many students in senior high school do not have this level of information and understanding.

Unfortunately, the results could not be compared with a control school. Since most children's magazines carried stories about the elections, it is reasonable to assume that many elementary schools covered the material. Neither do we know how many schools gave attention to the election or the degree of focus. But prior to the program, political affairs had never been given any systematic attention at King School. It can only be said that the unit achieved its own stated goals.

Staff awareness about children's interst in and ability to understand political life increased over the two-year period studied. The staff now includes election activities in the yearly curriculum program. It would appear that parents have an increased political awareness, although it is not known whether their actual voting behavior has changed. Parents, in any event, view knowledge of politics as very important to their children. Children understood, after a three-month interval, the primary concepts taught in the election unit and demonstrated an increased awareness of and interest in political life.

A banking unit was developed by three first-grade teachers. The purpose of the unit was to introduce children to the concepts of work, pay, purchase, and savings. The project involved the organization of a class bank and store. Children earned five cents a day for assigned tasks related to the care and maintenace of the classroom—leader of the classroom lines, picking up papers, maintenance of the activity areas, etc. The pay had no relation to either the academic work or behavior other than that related to the assigned task. Payment was neither given nor withheld as a reward or punishment, although no payment was made for days absent regardless of the reason.

Each child received a check every Friday which was cashed at the class bank and either wholly or in part spent at the class store or saved. The class store had a variety of items such as pencils, magic markers, writing pads, puzzles, small toys and games ranging in price from fifty cents to two dollars. The complete economy was a closed system—for example, money could neither be brought in from home nor taken out of the classroom.

In the spring, two of the classrooms were vandalized by outsiders. All of the contents of the banks and stores were stolen. The idea of "insurance" was introduced at this time. Other concepts introduced and explored were differential interest rates for saving and borrowing, differentiating between essential needs and wants or desires, discount buying, lay-away, and credit as alternatives to immediate purchase.

All three teachers made the unit a regular part of their work. Other teachers are now using it. Ninety-four percent of the parents returned the questionnaire regarding the project. All of them knew about the unit and gave it the highest possible rating for importance. Note that on this unit, no parent said it was not important! Sixty percent of the parents said that they had noticed that their child now handled money more thoughtfully at home. Thirty parents specifically commented on how the child's handling of money had improved as follows: twelve parents said their child could better differentiate between wants and needs, eight parents opened new savings accounts at their child's request, six parents said their child could count money better, and four parents said their child now saves his money to buy things.

Twelve children were randomly selected from each class in the fashion used for evaluating other units. The children were asked to count seven nickels and tell the total amount of money they represented; to read a check for twenty-five cents; to define the terms interest, deposit, withdrawal, and insurance. All thirty-six students correctly counted money, read the check and defined deposit and withdrawal. In the two classes that were burglarized, all students correctly defined insurance. Even in the classroom that had not been robbed, as a result of a teacher discussion about the theft and insurance, 83 percent of the students correctly defined insurance.

In one classroom there was a higher rate of interest for savings. In this classroom all children interviewed correctly defined interest whereas in the other two classrooms only 66 percent of the children understood the term. The behavior and learning patterns of children tell us a lot about ourselves; that things which touch us and affect our lives in some specific way have the greatest impact on our memory, thinking, learning, and behavior. Given these facts, this project or unit approach—utilizing meaningful social experiences—should be a highly beneficial way to teach.

A gospel choir unit was organized and led by a classroom teacher with the help of another teacher, a Child Study Center assistant, a parent assistant and a gospel pianist. Membership was open to all interested third and fourth graders. The choir gave twelve performances at various functions at King School, another elementary school, a church, and a New Haven administrators meeting. The latter program was televised locally.

The children experienced practice, preparation to achieve a goal, and the recognition and positive feedback for doing so. They had to plan, organize, and cooperate to select a program and put it on. They had to accept the responsibility of following through. Are these not the experiences that many middle-income children—and some low-income children involved in church and other social institutions—receive through day-to-day contact with their mainstream parents? These are the experiences and resultant skills and feelings of achievement capability that motivate children for demanding and sustained academic learning.

Teachers and parents felt that the choir achieved its goals. Enrollment in the choir increased from twenty-five to thirty-four members, with a waiting list. Attendance at rehearsals held between February (in the very difficult winter of 1976–77) and June had an average attendance of 95 percent. Two out of three parents attended all twelve performances!

The kindergarten teacher organized a language development program for children identified as high risk for reading failure on the Beers Screening Inventory administered to all New Haven kindergarten children each September. The teacher was particularly concerned about these children's poor fund of vocabulary for basic household and school objects. They spoke in incomplete sentences and showed limited verbal interaction with one another during play activities.

The teacher purchased a play family, safari, farm, village, Sesame Street house, and various construction toys and developed a list of 252 names of objects included among the items. This included a washing machine, dental chair, cement mixer, and gorilla. The toys were utilized both in the language program and as part of free-play activity from February until May. While the materials were utilized by all of the kindergarten children, the language program was specifically conducted with the nine children at high risk. These nine children were evaluated before and after by being asked to identify 55 of the 252 items, the names of which were randomly drawn from a bowl. On the pretest (February 25, 1977), the nine children achieved a score of twenty-four correct responses and on the posttest (May 30–31), the same children achieved a score of fifty-four correct responses. The differences were highly significant, at the .001 level.

While there was no control group, and the children may have learned the material elsewhere on their own, the specific names of some of the items (i.e., milkman, telephone booth, gorilla), as well as the relatively short time (three months) between the pre and posttest suggests that the change was due to the intervention. One of the children, on an unrelated individual psychological evaluation, failed to correctly identify any animals other than those used in the program.

The teacher rated the unit as somewhat successful. Her criticism was not based on a failure to achieve specific goals but toward the need to provide a far more comprehensive program for children at high risk of poor language usage. Such a program is now being developed.

The third/fourth-grade teacher took his class to a nearby planetarium as part of a unit on the solar system. It is interesting that while the children enjoyed it, talked to their parents about it, and wanted to visit again, the specific content of that visit had less of an impact than the material they learned relative to the solar system in the classroom. It should be recalled that the students helped to build the classroom solar system—to plan it, cut it out, paint it, feel it, use it, and understand the concept of a solar system. Again, this suggests that simple visual exposure and discussion is not enough for children of this age, and perhaps not enough for those with a limited amount of previous verbal learning experiences.

A second type of project was more difficult to evaluate. Here, proposals were presented for materials that were designed to enrich classroom life. The materials included certain games, manipulative toys and substances, and cassette tapes. The materials were used frequently, and the teachers felt that they were of great benefit to the children in one way or another. There was probably some value in having teachers establish goals for using this equipment; it became a more thoughtful process. But the goals—such as improving cooperation, and raising self-image—were too global. It probably would have been better to accept the proposition that well-selected equipment and supplies will enhance the overall program and pay more attention to the age and task appropriateness of the equipment.

Of the fifteen proposals received for projects, only two were not completed. One was for a math interest center and the second was to bring a variety of black performing arts groups to the school as a part of a fine arts program. The math materials were not used as stated in the proposal. One performance by a young dance group was highly successful, but no other performances were scheduled. In both cases the teachers apparently bit off more than they could chew. The projects, as they designed them, required a great deal of their time to organize and implement. This is extremely difficult for a busy classroom teacher to do— and one of the most important caveats when one is trying to implement a project program.

The impact of the Social Skills Curriculum program was reflected in school attendance, academic achievement, and improved social behavior and school climate. The Metropolitan Achievement Test scores in reading and math, routinely administered in all Title I (low-income area) New Haven elementary schools each spring, were analyzed to compare King students with students from New Haven's nineteen other Title I schools. Test results for students who had been in the King School two or more years were compared with those who had attended less than two years. Data were provided by the test division of Harcourt, Brace and Jovanovich, as prepared for the New Haven Public Schools. An observer instructed in acceptable testing procedures was assigned to each classroom for all testing sessions.

The results are given in the table below and those on pages 205 and 206.

All comparisons demonstrate significantly higher scores for King students than for other New Haven Title I schools.* The student who had attended King School for two or more years had significantly higher scores in both reading and mathematics compared to those children who had been at King School less than two years (reading, T = 4.771, P .001, mathematics, T = 2.823, P .006). The students with the longer stay at King were on the average eight months higher in reading and five months higher in math than children who had been at King less than two years. It is of interest that there was no siginficant difference between these two groups at the end of five years in the Baldwin-King program, 1972–73.

Metropolitan Achievement Test Scores: King School
Grade 4—1976 and 1977*

	1976		
	High Stay Group	Intermediate Stay Group	
	Students enrolled at King School for 5 years	Students enrolled at King School for at least 2 years	New Haven Title I Schools
Reading	4.6	4.1	3.5
Math	5.2	4.7	4.1

	1977			
	High Stay Group	Intermediate Stay Group	Low Stay Group	
	Students enrolled at King School for 5 years	Students enrolled at King School for at least 2 years	Students enrolled at King School for less than 2 years	New Haven Title I Schools
Reading	4.5	4.5	3.9	3.5
Math	4.9	4.8	4.2	4.1

*The fourth grade national norm, including all social status schools, is 4.9.

*The levels of statistical significance ranged between .025 to less than .001. Differences at .05 or below indicate that the differences could not have occurred by chance alone.

Metropolitan Achievement Test Scores: Comparison between King School and all New Haven Title I Schools; raw and grade scores, 1976 and 1977

Reading Metropolitan Achievement Test:

	National Norm	King School	All New Haven Title I Schools	Number of Students: King School	Number of Students: All New Haven Title I Schools
Grade 2 [raw]	2.9	70.3	66.7	55	400
(grade)		2.5	2.3		
Grade 3	3.9	73.2	66.3	49	373
		3.3	2.9		
Grade 4	4.9	65.5	53.8	59	388
		4.0	3.5		

Math Metropolitan Achievement Test:

	National Norm	King School	All New Haven Title I Schools	Number of students: same as above
Grade 2 [raw]	2.9	54.0	51.5	
(grade)		2.7	2.5	
Grade 3	3.9	85.9	80.4	
		3.6	3.2	
Grade 4	4.9	76.8	71.8	
		4.4	4.1	

King School—Grade 4: Standardized Test Scores*

Year	Test Administered	Number of Months Below National Grade Level Norms	
		Reading	Math
1969–72	Metropolitan Achievement Test	19	18
1973–76	No Testing	—	—
1977	Metropolitan Achievement Test	9	5
1978 (May)	Metropolitan Achievement Test	8	3
1978 (October)	IOWA Test of Basic Skills	6	3
1979	IOWA Test of Basic Skills	2	2

*In 1979 a total Language Score was computed on the IOWA Test of Basic Skills. King 4th grade students scored at grade level.

Unfortunately, data from other Title I schools relating length of attendance to achievement test scores are not available. It might be argued that children who attend a school two or more years are members of more stable families than those children who attend a given school for briefer periods. But in years past in the same school, there was no significant difference between children present two years or more and those in the school less than two years. It is more probable that being a part of King School and the Social Skills Curriculum over an extended period of time resulted in improved academic achievement.

The ten-year improvement in achievement is dramatic, particularly so after the initiation of the Social Skills Curriculum.

King School ranked second among all New Haven Schools in attendance for 1976–77 and third the year before, 1975–76. The average daily attendance at King in 1976–77 was 94.5 percent. Only three middle and upper-income area schools had slightly better attendance records over the two years! Attendance comparisons are not available prior to 1975. But the King School attendance record has shown significant and steady improvement since 1968–69.

Parental involvement was discussed in a previous chapter. In prior years parents participating in the school did so as volunteers. In the Social Skills Curriculum, they were paid. There were no apparent negative results from paying parents to work in the program. The pay appeared to facilitate an increase in parent participation. For example, a coffee hour for parents had been held in the school for several years. A "good" attendance, except for special events, was approximately fifteen parents. During the course of the Social Skills Curriculum, the average attendance was around twenty-seven parents, including those working in the program. The parents continued to turn out for evening assemblies, suppers, fashion shows, fourth-grade graduation, and so on in large numbers, sometimes over 200 people in a school with approximately 350 students and less than 200 families.

Parents and teachers felt that parent participation in the day-to-day life of the school was critical to the success of the classroom projects as well as to improved academic and social performance of the students. Probably because parents and teachers were involved together in planning and implementing programs, concerns about differences in status, race, and education—if they existed—did not surface. Because there were regular ongoing working and discussion sessions, differences of opinion could be talked about and resolved. The general climate of the school did not facilitate parents attacking teachers or vice versa. The spirit of interpersonal relationships between all of the groups involved was "we can work it out."

The principal, other staff, and parents are all powerful in the King School. The principal heads the School Advisory Council, now the name of the representative governance and management body. The parents continue in support of the school program through their Parent-Teacher Power Team and through representatives on the SAC. The Pupil Personnal Service continues to assist teachers' work with individual and small groups of children with social, emotional, or psychological problems and needs. The Discovery Room continues as a resource for such children. The social worker continues to coordinate the work of the Pupil Personnel Service and works with the principal to provide mental health perspectives and expertise to the work of the SAC group and works with the parents in support of their program.

Several education specialists—the reading teacher related to the FOCUS Program (for underachieving children), outside reading and mathematics consultants and others—have again been working separately from the Mental Health Team but cooperating with it since the onset of the Social Skills Curriculum. An effort is again being made to coordinate and integrate their work with that of the Mental Health Team and teaching staff working on the Social Skills Curriculum Program. Recall that this was done successfully in year four. This illustrates a point that I would like to emphasize—no problem or adaptive arrangement or solution is permanent in an ever-changing school and society. Old and new problems demand repeated attention. School work (management), like housework is never done.

New staff, new programs, new parents, new students, new levels of people and program development require a continuing program assessment or evaluation and response to new findings. In fact, the last SAC meeting I attended in the spring of 1979 focused on a report and recommendation from a subcommittee of parents and teachers to address a mild slippage in the quality of after-school behavior. After a lively discussion, the recommendations were approved. Those who disagreed were urged to give the recommendations a chance and eventually propose new ones if these didn't work; they agreed to do this.

Because the power to move the program is in the hands of the principal and shared with staff and parents, students are receiving good support for social and academic achievement, psychological and moral development. As a result, we have not had a major behavior problem at King in three or four years now. Handicapped children have been maintained in regular classrooms without being victimized by their classmates or being viewed as a burden by teachers. Yet in observing students in classrooms and in the hallways, it is clear that most have a good balance between personal control and spontaneity, enthusiasm, and excitement. The "action" is learning and achieving and not in disruption.

How does the Social Skills Program differ from other programs? Every piece of the program—classroom banks, stores, trips to the planetarium, parents working in schools, representative governance—has been a part of other programs, some successful and some not. The difference is in our focus on the process of elementary school living as well as learning; in addressing a school as a system rather than focusing on individuals, equipment, and programs as isolated pieces. In addition, the Baldwin-King Program, and then the Social Skills Curriculum, were based on well-tested child development, social science and systems principles and applied to live situations. Specific programs and governance and management arrangements grew out of school practice needs and insights and not from the fertile but removed minds of academic theorists. Programs were systematically reviewed, added, or dropped as the representative governance and management body saw fit. The decision was based on student, staff, and parent goals and needs at that time and not on whether an idea or piece of equipment was popular, prestigious, or inherently exciting. This general approach brought order and continuity to the system rather than the chaos that innovation after innovation—isolated and not a part of a total design—brings. At the same time, flexibility and the capacity for change in response to real need was maintained.

The Social Skills Curriculum does not reduce the attention given to teaching the academic basics. The same books and methods that are used in the rest of the system are used in King. The integration of the arts and other "free-time" activities makes time available for the Social Skills Curriculum. The small stipend mentioned earlier permits teachers to give some after-school time to this program. It also appears that learning the basic skills in the context of highly relevant and interesting school activities reduces their learning time for many children. We also believe that it is out of the context of relevant, real, and simulated world experiences that a child can be related to the more abstract and removed academic subject matter; for example, history had meaning in the context of the life cycle and biology had greater meaning in the context of the personal question such as "If I swallow a button will I die?"

The Social Skills Curriculum is designed specifically to create a social context that many middle-income children already have. But many do not. In addition, many middle and upper-income parents do not give adequate attention to teaching the social skills and exploring the issues young people need to be able to manage in order to function well in the complex society of today and tomorrow. The Social Skills Curriculum model can be applied to programs serving children from every income group.

Currently the Social Skills Curriculum model is being field tested in another New Haven elementary school. An indication of the kind of interest the model has attracted is the fact that the former New Haven mayor. Frank Logue, who participated in our first election project with two other candidates in 1975, was present for the field test program site visit by the National Institute of Mental Health. Members of our staff, social workers and psychiatrists, work more and more with various administrators, teachers, and others in the New Haven School System. The Child Study Center team is now working with the parents and staff of a 5-8 grade middle school.[3] We hope to eventually work with high school and pre-K parents and educators.

While every effort must be made to improve schooling at every level, the chances of doing so in a significant way are greatest with children from kindergarten, or the earliest time they enter school, through fourth or fifth grade.[4] During this early developmental stage, parents and staff can have a much greater impact with less effort than in later school age. And yet the elementary school experiences will not be enough without similar programs at the middle and high school. Programs at the higher age and grade levels will need to continue the process of relating young people to the larger social system—with the support of meaningful adults—and providing them with the social and academic skills needed to perform well in it.

While we will be guided by what we find at the middle and high school level, we will be operating from the knowledge of child development that young people are attempting to move from a dependent to a more independent condition in the world. Thus, we will be looking for ways in which the student can participate in school governance and management in a responsible way and in their own best interest. This will include guidance and support from mature, concerned, and meaningful adults.

The Social Skills Curriculum Program was possible in 1975 because King School was functioning at a reasonably stable level. *We warn you that this program will not work unless a school is already at a reasonably stable level or goes through a process of people and program "change" and movement to this level before instituting such a curriculum approach.* An effort to implement any "piece" or "package"—or any other program—in a troubled school could make matters worse.

PART III

Introduction

When I speak publicly about our program, four questions almost always follow. The first is "How did you [the university-based Yale Child Study Center] sustain such a long working relationship with the public schools?" The second is "How can a program such as yours be replicated or applied in other communities, particularly in larger urban centers?" Third, "What kind of teacher and administrator training would enable schools to add the improvement of community and in-school relationships —and the social, psychological, and moral-ethical development of students—to academic and intellectual development work?" The fourth question is usually about the cost of the program; however, since the original program costs are given in Chapter 4, I will only address this question in general terms when I suggest ways to replicate the program in Chapter 13. The chapters in Part III will address the first three questions above.

12
Sharing Expertise

I suggested earlier that in today's school one person can lead and coordinate a school program but that no one person can have the range and depth of expertise needed to operate effectively in all program areas. Thus persons with different areas of expertise must work together. This brings up the question of how the Yale University Child Study Center team has been able to maintain an expertise-sharing relationship with school people. Many school-university cooperative efforts have either not worked well or have failed. Indeed efforts to share expertise *within* a single school are usually very difficult and often do not succeed.

Let me be clear about the kind of expertise we attempted to share. The Yale Child Study Center's psychiatrist, social worker, psychologist, and special education teacher were trying to share mental health expertise with the professional and nonprofessional school staff and parents. The parents and school staff were trying to share knowledge about children and education

213

with the mental health experts. The school staff—teachers, principals, curriculum consultants—was attempting to share expertise with each other and trying to learn from parents, aides, and others.

There are structural and relationship reasons why such sharing often does not go well. The structural problem has to do with the training of school professionals and will be discussed below. Our first job as a Mental Health Team was to address the major relationship issues—including our own presence in the schools—which often interfere with the sharing of professional expertise as well as the sharing of knowledge about the children and community among staff and parents.

The rarely discussed but major and very powerful cause of public school–university conflict is perceived differences in status among the collaborators. Society does not grant public school careers status equal to university careers. For this reason many public school people feel angry, believing that others consider them second-class citizens of education, though they are relied on to do tasks as important as those of their colleagues at the colleges and universities. They believe that working under public scrutiny involves a great deal more pressure than college and university teaching, and often envy and resent the protected status of the academic.

University people have a long tradition of using public schools as a resource for training and research, while at the same time considering public school personnel less talented and less critical to education than university researchers. The same problem exists between those who deliver service and those who do research and train service deliverers in other professions—medicine, law, and social services. As a result, when college or university researchers go into a public school, tension is high, but the anger usually remains buried.

The inner dialogue sounds much like the tale of the farmer and his (house)wife. "If you had to do my job. . . ." Like the farmer and his wife, elementary, secondary, and college level educators often do not acknowledge to one another or themselves that their tasks are different, requiring different expertise and methods, but are of equal importance. For if the outsider (university person) succeeds, cannot one conclude that the public school people are incompetent? Public school educators have no way to prove themselves at the university. The defensiveness is further complicated when the university is Yale—known and respected, but a living symbol of "the Establishment." And, as the stereotype goes, "the Establishment" cannot be bothered with the average person and the problems of poor black people.

Another major obstacle to effective university-school collaboration and expertise exchange is difference in style or problem-solving approach. Social and behavioral scientists are trained to adopt a clinical or research approach to a problem, while educational practitioners are trained to apply a methodology or introduce new materials to solve the same problem. Each group bases conclusions and proposals for solving educational problems on what is known within its own sector. The experiences, professional language, and day-to-day working realities of the two groups are profoundly different, and their professional environments are rarely the same.

The reward system in colleges and universities—publication, recognition in the discipline, and promotion—often prevents professors of education from becoming intimately involved in the day-to-day problems and programs of schools. Academic people are more often involved in developing and refining theory that has been based on isolated aspects of school operations and programs or on theory developed from other settings and sources— clinical treatment centers, child development studies, experimental research studies, and laboratories where researchers study non-human animal responses. The academic tends to want to conceptualize, study, and address underlying issues rather than to confront the immediate and difficult problems of a school.

Elementary and secondary school educators-in-practice face great pressure from parents, politicians, the media, and others to produce positive outcomes. As a result they tend to turn too quickly to technological solutions—new programs, equipment, buildings. But this tendency also exists because careful conceptualization or diagnosis of school problems and highly selective application of well-tested programs or equipment is not included in teacher and administrator education programs. Untested fads and cure-alls abound—open education, back to basics, black English, new math, old math—some of which, if applied in the right place at the right time for the right purpose, are effective. When school and academic people work together on a common problem, they often talk past one another because their perspectives and problem-solving methods, their assumptions and experience are so different. Each group characterizes the other as unrealistic and naive, which precludes the opportunity for trust and respect to develop.

Stereotypes nothwithstanding, the philosophy of the Yale Child Study Center is that research and theory-building should grow out of direct experience with the realities of public school life. Thus we entered the project having decided not to design a rigorous research project, and we communicated this to the school personnel. We were gradually accepted as participant observers.

One advantage in participating without the backdrop of a formal research investigation was a chance to understand the questions before we had to provide answers. To increase the chances for trust we made a commitment to parents that we would not write about the project until we had evidence that our findings might benefit their own or other children elsewhere. This helped alleviate the initial fear that we would exploit the school for our own research purposes and then leave right away. At the same time, because we were clinicians—social workers, psychiatrists, psychologists, special education teachers—we had skills that we were able to use to be helpful to students, administrators, teachers, and parents immediately. The ability to be useful in a tangible way reduced distrust.

First we had to confront preconceptions about academics. Telling the school people that we planned to do what was in their best interest would have been suspect; so we decided to let experience be the evidence. Thus the program was deliberately structured as a Yale Child Study Center–New Haven School System co-venture with separate funds and equal responsibility for the outcome. We hoped this format would facilitate both independence and intimacy. The schools had ultimate authority, but we agreed from the outset that program success or failure belonged to both school and university, not one or the other. Professional staff at the school were given research appointments at the Yale Child Study Center and were welcome to attend conferences. Because release time was not supported and the number of Yale Child Study Center programs of interest to teachers was limited, the teachers did not come to Yale very often. But the appointments contributed to the notion of collaboration and sharing.

The specific Child Study Center–New Haven School based programs were planned by representatives of all groups. We believed that everybody had the power and skill to develop objectives and identify and contribute to the solution of a problem.

Another contribution to trust was our stated assumption that within a short time teachers, community relations workers, and aides would all become able to handle many behavior problems without advice from Mental Health Team workers. Within a short time, beliefs that the outsiders wanted to take over were weakened. This approach eventually extended the range of skills of the staff and parents. Confidence and trust grew. Soon others who were not the primary school staff, such as consultants and student trainees, were accepted quickly as long as they demonstrated respect for the people and ways of the schools. One professional consultant was asked not to return because she insisted on removing a child from the classroom who displayed behavior problems that teachers felt competent to address in the classroom with support of mental health staff. Helping children with problems to function adequately in the classroom was an important program goal.

Another important strategy as our school-university relationship developed was to be modest in defining expectations for change and to establish trust first within small groups. That was the reason we had initially decided to work in two schools rather than with an entire system. In addition we found that didactic lectures were less effective than teaching and learning that took place around a specific issue or incident. Very early in the first program year we attempted to lecture to teachers about child development theory as it applied in the classroom. Some of the teachers who agreed most with the ideas presented in the lecture were least able to apply them in their classrooms. Some were apprehensive about trying them at all. This is even more the case when the consultant or expert is not known and the lecture setting is large and impersonal.

Our decision to work slowly and only in the two schools also enabled us to be available to support teachers who were trying new methods that had been proposed. Encouraging a teacher to try a new approach and then not being available to support him or her is a quick way to lose credibility, trust, and respect; and to lose the opportunity to share expertise in the future.

We set as low-key a tone as we possibly could while making every effort to report the program as a joint effort. Early evaluations by professional evaluator groups, newspapers, and television reports can be devastating to a struggling new program. Extensive newspaper reports in the first year of our program would have destroyed us. Statements made in public forums taken out of context or just reported inaccurately could have hurt budding trust. Because school system people are often under attack they expect it from everybody until there is evidence that this will not be the case with a particular group. Notions that the program leaders are getting all the glory "while we do the work" can also develop and hurt relationships. When we did begin to report on program development, parents, teachers, and principals participated, even to the extent of making presentations at several conventions held by mental health professionals. Reporting to others enabled the staff to better identify and take pride in their achievements as well as identify areas needing more attention.

The Yale Child Study Center attempted to maintain open and honest communications with key people in the New Haven School System by describing our efforts in private meetings, inviting key staff to some of our programs, and by trying to establish a program in which curriculum supervisors could give consultation and leadership to the Baldwin-King program and by participating in school system initiated conferences. Not everybody in the system agreed with our methods or even approved of our involvement, but most of them were cordial, and helpful when asked.

Sharing expertise among persons of different disciplines within a school is also a considerable challenge.[1] The reasons for impediments are similar to those in the outsider-school relationship. For the purpose of examining the problem of sharing expertise within a school, let us make an artificial distinction among the various activity areas of schools. The areas are administration, teaching, mental health and child development, and curriculum development. Professionals who have overlapping responsibilities are active in each area, and as they do their jobs, opportunities for cooperation and conflict emerge.

Administrators are the system superintendent and his or her staff (including subject area supervisors), and building principals and their assistants. The major task of the superintendent's office is to plan, implement, and evaluate every aspect of the school system program. This includes finances and facilitates management, personnel management and staff development, instructional activities, evaluation, research and dissemination and the promotion of staff, student and community cooperation and achievement.

The building principal is a branch manager. He or she is responsible for implementing system policy at the local level. This includes modifying policy, (consistent with the system policy), as required, to meet the needs of the local staff, students, and community being served. The principal keeps the superintendent and central office staff informed about changing conditions and needs at the local level, thereby permitting continuing program modification.

As manager, the principal has primary responsibility for operations and facilitates management. The principal is ultimately responsible for staff performance, although often department chairmen act as middle-level managers. He or she could serve as, or create and lead, a governance and/or management mechanism which permits the efficient and effective sharing of expertise in the planning, implementation, and evaluation of a school program. The principal authorizes and coordinates community participation, particularly parental, in the service of meeting the academic, intellectual, social, psychological, and moral development of each student.[2]

The school administration must enable teachers to feel free, and know where, to contact education and mental health resources and not view the need to do so as a poor reflection on their ability.

Teachers should be encouraged to participate in curriculum development, special service and administration conferences, and committees working to tailor programs to the student body, staff, and parents. Such participation is the most important element of the feedback system that should run through the office of the principal, supervisor, and on to the staff office of the superintendent and to the superintendent when necessary.

A competent subject-area supervisor has in-depth knowledge of theory and content in a specific subject area, and can apply theory to curriculum development and to classroom practice. Supervisors should help design and implement staff development programs initiated by the superintendent, principals, and school staff, and provide assistance to and evaluation of teachers. Subject area supervisors usually inform central administration about change at the local level.

Teachers deliver the critical service in a school and are most responsible for the success or failure of the school in meeting its mission of student learning and development. *All* other staff and non-staff involved in a school program are assigned to support the classroom teacher.

The competent classroom teacher is an expert in subject area content and delivery. Teachers of primary grades know the spectrum of subjects for the grade levels they teach—reading, mathematics, science, social studies, the arts, and athletics. The competent middle or junior and high school teacher is an expert in one academic area. We suggest that teachers should also know teaching and learning theories and alternative teaching methods and techniques, although often these aspects of education are not required areas of expertise for completion of the teacher training programs.[3]

Successful teachers are also careful, objective observers of children and are able to spot problems. Teachers are able to recognize when physical problems such as vision, hearing, and other disabilities are interfering with learning. They should be able to identify social and psychological problems that interfere with student learning problems such as fear, self-doubt, low self-esteem, anxiety, depression, inappropriate aggression or withdrawal, racial, religious or class antagonisms, drug and alcohol abuse, and most rarely, neurotic and psychotic behavior.[4] Also, teachers should know when to ask for help with student problems.

In most school systems there is a Department of Special Services. Most of the experts in this department are in the mental health, child development, and systems operations area. These include social workers, psychiatrists, psychometrists, psychologists, counselors, special teachers, and other personnel to support classroom teachers and students. These people should be experts in understanding and promoting, and assisting others in promoting, individual growth and cooperative behavior, and smooth operation. Various members of this department should be experts in special education, since most schools include one or more children who are handicapped, retarded, gifted, bi-lingual, physically and psychologically disabled, delinquent, truant, or otherwise in need of extra help.

The major task of a curriculum specialist is to develop system-wide curriculum, select books and materials, and modify existing curricula as appropriate. Many curriculum experts work with teachers and administrators as they develop curricula. Some curriculum specialists work directly with teachers in the classroom. Curriculum specialists often help evaluate student academic achievement, and, based on achievement levels, modify curricula.

Many small school systems do not hire curriculum specialists because of budget constraints. Thus in many systems subject-area supervisors serve in this capacity, and sometimes teachers work on curriculum development. On the other hand, some school systems are in fact overburdened with specialists who carry out uncoordinated and often overlapping tasks at the central office and local school levels. In such instances there is a greater need for personnel management by the superintendent or subject-area supervisors in order to minimize potential confusion.

Schools, then, are complex networks of human interaction. They are administered and operated by individuals, each with different tasks to accomplish. And school systems have a larger common task, which is to educate children, and therefore the personnel must have a common base of knowledge about children, systems operation and management; and the learning processes. Each expert must understand family and neighborhood systems and the impact of these environments on the child's growth, learning, and behavior. The experts should ideally understand societal functioning and its impact on local families and neighborhoods—but should not excuse poor teaching and learning because of local conditions.

Each actor/expert needs to understand the institution he or she is in—how it is organized to achieve individual and institutional tasks; the relationship of tasks to the system's mission; the reason other experts are there and what each is trying to accomplish. With an appreciation of the larger picture, each expert will then better understand the potential and limit of his or her own knowledge and skills. Experts should know when and how to use the expertise of others and feel enhanced rather than diminished by doing so. Experts must know how to use other experts within and outside a particular program and must be able to participate in the process needed to make coordination and sharing efficient and effective.

In addition, school staff should be able to work with parents and other community people who are concerned about the education of children. School staff should be able to work with volunteers and to tap the resources of the neighborhood storekeeper, local minister, policeman, and business person to give vitality and practical significance to the classroom fare, particularly in the early grades and with students who are not motivated toward academic achievement, and where the relevance and benefits of such learning are not clear to the student.

As discussed in Chapter 1, many people hired as experts are not well trained. They are often working in environments where hostility and suspicion block cooperation, where their training gaps become evident. In circular fashion, because governance arrangement and management approaches often do not promote mutual trust and respect, staff, students, and parents often feel powerless, frustrated, and act-up in subtle and overt ways. The possibility for sharing expertise and mutual support is reduced, and good teaching and learning is lessened. In such a climate, issues of professional status, class, and race grow to be pre-eminent and disruptive issues; trust, respect, and, in turn, sharing, support, teaching, and learning become even less and less possible.

A number of Baldwin-King program activities were designed to tumble the blocks to sharing by interrupting this harmful circular process and setting a beneficial one in motion. The regular meetings among principals, mental health, and education program co-directors enabled us all to consider both the disadvantages and benefits of sharing power, and the relationship of good management practices to the behavior of staff, students and parents. The mental health and education administration experts shared their understanding of systems, individuals, and group behavior, and applied it to day-to-day management of the schools.

For example, we observed together that too little attention to a personnel recommendation by parents reduced the parents' interest in attending committee meetings; but that even difficult and limiting decisions and policies will be tolerated when they are goal-directed, well reasoned, stated openly, and justified; that parent participation in decision-making protects principals against unjust criticism; that a seven year old can tolerate an hour assembly but many become disruptive beyond that point; that staff morale in January and February or during the post-holiday "blahs" can usually be elevated when plans are being made for a major activity in late February or early March.

We planned activities based on a consideration of how people and systems function. Goals were established with human and system needs and capacities in mind. Such conceptualizing and planning prevented many time-consuming problems and made administrative time available for carrying out program objectives, thereby increasing the opportunity for all other staff and parents to share their information and expertise with each other.

We found that sharing expertise in child development, human relations, and systems operation with school administrators is the most important aspect of sharing in a school program. As I have said many times in this book, behavior problems can seriously interfere with teaching and learning. To prevent and handle behavior problems, administrators should have considerable knowledge and expertise in child development and human relations. Administrator training in these areas is typically limited to theory, and usually is not taught through well-supervised school-based practical experiences. While administrators often receive information about systems operation in training programs, the impact of the operation of a system on the development and functioning of children and adults working in it receives too little attention.

This deficiency in administrator training is problematic. *My impression is that the majority of staff, student, and parent participation problems are secondary to systems management practices which do not incorporate human relations, child development, and organizational behavior perspectives.* The inadequate orientation of new teachers, parents; meetings that are too long or poorly planned; little consideration to the mechanisms needed to permit expression of discontent and problem resolution and many others are examples of management without human relations and child development, systems behavior consideration. Recall the child in our program who transferred from North Carolina and reacted by kicking his teacher.

It has been my experience that the majority of students referred for acting-up behavior problems are not psychologically ill. Most are reacting to school programs that are not managed and based on what is known about human relations and child development. Certainly the behavior of some acting-up students, particularly beyond the elementary school level, is a product of difficult social circumstances and range from problems in the economy to problems with parents. But remember that even in the most difficult schools certain teachers and principals are successful.[5] Success usually comes for people who are intuitively expert in human relations. Many more could be expert, given training.

Mental health personnel working in schools should be a major resource for principals and other school managers. Their expertise could be shared with managers to apply social science and behavioral principles to every aspect of school programs. For a number of reasons this is usually not the case.

First, many mental health people are highly enamoured with the high-status methods of working one-to-one, or working in small groups with children. Yet of the eight children I evaluated in a one-to-one setting in the first chaotic year of our program, not one had a serious psychological problem. In the case of one eight year old who was extremely active, I recommended that he be placed with a firm, well organized but warm and enthusiastic teacher the next year. That was done and the youngster became an academic star who did not act up at all. Many children appear to have serious psychological problems in difficult social settings but function adequately in good social settings.

The major problem is that most mental health people are not trained in systems operation or application of their knowledge of human behavior to the management of a school.[6] In fact many are trained in programs where they receive no specific preparation to work in schools. But even those trained in school psychology and school social work programs often have very little contact with teachers and administrators until they do an internship program that focuses on diagnosing and treating the problems of children and families. Very few programs—I know of only one—

ever train teachers, administrators, social workers, psychologists, and other school professionals in a core curriculum. Each professional is trained narrowly, learning to use different language and decision-making models. This contributes to a "Tower of Babel" effect when experts try to share expertise in schools.

Isolated training also leads many administrators to ignore mental health personnel as a resource in management, educational leadership, or even in general human relations, and leads teachers to ignore the dynamics of interpersonal relationships. For example, social workers are trained in conference and group work but often are not called on to share their skills with teachers so that teachers might better relate to parents and community.

Mental health persons and academic consultants or specialist groups in most school systems serve students directly, thus contributing to underutilization of such staff in the support of administrators and teachers. Mental health and education consultants often report to one person on the superintendent's staff, and the principal usually reports to someone else. Communication and cooperation among these respective staff persons is often inadequate. Changing the reporting relationship so that those who must work cooperatively at the level of the school report to a single individual might facilitate more appropriate utilization of mental health and education consultation. Too often the consequence of not applying human behavior principles to school management is that students are traumatized by inappropriate or useless rules and practices. The mental health workers sit at the end of this process, treating the wounded instead of working to prevent problems.

While mental health knowledge is absolutely critical for administrators, improving relationships between parents and school is a second, equally important task. It was important for us to have relationships in which parents share with the staff knowledge about their children and community. To do this, it was necessary to reduce social and psychological distance and increase the trust and respect among parents and professional staff. Knowledge of systems enabled us to structure our program so that there was joint parent-staff planning, program implementation, and evaluation. The task-oriented support of parent leaders (for example the social worker aiding a president of the

Parent-Teacher Power Team in preparing the Team agenda), promoted collaboration, not confrontation, among parents and staff.

Parent concern and knowledge about their children can aid the school program in a very subtle way. The normal group process can cause organizations, groups, or systems to protect their own members and programs, often to everyone's disadvantage. The presence of parents with power in the Baldwin-King program forced staff to see and face up to difficult problems (for example, a teacher in our program who wanted to stay in the elementary school but was better suited for the high school). The disagreement, anger, hostility, and acting-up behavior that develop when such problems are not addressed, negatively affect school climate. A climate and mechanisms that permit parents and other staff to identify problems and support corrective action can help prevent otherwise harmful outcomes.[7]

Student behavior problems often put parents, teachers, and administrators on the defensive and are a major source of parent-community and school conflict and alienation. Helping teachers to handle behavior problems increases a teacher's energy and reduces the likelihood of conflict, distrust, and disrespect between parents and teachers, and in turn, between teachers and students. When staff energy was increased in our program, it was available and used for curriculum development, for identifying learning problems, and for developing appropriate programs to address them. Because conflict between school, home and community was reduced, community resources—the church choir, the mayor, artists, fishermen—were willing to participate and be useful to the staff. All of these developments increased trust and respect, and set a positive process in motion that increased sharing and cooperation among parents, teachers, administrators, and mental health personnel.

Incidents described throughout this book show how sharing expertise, knowledge, and concern benefitted students.

Let us look more closely at what happened when the youngster from North Carolina panicked and kicked his new teacher. He entered a system that could meet his needs because a great deal of sharing of expertise had gone on, and trust and mutual respect had developed. His teacher was the same one who had previously said she could not help but feel under attack when encouraged by administrators to look at other classroom styles and ways. She was also the one who later commented in a workshop that it was important for staff members to be respectful of each other's problems before they could open up, expose their problems and shortcomings, and share ideas about how to resolve them. This observation helped to establish the climate for doing so.

When she was kicked she was furious but was by that time a disciple of exploring, conceptualizing, and developing a solution based on behavior principles and developmental needs. She was able to restrain punitive impulses with the knowledge drawn from several years of evidence that there were long-range benefits for her and the children by not being punitive. The existence of a mechanism for behavior consideration and understanding in the school, the Pupil Personnel Service, was supportive.

By that time, the Pupil Personnel Service meeting where the problem was addressed had become a volunteer seminar for teachers and all interested parties. Her principal and most of the other teachers were there to share their experiences, information, and expertise. They were able to do so because they understood the total school picture; that there was a principal who would mobilize the available resources; that there was a school effort to improve the climate of relationships in order to decrease behavior problems and increase teaching and learning opportunities; that the way they respond to children can improve or adversely affect the school climate; that there were behavior experts to assist them; that if they participated in sessions such as this seminar they would gain skills which would enable them to handle such problems in their own classrooms and would need less and less assistance.

The teachers understood, or were easily reminded, that child behavior is greatly influenced by the level of psychological and social development and the immediate and general social environment or conditions. Thus it was not difficult for them to empathize with the youngster. They knew the neighborhood and the fact that such transfers are frequent; understood the thinking of parents and relatives; understood the aunt's need to drop the youngster at the school and keep on to work.

No one spent time and energy on blaming. Rather, attention was immediately focused on an in-school solution. Teachers were free to share their experiences with similar problems and came up with a number of acceptable ways to help the student make it in the system.

Workshops, seminars, and experiences over time had created a unified approach to education and child management. The belief system of the school personnel included the notion that students can learn at a reasonable level regardless of their social circumstances; that having a problem in the classroom is not a mark of incompetence; that knowing when to seek help, and share it, in the process of solution is the mark of competence. Most important, the belief system held that there is no simple answer to any problem, that problems are resolved when people are brought together who want to resolve them and want to share skills. In fact, I believe that the concern and desire to resolve a human relations problem is as important as the approach.

The child whose behavior and learning problem were related to the expression of sexuality and aggression—who used but was fearful of "bad" words—came into a system that permitted a clinical support mechanism, the Discovery Room, to operate. The methods used are not a part of usual teacher training. Differences of opinion and misunderstandings about the objectives, methods, and outcomes of the service did threaten its existence at times. This required sharing the concepts underlying the operation with staff, listening to their concerns about the wisdom of rewarding children who were not performing well; modifying, changing or maintaining the Discovery Room methods as indicated by on-going evaluation. Sharing expertise among all to create the climate which permitted teachers to raise questions, receive explanations, and continue to work cooperatively with the Discovery Room teacher was necessary before the Discovery Room could become an effective service for the children.

Too often such misunderstandings and differences in opinion spark confrontation among adults who could otherwise be working cooperatively. In such cases teacher and helper often go through the motions of working together or openly work against one another, sometimes using the students to express that dissatisfaction. The student always loses.

The students benefitted from an academic program tailored to their needs because their parents, and the educational and mental health staff worked cooperatively and collaboratively over time. Integrating the arts, social skills, and academics in a single curriculum grew out of the sharing processes. It is only in a system with a reasonably high level of trust and respect that a teacher can admit that he or she is weak in a subject area and seek assistance from consultants and educational leaders. Only in a supportive school climate can teachers consider ways to use arts, athletics, and neighborhood resources to strengthen their teaching program.

I am told often that what we did in the Baldwin and King Schools has been tried or exists elsewhere. So what is new or different? Only one thing: we established trust and mutual respect among participants. A newspaper reporter spent a week in the King School and made an observation that supports my point. He observed that we did not do anything that is dramatically different than what is done in most schools, but the way things are done results in a better outcome. The "way" he is referring to is the application of social science and behavior principles to all activities in the school.

There are important areas of school expertise that did not recieve adequate attention in our program. Communication and public relations are such areas. We were aware of the benefits of establishing and maintaining good communications among program participants and with the larger community. We were aware of the need for good public relations. But we were ambivalent about publicizing our activities beyond the program because of the difficulties of the early years. No one wanted to draw hasty conclusions or sound praise prematurely.

Conflicts among principals and Child Study Center staff occurred because of breakdowns in communications. Similar breakdowns occurred among all groups from time to time. They occurred between the Baldwin-King program unit and the larger school system from time to time. We worked continuously to improve internal communications. We made sporadic efforts to improve communications so we would be perceived more accurately by people outside the program. But so much program energy and time went into overcoming the legacies of a difficult start that we could not give these efforts adequate attention. In addition there was some danger that opening the program to too much attention and feedback could happen before the people involved had a good sense of where they were going, how they were going to get there, and the confidence that they could achieve long-range goals. On the other hand, one of the major reasons there was little interest in our program at the end of the first five years was that we did not do a very good communications and public relations job with people outside the two schools.

Had there been careful planning before the beginning of the program to utilize the expertise of people with communications and public relations skills, we might have avoided some of our program difficulties. These people could have worked with us to advise us about the timing and flow of information based on our assessment of program progress.

It is possible, then, for a staff of professionals, each having in-depth training, much special equipment, and special programs to fail to educate students. In order to provide good learning experiences for students, trust and respect must exist so that behavior, teaching, and learning issues can be addressed. Such a climate cannot be imposed; it must grow out of governance and management arrangements and ways of working based on knowledge of social conditions and human and system behavior.

13

Program
Implications,
Replications,
and Applications

New Haven is not New York City, Atlanta, or Los Angeles. Can a program like ours be replicated in large and complex cities? Are such programs needed in middle and upper-income suburbs and small towns, and if so, how can the program be modified, adapted, or replicated for neighborhoods or school systems outside New Haven?

Let us begin with the implications for student development within such a program, and then I will discuss questions of need, replication and application.

The improved academic achievement among King School students seems to contradict findings of a body of research literature which indicates that most poor minority students are doomed to low achievement regardless of the effort made by educators.[1] Such studies missed the mark because they focused primarily or only on family and community conditions as determinants of student achievement but ignored the internal environments of schools.[2]

Our findings in the Baldwin-King Program indicate that by adopting management, relationship and teaching methods consistent with current social conditions and concurrent needs of a particular school, social performance and learning can be significantly improved among low-income, minority group students. We were able to eliminate serious behavior problems among students, and problems common among most groups of students were managed adequately. The implication is that behavior and learning problems which derive in part from historical conditions need not preclude normal school success.[3]

We concluded that focusing on the environment external to the school is shortsighted and may lead to faulty assumptions and conclusions and that the major educational catalyst, the school staff, is a critical variable that has been ignored.

Our findings show that school staff desperately want to be successful. However, because administrators and teachers are not trained to manage in systems and address the social and psychological development of children adequately, staff are often frustrated, knowing what needs to be done but not able to do it. Educators are as much victim of the educational system as students. We found that when given the know-how, administrators and teachers eagerly shared their skills, and in the process gained human systems management, child development and relationships skills. We strongly advocate that such skills be taught at the pre-professional training level and that training should continue in-service for school personnel at all levels of responsibility.

Recommendations, and in some cases mandates, for increased parent participation in schools have been made by government and private groups for a decade or more now. Yet in too many schools parent interest and participation remains crisis-oriented and marginal. We discovered that parents are likely to sustain and make a major contribution to healthy school life if they are adequately prepared for participation and are then invited to share in making important decisions.[4] The critical prerequisite for success, however, is that decision making be shared willingly, not on a token basis, because the parents know when they are being used; and under those circumstances they will contribute to rather than reduce anger, tension, and blocks to progress. Our findings have shown that many highly competent parents can be threatened by school staff; that parents with little education, income, and social achievement are particularly vulnerable. We also found that many staff are more wary or apprehensive about parent participation in school than strongly and unalterably opposed. By deliberately structuring our program to decrease threat, through carefully planned and supported parent and staff social and task interactions, sharing among parents and staff leaders became possible. The implication is that nobody can simply invite or mandate parent participation and expect it to be sustained.

I am not suggesting that our model or methods be used to address school problems everywhere. Nor has our program been the only successful one in inner-city schools. A number of inner-city school programs across the country have been successful. What are the elements those and ours have in common?

In a study of four successful inner-city elementary school reading programs operating in geographically distant parts of the country, George Weber, an educator and researcher, identified eight factors common to the four programs: strong leadership, high expectations, positive attitude, strong emphasis on reading, ancillary reading personnel, use of phonics, and individualized instruction and evaluation.[5] These are the factors which, with two partial but significant differences, we found to be important.

First, our notion of leadership strength differs from the usual or traditional in that we advocate strength through shared or consensus decisionmaking; taking care not to paralyze the principal. The second difference is integrally related to this point. While the reading approach now utilized at King School has a strong phonetic orientation, that reading program grew out of a careful assessment of King children by King teachers and Child Study Center consultants rather than out of any particular dogma about reading. Our reading program, like all aspects of the curriculum, is continually assessed and modified by the staff to meet the needs of our particular children. This approach fosters constant diagnosis, permits change in response to need, and avoids overinvestment in one method or another related to adult, institutional, or commercial interests and not the needs of students.

Successful schools are often led by principals who are unusually gifted and have the temperament and intuitive skills to apply child development and human relations principles to their school programs. Such administrators establish reasonable levels of parent-staff-student trust and mutual support, even if it is simply parent support for student compliance with school expectations. But since this is possible, why involve parents and share power? Why not select more such principals?

First, such persons are very rare. They often do not survive the vagaries of the principal selection process. Too few programs are able to train persons who do not have these skills intuitively. Even where principals are able to create a good school climate without sharing power, it is often at the expense of promoting leadership skills among others. Finally, in too many instances "strong" is a synonym for controlling and authoritarian.

A controlling and authoritarian leader operates as if there is one best way to do things. Thus accountability, flexibility, and a sense of program ownership and investment among staff are reduced, with consequent reduction in overall program success. The authoritarian, controlling approach in administrator and teacher training programs and practice has contributed to the "we teach, you learn" way of working with students which has for so long been prevalent in schools.[6]

This approach can suffocate creativity and can mask what we believe is the true value of education—learning to understand that everything is always in flux and that most questions have many answers. The result of the "single answer" approach is a curriculum based on "fact" learning doled out by people following rigid patterns rather than what we advocate: a dynamic system of planning, teaching, and process evaluation followed by searches for better ways of teaching. It ignores the relationship of the school setting or environment to student learning and social/psychological development. This is not true of all educational institutions or teachers, but it is still the preeminent style.

In our program we demonstrated that when leaders share power wisely and appropriately, both parents and teachers can develop a sense of program ownership and pride. I have observed an additional benefit: when staff have participated in school program development and the principal leaves, school operations and student performance do not suffer as severe a setback as when staff have not participated and have not gained leadership skills. *Indeed an important implication of the Baldwin-King Program is that no particular model, technology, method, or*

person is as important to improved student behavior and learning as a process that places highest priority on flexibility, accountability, shared expertise, open communication, trust, and
respect.

What is a process model? What are the principles of research and intervention on which it is based? Can it be replicated?

In such a model specific methods, technologies, equipment
and materials are less important than systematic planning, identifying problems and opportunities, or mobilizing and utilizing
resources. The methods, technologies, equipment and material—
bought, borrowed, or created—are mixed or blended by program
participants utilizing knowledge of system and human behavior
to create the social and psychological climate needed to promote
child development and learning in their particular setting.

In a process model all levels of school personnel, directly or
through representatives, participate in making decisions about
all school issues. The principal facilitates the process through
his or her leadership. Individual problems, opportunities, and solutions are not isolated but are considered and addressed in the
context of the total school operation.

The process model is consistent with the principles of intervention research and an ecological perspective.[7] Human ecology
is the study of how people and environment interact. In intervention research it is important to understand the principles of
human interaction in a particular environment—in this case the
school—and develop processes to improve the quality of these interactions in the service of achieving established goals.

The processes developed in our program, though not necessarily the methods, personnel, materials, and equipment, can be
initiated in any school; though each school operates at a different
level of development, each represents a unique combination of
assets and deficiencies, and each requires processes that address unique problems and opportunities. To achieve success in
a reasonable period of time, the initiative for and commitment to
a school system process of change should come first from building administrators and should be sanctioned, if not initiated, by
school system administrators. The requisite for system support is
critical, for without that support the school system cannot be the
psychological as well as legal owner of such a program. Programs developed or largely influenced by outsiders are less likely

to be rapidly or successfully internalized.[8] In the Baldwin-King Program too much of the initiative and interest was from the Yale Child Study Center, and we spent precious years trying to get the attention and interest of school people. In the last three years the New Haven School System has been taking major change initiatives and the Center has been supportive wherever possible.

One key component of our program was the mental health team. Due to the circumstances of our environment, the mental health team was initially brought in. However, two other organizational designs would be suitable. One is a system in which mental health and educational supervisory leadership already employed by a school system would provide intimate, comprehensive, and coordinated support to the particular school staff involved in a change program. The other is a combined internal and external mental health and educational team effort.

The drawback to the first is that busy school people charged with total system responsibility usually do not have as much time to study new approaches in depth as an outside group whose mission it is to do just that. Even with good intentions, daily responsibilities nibble away at time and energy. Moreover school staff are usually expected to follow established practices. Bureaucratic conventions often interfere with new approaches. When school mental health and educational supervisory staff collaborate in a special project with an outside group, however, the blocks to change must be confronted.

Many change-oriented or school development programs don't get off the ground because the program designers involve too many people at once, evoking widespread anxiety and even active sabotage.[9] We concluded that a few schools in a system can be established primarily as development units. Such units could become the models for change throughout the system. We believe this could become effective in school systems of any size as long as one person were given explicit authority to implement and monitor the process.

A demonstration unit within a district or system is the least threatening, least painful way to initiate change. Properly designed it can permit administrators, teachers, and parents to observe that when power is redistributed in an atmosphere of trust and respect, positive change can take place. This should permit other schools in the system to consider and undertake change efforts with less apprehension than they might otherwise experience. Attitudes about what is possible and new ways of working will infuse the surrounding education community gradually. Of course some systems are so rigid that severe shakeups would be in order before system change could begin.

Many school systems already have demonstration units. However most traditional research and development units focus their activities on isolated program areas such as personnel, curriculum, hardware, and software. I am suggesting a research and development design that incorporates and integrates all aspects of school operations at once. In this way, the relationships between various program elements and people would be considered and addressed through planning, implementation, evaluation and redesign stages.

The demonstration unit could become a comprehensive research and development model. Such a program might take place in four or five schools over a period of three to five years in each. Mental health and education support services to the principals and staff of these schools would be concentrated until a sharing of skills had adequately occurred, behavior problems were reduced, and teaching and curriculum strategies had been developed. Each could perform peer review of the other's process. This would help to maintain program accountability and uniformity within a system.

An alternate method of initiating change is to orient an entire system to change but concentrate efforts in four or five schools. At in-service workshops, administrators and teachers throughout the system could be introduced to system goals, desired administrative and management practices, and child development and human relations principles. They would then be better prepared to utilize mental health and educational support services when staff became available for a concentrated effort at their schools.

Where few mental health and educational support services are available, the process could be implemented by different or fewer people. A principal who is trained in, or adept at, human relations management could lead his or her staff as they analyze school problems and make staff adjustments and program changes following evaluation. Should sustained parent participation be identified as an important goal, a capable and committed teacher could coordinate the parent participation program and be the liaison to both the parents and the administration. A very successful teacher who is respected by and works well with his or her peers might coordinate the teacher and curriculum program and relate it to the overall school goals. The entire staff could develop a plan to integrate arts, athletics, and subject area curricula.

Utilizing school-based staff in place of consulting experts is not the approach we recommend, however, because change strategies and group management methods are usually techniques developed over time through graduate education. And although some, perhaps many, educators intuitively understand when and why groups are in trouble, the particular skills needed to reduce conflict or stress are often not available.

But no matter what form the school development effort takes—no matter how large or the level of staff training—the plan should focus on the whole school, and the process should involve all levels of staff. A number of people have tried to adopt components of our program—the crisis unit, the "Spring Fling," the banking unit—and have reported that it did not work nearly as well as ours did. The difference in outcome is due largely to the fact that their particular effort was not a part of a comprehensive school plan established by parent-staff consensus after mutual trust and respect had been established among parents, staff, and students.

Whether the process model is with or without mental health and educational consultation, the principal is a critical figure. The principal who heads a research and development unit must be highly motivated to do so. He or she must know when to utilize mental health and education consultation and not feel diminished or threatened by doing so. His or her role is to lead but not to control program direction. If the principal is not philosophically committed to this approach, and in fact "goes along" because he or she has other personal and/or professional objectives— approval of superiors, promotion—he or she can at the same time undermine the program.

Selecting staff for demonstration units is a difficult task. If possible the staff of this model unit should be realistic about complex systems and about the time required for change. A missionary zeal will not be enough. But a strong commitment to success and a high regard for parents and students is important. A missionary zeal will only work with the underpinnings of long-term planning and knowledge of educational development and technology. The question is not, as some have tried to demonstrate, either high expectations or a particular technology. Rather, success is predicated on high expectations supported by knowledge of many methods.

Demonstration units could become training sites for those who do not yet understand the process of change within complex systems. Public schools now providing internships for student teachers and administrators are rarely units in which the entire educational program is being continuously evaluated and modified. Often the status quo is transferred and those in training do not know how to work for change when they enter full-time service.

Once a research and development or demonstration unit is working well, educators can help future teachers, administrators, and other school workers learn how to facilitate and manage orderly change. In troubled settings student teachers are a burden and often create additional administrative and classroom problems. In stable but flexible settings student teachers can add an additional dimension of curiosity, searching, and learning which benefits a school.

Personnel trained in the kind of demonstration unit I have described would be prepared to work toward change in other schools in the same system or elsewhere. Early in our program the notion of periodic assessment was not well accepted by our staff precisely because assessment was not a regular and important part of the teachers' or administrators' initial college training.

Inviting college/university researchers to use development units as a research setting would give the academic theoreticians a realistic look at public schools and thereby help to reduce the suspicion that exists among school practitioners and public school personnel. Social work, psychology, and education programs often exclude cross-training. If these trainees worked together at a public school research and development unit, those who eventually work in school systems would serve the schools better than they are able to now, and teacher and administrator training could be redesigned to include evaluation of research that was conducted in the real world of public schools rather than of research done in isolated settings. Innovative methods would accommodate local conditions and would less often be based on questionable or biased research conclusions.

Will unions and politicians permit the kind of changes in governance, management, and curriculum that took place during the course of our program? If programs to improve schools are based primarily on issues of power and control, unions may be opposed. However, if programs for change designed to create a good school climate do actually improve conditions for their members as well as the students, only the most unenlightened union leadership will oppose. Teacher union members in our program are among the most dedicated teachers, serve on governance committees, and are not concerned about the letter of the contract when it comes to extra time and effort as long as the spirit of fair play exists.

Unions and politicians really have nothing to lose and everything to gain when social and academic operations improve, and a politician who supports improved schools will usually find that such support is in his or her own self-interest. The difficulty lies in finding a politician who will risk support before the data on success are in!

Most importantly, schools are not going to be improved significantly by legal or adversary procedures and antagonistic attitudes toward individuals or unions. Careful need assessment, resource identification, program planning, implementation, and evaluation accomplish this much better than accusatory confrontations and legal action. Incompetents leave, shape up, or find systems that tolerate incompetence when the climate they are in begins to call for excellence and dedication. A demonstration unit can permit this to occur without posing an across-the-board system-wide threat to anybody.

What will it cost in dollars to initiate a demonstration program, and is it necessary to add a large number of people to staff such a unit? Perhaps you are not certain which program elements are most important, when and how to introduce them, and whether special materials, equipment, and supplies would be essential.

The cost will depend largely on the composition of your existing staff. Major new commitments to expenditures for personnel are not absolutely necessary. Normally some mental health professionals are on staff at most schools or within a system. We recognize that their time is usually spread thin and as a result they are often minimally or ineffective. However large or small their number, though, the critical consideration is to involve mental health professionals who will contribute to good management, teaching, and curriculum development, who understand how to help staff share power or who have group facilitation skills. Hopefully you will also apply similar criteria to identify educational supervisory staff or subject area specialists. Normal staff turnover might permit you to replace existing staff with persons having the necessary skills at no additional cost against the salary line of the school's budget. In every school we have ever visited, we found at least one, and usually three or more energetic creative teachers who supported our approach. These teachers are excellent potential sources of leadership.

Most schools in low-income communities already receive government financial support for special personnel and programs. As noted in our "Update" chapter, our cost for ten parents of children serving as aides for fifteen hours per week was $13,500 in 1975. Teachers received $200 each for forty extra hours per week. It may well be that no need exists for equipment and supplies beyond those already supplied by school systems, though allocation and consumption patterns might have to be changed. Often we have seen schools order costly gimmicks and kits, when a school-based needs assessment would have resulted in a low-cost package of ditto masters. Costs, then, are more likely to be in energy, decisive and perhaps controversial action, risk management, and time instead of in dollars.

Who should coordinate, manage, and supervise the program and its components? In our experience, the director of the research and development support group should probably either be a social worker, a clinical psychologist, or a psychiatrist who has special training or expertise in systems intervention.

It is the director or coordinator's job to faciliate group discussion so that staff and parents are able to formulate both long and short-range school goals and strategies to meet these goals. Personnel resources will vary from school to school. At King School, the program has traditionally been managed by a social worker provided by the Child Study Center. At our field test school, where a social worker was not available, the program was managed by the principal, with specific functions delegated to teachers. One teacher was responsible for coordinating parent activities; another for pupil personnel and curriculum development. These teachers were paid a small stipend, comparable to that paid for after-school activities.

The director should have enough respect and status to be taken seriously by the school principal, the superintendent and his or her staff, the school board and other public officials. The director should have good communication skills—oral and written—or be able to utilize the skills of experts in this area when necessary in order to disseminate program findings. It can be useful if a writer or person with communications and public relations skills is a member of the team or available as a consultant.

The key needs are coordination and relatively good agreement about purpose and methods. Confusing reporting relationships and allegiances among the staff in a school will complicate and fragment the effort. An example of this would be an organizational arrangement by which a staff person had little contact or responsibility to a principal and reported to a central office person who had little contact or knowledge about a particular school. On the other hand, principals need central office direction. Principals should be under a strong mandate with clear directions from the superintendent and the board of education.

This brings us to the issue of in-school governance and management and the question of the relative importance of various elements of a school development program. *I believe that the governance and management mechanism is the pivotal element of a comprehensive demonstration school.* Our governance board contributed to our eventual success in four ways. First, it provided an efficient way for everyone to be informed and to contribute ideas about planning, implementation, and evaluation. Second, the program governance board established priorities, identified problems, created programs to redress major weaknesses, modified or eliminated programs that did not work or were no longer needed, decided when an outside program might be helpful or might overwhelm the resources of the school, and more. In fact, it coordinated all the major activities in the school. Third, when there was real or potential conflict in the system over group and individual interests, the governance and management board acted to resolve the issue before disappointment or a sense of being cheated or abused led to serious intergroup and interpersonal difficulties. Fourth, the existence and work of the board gave a sense of coherence and direction to the program staff.

One question asked often is about the likelihood that change programs can be successful in poor neighborhoods. It is often reported that poor people are hard to work with because they are often angry and alienated. This is true, but understandable. Low-income, urban, minority people have repeatedly been the recipients of broken promises. They are often wary and will test those who make promises before approving or joining their efforts. The first task for the development unit team is to demonstrate the commitment and resources to carry out promises.

During the first year of the Baldwin-King Program, there were days when I felt under personal attack. There were many nights of fitful sleep after which I asked myself, "Who needs this?" It eventually became clear that parent criticism and attack was not against me or anybody else in particular. It was against "the system," "the establishment" whose members enjoyed prestige, power, and privilege but who did not improve the quality of educational opportunities or the conditions in schools. Our strategy of responding to confrontation without reacting as if the criticism and attacks were personal, while at the same time addressing the real problems as quickly as possible, proved to be productive.

Because the blocks to positive attitude and acceptance have become so pervasive in most communities, and so many people are cynical, I will repeat several principles already discussed. The school or school system should not begin a change effort such as ours unless the authorities are prepared to provide personnel and reasonable financial support over a reasonable period of time—at least three, preferably five years or more. Even then it is important not to promise too much.

Improving schools in communities experiencing severe social stress is almost impossible without influential parent involvement. Thus the staff should be selected not only for their professional competence but for their human relations skills and appreciation of the strength in all people. The staff must be particularly committed to the concept of sharing power and expertise. People who are highly controlled and relatively powerless in a social system—most often low-income and minority group people—are more often themselves controlling and in search of power in smaller social systems such as home and school. When people are in search of power, the potential for conflict is high but energy is available for constructive work. On the other hand, they may be overwhelmed and apathetic. When people give up and become apathetic, the potential for parent support of a school program on a sustained basis is low. Thus the school principal, program director, or coordinator should work toward generating parent energy, but must know how to keep it goal-directed and positive.

To channel energy, it is very important to immediately establish and maintain a representative governance and management mechanism. Energies that are not goal-directed can quickly be discharged around petty personal issues related to differences in education, race, or income group. Because poor people face seemingly hopeless situations so often, discharging energy through anger and protest can become an end in itself, with some of the gratification that long-range goal achievement brings. The effective operation of the governance and management board—parent-staff planning, implementation, evaluation—can turn energy toward achievement and away from destruction.

Early in the Baldwin-King Program, enthusiasm for the project methods occasionally waned, and operations became haphazard. Meetings were not called regularly; officers were not selected on time. Serious communication and other problems usually developed. Repeatedly we traced these problems to breakdown of governance and management board functioning, and maintaining the board became our highest priority.

As a program develops in an urban area it will be necessary to spend a significant amount of time working with public agencies outside the school—public welfare, employment agencies, nursing and hospital agencies, mental health agencies, juvenile authorities, and adoption agencies, for example. For this reason, communications and public relations are important. We have had excellent cooperation from public welfare, mental health, and other agencies. We received such cooperation, in part, because most people who staff public agencies are frustrated by their after-the-fact responsibilities; they welcome an opportunity to support a preventive effort with parents and students. Workshops and other activities that served to familiarize personnel at these agencies with our work also promoted good relationships.

The process model can be utilized to develop schools at every grade level. But to be successful at the middle and high school level, educators at this level should be reinforcing academic and social skills students have already developed. Thus, if a school system must make a choice for economic or other reasons, it is best to start with pre-kindergarten and elementary school and expand the program to include middle and high schools whose students have already been exposed to such programs. In middle income or suburban schools, the program may be successful among older students because they already have better academic and social skills.

In high income and suburban school districts, serious behavior problems may or may not exist, but over time, these communities tend to sustain resistance. In many middle-class schools, large numbers of students are academically successful, and the community often underestimate the number of students who are having serious academic problems and who suffer the same or worse problems of self-esteem, as those in low-income schools. These low achievers in suburban schools are usually responsible for much of the violence, vandalism, and drug and alcohol abuse in such communities. But there are also problems among "the brightest and the best."

Recently, in one of the most affluent high schools in the nation, the graduating class valedictorian focused his speech on "The Great Drug Bust" of his senior year. He stated that in effect authority figures can arrest students but cannot stop them from using drugs. He went on to support generally anti-authority student behavior. His speech did not touch on the notions of promoting fair play, justice, service, personal responsibility, mutual gains, and other cooperative behaviors that sustain a society. He may not be representative of class valedictorians across the nation, but he is representative of large numbers of high school and college students.

These are youngsters who have received tremendous amounts of information about the world without adequate help in understanding its complexities, contradictions, and human frailties; without help in imagining their role and their future in it. Drug use and the graduation speech alike express the disillusionment, uncertainty, confusion, anger, and apathy so many young people from all socioeconomic levels feel today. Despite these very serious consequences of ignoring troubled students, many observers explain that underachievers are less able, or less motivated than those who achieve academic success. Too few see the need to adjust the school program itself.

The task for suburban and middle-income parents and school staff struggling to address problems is first to help others acknowledge that they exist; that the schools can, and have a responsibility to, begin a change process. As I have already stated, valuing academic or intellectual undertaking alone is not enough. The climate of a school must provide for staff and students the opportunity to trust one another, and to develop and contribute skills and talent.

The process needed to create this climate need not be remarkably different from that used at Baldwin-King. Personnel, emphasis, the order of events, technology, and methods vary. But the representative, collaborative, comprehensive school development process carried out by all the parties involved in a school program can usefully underlie any effort in these directions.

The same problems exist and the same basic approach can be used in small towns and rural areas as well. Mass communications, high mobility, and other technologically based changes have bombarded the young with information and affected life in rural areas and small towns as much as it has elsewhere. Many young people in these areas will choose to live their adult lives in urban and suburban settings. All schools should be exploring and improving ways to prepare their students for this complex age.[10]

Sometimes I am accused of being too optimistic. I am told that racism and classism will prevent sustained improvement of schools; that social conditions outside of school will overwhelm low-income and minority-group students and preclude improved achievement over time; that schools cannot improve the opportunities and achievement of the poor.

Certainly many schools serving the poor, operating as they do currently, cannot improve the opportunities and achievement among the students they serve. But they need not continue to operate in the same way. Troublesome negative attitudes about race and class will never be completely eliminated. But in schools where improved relationships permit improved academic achievement, the consequences of these attitudes can be reduced.

Improving the relationships and the quality of an education program within a school is only one part of what must be done to improve social and academic performance of students from the most difficult communities. Community development is even more important. But the best chance to promote community development is to provide students and parents with knowledge of skills necessary to make an impact on the larger social system and carry out needed development programs in their own areas.

It is easy to despair about the future of public schools. The problems in many areas appear overwhelming. But I believe that the future of America rests heavily on the future of the public school. Alternative and private schools can serve only a few— often those who have had a privileged developmental experience in the first place. De-schooling or replacing the schools with some other institutions would be catastrophic unless the transition were from successful public schools to new and equally successful alternatives.

Despair is paralyzing. I urge you to remember that chaotic, distressed, impoverished, and underachieving schools have been turned around by individual efforts just as our distressed and underachieving students were able to become productive through individual efforts. I am suggesting that most schools and school systems can become more productive and happier places to be than they are right now. But to be successful, school programs will need personnel who are trained differently. In the next chapter I will describe the education and training changes needed to meet the needs of the modern school.

14
Pre-Service and In-Service Education

In the previous chapter I described some ways schools and school systems can operate to reinforce and strengthen positive attitudes toward self and learning among students. In this chapter I propose the structure of the pre-service and in-service eduction needed by education personnel to better integrate the social/psychological and academic components of their jobs.

Introduction

While some educators still argue that their only job is to teach academic subject matter, most do not. The 1975 report of the National Association of Secondary School Principals Task Force on "Secondary Schools in a Changing Society" clearly indicates that schools have a major responsibility for each student's personal development and preparation for living as constructive citizens in the larger society.[1] The Task Force indicated that, in order to do this job, school personnel must be able to work with families and other community people to determine goals and establish priorities; that consensus about school operations must be achieved among school and community groups.

The NASSP Task Force expressed some concerns about the ability of local school people to work in this necessary way. The first concern is that organization of community opinion to determine goals and establsih priorities for education is an unfamiliar role for educational leaders. The second is that a majority in most communities now expect the schools to address social, emotional, and psychological needs of students—tasks most of the teachers and administrators were not trained to do. The Task Force urges that pre-service and in-service programs for administrators be developed so that local administrators can help the community achieve consensus. The same is needed to enable school personnel to aid student development beyond the academic area.[2]

There is other evidence that many educators are not skilled in creating and maintaining effective interpersonal relationships. Among two thousand Ontario, Canada, administrators with varying levels of responsibility, 41 percent felt that their pre-service administrator training program had not helped them acquire the interpersonal skills needed to do their jobs. No other skill area was identified as a deficit area at a level much over 20 percent.[3] Thus our own work, the opinion of the National Association of Secondary School Principals Task Force, and other studies suggest that the most critical gap in school personnel training is human relations competency.

Over the past two decades experimental pre-service and in-service training programs have been developed in response to school personnel needs for focusing on better interpersonal and student development skills. Unfortunately, these programs are often unpopular. They sometimes supplement traditional administrator and teacher education courses. Rarely do they inspire or serve as a catalyst to major and permanent changes in academic and mental health training. Nevertheless the content of many innovative programs could become the basis for an undergraduate and in-service training model that would serve the best interests of school personnel, students, and the community, and provide guidelines for integrating academic and mental health training.

Child development and the social and behavioral sciences have become an increasingly large portion of the teacher training curriculum, but the instructional methodology has remained static. The traditional lecture, reading, and note-taking are useful and rewarding in some circumstances but are probably the most ineffective way to develop personal and interpersonal skills. In such classes, future practitioners cannot experience the problems, and have little or no opportunity to apply the theory they have studied. The traditional classroom methods are probably the least effective way to motivate people to become active, open, self-motivated learners.

Teachers usually teach as they were taught. Where little attention is paid to what students think or feel, to what is confusing, or to what is debatable, the students will usually pay little attention to those components when they themselves assume a teaching position.Once a somewhat rigid style is established, changing it is very difficult, even when there are indications that it would be helpful to do so and where an individual would like to do so. Thus the findings of the following research project are not surprising.[4]

A film series about teacher/student interaction was presented at an in-service teacher workshop. The presenters hoped to stimulate teachers to be more humanistic in their relationships with students. All the teacher participants were impressed by the film and said they agreed with its message, but only 25 percent showed any appreciable pre/post gain in attitude test scores. Most showed no change. Eighteen percent showed a lower score. Very few positive shifts occurred in the students' attitude toward those teacher participants, suggesting that those who had attended the film series had not changed their own behavior very much, if at all.

The teachers were willing and the films were clear and potentially effective. However, the teachers' pre-service training did not prepare them to become lifelong learners; to be flexible and able to change. Only people who, by virtue of their own temperament and personality, are flexible and secure are likely to be able to change significantly in response to lectures, films, and other techniques frequently used in in-service training programs. I believe this is one reason research findings and new training approaches are so difficult to integrate. Thus it is very important that the pre-service education program prepare future teachers for flexibility and lifelong learning.[5]

A review of the typical teaching tasks leaves no doubt in my mind that pre-service school personnel training falls short in preparing them for their immediate and future world of work. Let us again review the work or service delivery expectations and demands of school personnel.

Tasks

Principals need to be experts at system management, instructional leadership, and human relations. Ideally, they should be able to facilitate the work of the teaching and mental health teams. They must lead the staff in identifying teaching and learning problems and opportunities, planning and developing problem-solving strategies, facilitating harmonious relationships among diverse groups, and evaluating and modifying programs. They are expected to understand the relationship between management practices and staff morale; school organization and student achievement; their management of desirable student behavior and future behavior and personality development.

Teachers must be able to facilitate the academic, social, psychological, and moral development of their students. To do so they must understand child development and how to develop curriculum and utilize materials and activities to facilitate it. Teachers are expected to be able to work with parents to facilitate the education of children.

Teachers are being asked to share in the school management effort—planning, establishing purpose and goals for the school, implementing programs, promoting good home-school relations. To do so they must serve on committees, run meetings, plan programs, give demonstrations and talks. Teachers are being asked to individualize the curriculum for a particular student, group of students, or a particular subset of a school community; for example, students with different interests or modest ability in college oriented schools. Teachers are expected to work with mental health and education specialists to best meet the needs of students.

Mental health specialists are expected to support teachers and administrators. To do so they should have the skills to address the needs of the individual or a small group of children, staff members, or parents. They should also have the ability to apply the principles of their discipline to every aspect of the school program. Pre-service programs should provide mental health students with introductory knowledge and skills in all of these task areas as well as permit them to practice and apply them in a supervised field experience.

Most of these tasks are not adequately addressed in pre-service programs. When they are, there is usually no supervised field experience to enable students to learn to apply the knowledge they have acquired, mostly from lectures. Where there are field experience supervisors, they are often the least powerful in the academic setting.

Competencies

A Task Force of the Southern Regional Education Board, composed of educators and mental health experts, classified the mental health competencies school personnel need to be able to meet the expectations and carry out the tasks outlined above.[6] The competencies fall into three categories: personal, interpersonal, and environmental organization.

Intrapersonal skills are defined as those which enable a person to deal effectively with his or her self; to know his or her own values and needs; and to respect those of others. The competencies needed are self-awareness, ability to clarify values, an ability to anticipate problems and opportunities, a good decision-making and action-taking process and an ability to keep anxiety at an optimal level.

Interpersonal skills are defined as those which enable a person to relate to others in a satisfactory way. Communication, assertiveness, conflict resolution, insight, and feeling for the position and circumstances of others, ability to sense what is going on with others and relate to it are a few of the skills required here. It also requires an attitude of positive regard for the work and dignity of others regardless of their academic skills, socio-economic, racial, ethnic, or religious status.

Environmental organization—physical and social—skills are defined as those which enable a person to create, within a particular place and social system, such as classroom, school, or factory, a climate that fosters social, psychological, and moral development as well as cooperative and supportive relationships. Social environment (governance, rules, lines of communication) management and evaluation skills are more important than physical environment management. What was clear from our program experience was that administrators, teachers, and parents could not feel free to expose their feelings and needs in an environment that did not permit trust and mutual respect.

Screening and Selection

Before discussing pre-service training models, I must present two issues for consideration—personnel selection and early exposure to schools. While many people in education represent the most humanistic and intelligent among us, too many select the field because it is the only occupation to which they have really had any exposure. And the standards for admission to many teacher training programs are so low as to be almost meaningless, though society expects teachers to be talented and thoroughly trained. In addition, some people will not benefit even from greatly improved pre-service and in-service education. They simply do not have, and probably cannot develop, the temperament and skills necessary to be successful in human service professions; yet in general no screening process exists to help aspiring teachers and the institutions make informed choices.

A screening process would permit some to choose other fields. It would permit educators to select for appropriate aptitude, interest, and abilities. An early and continuous field experience would permit others to select themselves out or be counseled out by supervisory staff before a major investment of time, money, and energy had been made. Where it is not possible to screen or select applicants, pre-service educators should explain in detail to applicants the realities about the status of teachers, school and community expectations, and the tough relationship issues they will have to address one way or another.

It is important that prior academic achievement standards for selection to pre-service education programs be maintained at a reasonable level, and in some cases, raised. But raising them to unrealistic levels as a device for raising status would eliminate some highly qualified people. Teaching is both an art and a science. A reasonable intelligence and achievement level combined with good relationship skills is the mix which makes good teaching most possible. The focus of admissions process must include a quest for people who have reasonably good academic achievement records and are interested in working to establish and maintain smooth working relationships with colleagues, parents, and children; for people who have or can develop good intra and interpersonal and environmental management skills.

In the next part of this chapter I will describe programs I believe are needed for administrator, teacher, and mental health personnel training—programs that would provide the perspective, attitudes, knowledge, and skills needed in the modern school. I do not presume to know whether existing pre-service curricula across the country are adequate to prepare teachers to teach academic subject matter. Other people are more qualified than I to discuss the changes needed in specific content areas. Therefore, while I will outline a comprehensive program of pre-service and in-service training, I will concentrate my discussion on those aspects of training related to preparing educators to become continuous learners, able to support social, psychological, and moral development among students.

Clearly the competencies and skills that school personnel will need overlap disciplines. But I will separate the disciplines for purposes of analysis and discussion. I will begin with the pre-service education of teachers, because they are key people in schools and the most important part of teacher education is the undergraduate program. Pre-service programs for administrators and mental health people should be adjusted, where necessary, to mesh with teacher pre-service program content and organization.

A Teacher Pre-Service Program

Teacher pre-service training programs, which are typically part of the four-year undergraduate college or university programs, are usually sufficient in time though deficient in substantive content. In my opinion, most existing programs should be refocused and restructured to better meet specific future work expectations and tasks. The goal of the first year-and-a-half of study should be to broaden a student's perspective and establish a foundation on which future specific skills can stand.

To provide an appreciation for the purposes of education, all teacher training programs should include instruction in economic and social history, and should include the history of education in America. This is probably best acquired through liberal arts courses such as history, literature and the social, behavioral, and natural sciences. Courses in child development and introduction to teaching would be most helpful if taken during the first year of training. The child development course should include knowledge about how children acquire and express cognitive or thinking capacities, social, psychological, moral and physical skills and competencies at each age level. In addition, the implications of cultural, racial, and ethnic diversity as they pertain to human relations and learning should be considered during the first year.[7] The introduction to teaching course should expose future teachers to the training and service expectations of the profession. These two basic courses would be the foundation on which task-oriented knowledge and skills are laid throughout subsequent training.

A supervised field experience of an hour a week should be mandatory during the first year. Closed-circuit or taped television exposure to school settings could replace field experience if necessary. Television can more closely approximate a field experience if students participate in simulated games or role-playing exercises in small groups after television viewing.

The traditional instructional methods used in course presentation is satisfactory for the first phase non-field experience part of teacher education programs, but staff trained in the behavioral sciences should be available to accompany students to the field. Observations of teachers in service should focus on lesson organization, teaching style, student management, and other relationship issues.

The behavioral and social science courses might be given as an integrated package based on concepts presented in the child development and introduction to teaching courses. This might serve to integrate notions about social conditions, child-rearing and development, school management and teaching.

The goal of the second phase of pre-service education should be to begin to apply general academic knowledge to specific teaching tasks. This phase should be about an academic year in duration. The curriculum content and methods I am recommending here represent a significant change from the format of traditional pre-service programs. Students should be preparing for the extended supervised field experience by taking subject area content and methods courses as well as courses which will help them develop intra and interpersonal and environmental man-

agement skills. Courses in educational diagnosis should be offered to help students learn how to assess self, the school, the
student, and his or her out of school environment, so that source
and relative contribution to learning and development difficulty
of each can be understood and serve as the basis for developing
a useful response to pupils. Course work should enable future
teachers to understand the proper use and limits of diagnostic
tools such as reading level, achievement, intelligence, coordination, and maturity tests. Courses should be offered to help
teachers learn to evaluate curricula and materials and utilize
the most appropriate for a particular kind of problem; to supplement existing or develop or build their own materials and curricula when necessary.

Future teachers should be taught the basic principles of
school organization and management. Either as part of such a
module or as part of the concentration on teaching methods,
future teachers should be taught classroom organization and
methods. They should have an opportunity to learn to plan and
organize classroom activities—trips, plays, athletic contests, assemblies, meetings—and to appreciate the impact of poor and
good planning on student, staff and parental attitudes and behavior.

Future teachers should have an opportunity to learn realistic
alternatives to negative disciplines or scolding, punishment, and
exclusion. They should be shown how troublesome behavior de-
rives from problems such as poor transitions, inappropriate materials, poor planning, student concern about staff attitudes; how
to use any and every activity in the school—including ideas and
information in curricula materials—to enhance a student's
sense of belonging; how to settle fights and manage various
transitions. They should understand the specific way their responses and decisions either work to enhance or defeat growth—
their own and their students' growth.

Future teachers should be taught that parents are usually
anxious about school, and some of the reasons; that the parent-
teacher relationship is often stressful because of parental expectations. They should have simulated interviews with parents,
hold mock parent-teacher conferences, and eventually work directly with parents involved in school governance. Advanced students might even present workshops for parents. Future
teachers should be taught about the kind of ambivalences

teachers, administrators, and mental health support staff have about parents and about one another and how to facilitate cooperative working relationships.

A course or course concentration should familiarize teachers with the signs and symptoms of learning disabilities, organic brain problems, social and psychological problems related to drugs and alcohol abuse, psychotic behavior or social stress, such as family, racial, class, or other problems. Teachers should know when and how to work with minor or temporary problems and how to work with support staff to aid students who have more serious or disturbing problems. The teachers should learn when or on what basis it is appropriate to refer a student to support staff; and that doing so is not a sign of failure. Teachers should learn how to manage their attitudes and feelings about and their behavior toward problem students; overinvestment or underinvestment in a student can both interfere with his or her development and the teacher's performance.

Instructional methods and technologies during this second phase should permit the pre-service student to be active and to experience simulated teaching duties. Opportunities to observe a range of appropriate teaching, organization and management, and mental health support staff techniques should be available if a cooperating school can be identified. For example, opportunities to observe skilled teachers teaching, psychologists or psychiatrists doing evaluations—with proper respect for patient or subject privacy—would be useful. Student teachers might observe or participate in school governance and management procedures in their own classes or under supervision in the community. Closed-circuit and taped television can be used when live participation is not possible.

Future teachers should have a chance to learn to lead a discussion or plan activities in simulated classroom settings in order to promote independent thinking and participation in groups. By using videotapes and diagnostic tools, teachers-in-training can learn to recognize when they are waiting too long, not waiting long enough, putting down a person's idea, not exploring, playing favorites, and other responses that discourage constructive participation and often promote negative behavior. Teachers can be shown how their classroom practices enhance or deter development of the goals of education they identified during the first year and a half of training.

Situation simulation and/or role-playing can approximate the live conditions of school. Case-study methods can be used to consider and develop strategies for managing a variety of school situations. Psychodrama, relation techniques, listening, communication, and empathy and assertiveness exercises can help future teachers acquire intrapersonal and interpersonal skills. Small group workshops or laboratories could be used for many of these activities. Many instructional methods and techniques are available to the creative staff and students; indeed, students should learn to create instructional techniques and methods from chance opportunities and materials not ordinarily thought of as instructional. Experiential learning should replace the lecture when possible and appropriate.

In addition to teaching methods, staff with organization, management, and mental health knowledge and experience should teach courses or supervise students during this second phase. Such staff could include psychologists, social workers, psychiatrists, and/or others with social and mental health training and expertise.

A very important word of caution is needed here. Mental health personnel generally use individual and group exercises and techniques to help people develop personal, interpersonal, and social system management skills such as role-playing, sensitivity groups, simulation, and psychodrama. These techniques can be very valuable when combined with or integrated into a curriculum. But too often they are offered as as substitute for rigorous management and teaching training rather than as complementary training. I have talked to teachers and administrators who complained that their training programs were dominated by "touchy-feely stuff."

Mental health people teaching in pre-service programs must understand the big picture, or total school social system dynamics, and not be unduly enamoured with any particular segment of it or any particular technique. They must understand that good management skills are necessary to create a positive school climate; that relationship skills cannot be a substitute for good management and effective teaching. Used in isolation, mental health techniques can be gimmicks—stimulating and pleasurable, but of no real value to a future administrator or teacher.

Because many mental health techniques appear neat, clean, and quick, they appeal to people who want to work differently without really going through the pain and pleasure of a change and growth process. Because mental health techniques can be easily packaged as treatment or behavior modification programs, they are often commercialized and oversold, utilized by persons not qualified to determine when they should be used, who should be involved, and what outcomes are possible. Adverse effects are possible and potentially damaging. For example, putting people in touch with their feelings before there is a supportive environment or before they have developed healthy defensive and adaptive mechanisms can be traumatic. Thus mental health staff should be selected carefully, and the mental health component should be an integrated part of the education program.

The field experience during this second stage should be slightly longer than during the first—perhaps an average of two hours a week—in a block or over an academic year. This experience should be carefully planned to achieve specific goals. For example, a goal for student observers could be to study planning, organization, cooperation, self-esteem promoting and achievement motivation strategies and activities in a classroom and school.

During all the simulated and field experiences, instructors should discuss strengths and weaknesses with individual students. People who are not likely to overcome serious weaknesses should be told so, and should be counseled into another field.

The third phase of the pre-service program for teachers should be an extended supervised practice period in a school. This experience should give the pre-service student an in-the-field opportunity to apply theory, knowledge, and skills acquired through non-practice situations and simulation, and from the previous brief periods in the field. The end of the third and the beginning of the fourth year is a desirable time for a practice period. The student teacher would be exposed to classes, beginning and ending or transition activities, and would have a break in the middle to reflect, recoup, and even reconsider his or her interest in teaching. A decision at the end of the third year not to pursue teaching as a career is easier than at the end of the fourth and final year in college.

During student (or practice) teaching, the students should have an opportunity to observe a highly competent and successful teacher organize and manage a classroom, teach subject area material, and facilitate the social, psychological, and emotional development of students. This should include academic, social, and psychological diagnosis or evaluation of students, self or other staff, school or community problems, and opportunities interfering with or facilitating learning. The experience should enable the student to observe the teacher working with the administration, support staff, and parents around school governance, management, and other matters. The student teacher should have an opportunity to do all of these things, under supervision, him or herself.

The instructors should include staff of a local school as well as college or university staff, including teaching, administrative, and behavioral science personnel from both. Again the instructors should work together to carefully plan a student teaching experience so that specific goals are achieved.

The fourth phase, or the last half of the fourth or senior year should be an integrating and preparatory period. The student has acquired information through a variety of methods and experiences. While great effort should have been made to make it as coherent a process as possible, it is an inherently fragmented one. An integrating course and/or an organizing, integrating paper or project could be useful in preparing the student for a future service position. A course that reviews the relationship between social conditions, child rearing and development, teaching and school management would be as useful here as it was during phase one and equally critical. In some places such an activity might serve as a bridge course for teachers, administrators, and mental health personnel. This would permit pre-service personnel from all areas of education to acquire a common professional language and to feel related so that they can work together on the job.

The pre-service programs for elementary and high school teachers should reflect the developmental stage and needs of students. The elementary teacher should be prepared to help the youngest students feel cared for, adequate, and secure. The teachers of older elementary and high school students must be prepared to help them feel the same but also to develop greater independence and responsibility, personal or inner control, motivation, and direction. Elementary teachers should be made aware of their greater potential to influence the academic, social, and psychological development of students; they should also be aware of the way student motivation is more directly tied to the quality of teacher-student relations at this level.

Pre-service programs for future teachers in the arts and athletics have more potential to influence the psychological, social, and moral development of students than other subject area programs. In these areas there is an opportunity for students to achieve and to acquire self-esteem and gratification based on more personal, less rigid attitudes and standards of performance than in academic areas. Arts and athletics provide opportunities for students to learn about winning and losing, competition vs. exploitation, cooperation and collaboration vs. excessive individuality, control vs. lack of control, appropriate levels of enthusiasm and sponteneity vs. concentration and discipline, anxiety management, tension discharge, self-control, planning, practice, creative expression, nutritional and physical fitness, mental fitness, and fair play. Games and activities can be designed to more directly teach these values and skills.

Unfortunately, as presently taught—with emphasis on performance or a finished product—the arts and athletics are not providing the benefits they could. Many local communites are calling these important activities "frills" and often sacrificing them first when budget cuts are made. Pre-service programs should help future educators appreciate that the arts and athletics are an essential part of any school curriculum, and must include methods of using them in other subject area classrooms. Special courses and teachers in the arts and athletics are desirable but not always possible.

The teacher pre-service program I have outlined above should go a long way toward preparing teachers for the real world of education; yet it cannot give them experience. Thus the new teacher in a school needs an in-service and special support program to minimize the problems of inexperience and facilitate adjustment. I will discuss this matter in the section on in-service programs.

Administrator Pre-Service Programs

Principals have the greatest need for intra and interpersonal and environmental management skills. When a principal lacks such skills all the time, money, energy, and programs above and beyond the level of the local schoolhouse are of little benefit. Research findings, modern hardware, and the plans and expectations of well-trained, highly motivated school superintendents and even local school staff cannot be effectively utilized when the principal is unable to manage well.

Principals and other administrators need a pre-service program that concentrates most on school organization and management but includes curriculum and instructional development and mental health studies. Although requirements and programs vary from state to state, in recent years administrator training programs appear to have been more integrative and more geared to mental health skills than teacher education programs. Many pre-service programs above the master's level include courses in school administration, law, and finance; curriculum and instructional development, supervision, test, measurement, and statistical methods needed for evaluation; educational psychology; and sociology, philosophy, guidance, interpersonal relations, and social issues.

The best administrator pre-service programs above the master's level utilize a combination of lecture and simulated experiences—role-playing exercises, case-study methods, closed-circuit television, and video tapes. Some programs are designed to have students of administration work in simulated projects with actual parents, teachers, and students. The faculty of such programs generally include people with education, administration, and mental health backgrounds.

Some master's level administrative training programs offer similar courses. Unfortunately, master's level programs for administrators are more often given in a predominantly reading and lecture format. The content and balance between organization and management, curriculum and instructional development, and mental health is often not related to the realities of practice. In addition, few master's-level programs require a well-planned, carefully supervised, extended field experience.

Some states have complicated the problem by requiring master's-level training for teachers after a realtively short work time, generally five years. Master's-level administrator certification can be gained by taking electives in administration in a student's subject area master's program and tacking on ten to twelve additional hours of training in administration. This serves to bring many people into administration who have little real interest in it, people who do not show promise in this area and who are often poor teachers trying to escape the classroom.

Because there is little screening and selection at the teacher and administrator pre-service program level, training in personnel management is extremely important. Perhaps the weakest aspect of administrator training programs at all levels is personnel selection, evaluation, and development. Thus, too many teachers enter administrator training programs who do not have the needed skills. And most master's-level administrator programs rarely provide them.

In too many school systems, the problem is further compounded by political patronage factors involved in the selection of personnel. While this is a political or social policy issue, it is related to training. Persons who recognize their limitations as teachers and future administrators often take courses leading to administrative certification because of their political connections. This adversely affects the participation and motivation levels of able students and staff of administrator pre-service programs.

Requiring teachers to obtain master's-level certification has another negative effect on teaching. There are salary and prestige rewards for master's-level training. While teachers gain knowledge in such programs it is often not directly job related. Knowledge is transmitted in the abstract and, at best, through simulated experiences. Teachers are not rewarded for improving specific task-related skills through in-service training and staff development programs. Out of school training—with courses at night and on weekends—often interferes with staff development efforts in a particular school or system. The latter often requires after school time.

In short, the pursuit of degrees rather than job-related skills works against the development of the latter and leads a number of people into administration who are poor candidates for it. Reducing the emphasis on advanced degrees for teachers or awarding them based on work and participation in in-service, task related training programs and making master's-level administrative training more autonomous from subject area programs is indicated. Finally, as previously mentioned, I know of only one pre-service program—not in a school of education—that has a bridge course to bring together administrators, teaching, and mental health personnel. The difficulty such staff have in working together in a school is a major contribution to school problems. Administrator training programs very much need to provide bridge courses for future administrators.

Mental Health Pre-Service Program

Social workers and psychologists are the key school mental health personnel. In some settings, guidance and special education personnel are mental health staff, though in other settings they work exclusively as career counselors or in clearly delineated academic support roles. Few psychiatrists do more than provide evaluation services in school. For this reason I will confine this discussion to school social work and psychology training.

Social work and psychology pre-service programs should concentrate on school-related mental health issues. But the training should also provide students with a good understanding of instructional methods and the basic principles of school organization and management. School social workers and psychologists should have survey courses that teach them some basics about how children learn to read, do mathematics, and acquire other basic skills. They should be taught how the curriculum can be used as a tool for promoting social, psychological and moral development of students as they learn basic academic skills.

Pre-service programs for school social workers and psychologists should include a course in the history of public education with emphasis on parent-school relations, the development of administrative bureaucracy and the unions, and the use and role of mental health professionals in schools. Future school mental health workers should have an opportunity to learn about the tensions and potential for mutual support among mental health, administrators, teaching personnel, and parents in schools and how to cope with it as well as how to help others minimize relationship problems.

The organization and management course should show psychologists and social workers how management affects the attitudes and behaviors of all the participants in the school enterprise. It should help them learn how to utilize planning, orientation, transition, personnel selection and development, and other management functions to prevent or reduce interactional problems. Training programs should teach school mental health personnel how to transmit their in-depth knowledge of child development—cognitive, psychological, social, moral—and rearing and general mental health skills to other school staff, parents, and students as appropriate.

Mental health pre-service personnel would benefit from a bridge course with teachers and administrators. In addition they should have a field experience in schools prior to taking a professional job. Educators and administrators should teach or assist mental health faculty in pre-service programs for social workers and psychologists who will work in schools.

The curricula of school psychology programs comes closer to preparing students for practice than most social work programs. But most school psychologists are not trained in school psychology programs. Most acquire certification by taking a number of required courses in psychometrics, child and general psychology areas. Many people titled "school psychologists" are actually psychometrists—able to administer a variety of diagnostic tests but not really able to evaluate home and school conditions affecting development and learning, and work with a teacher to develop and carry out a management plan. They are not able to apply the principles of the social and behavioral sciences to all aspects of the school program.

Few schools of social work specifically prepare students for work in schools. Most have relatively few courses related to children and schools. A significant number have no courses related to schools or children in schools.

In-Service Programs

In-service training should meet the continuing education need of teachers, administrators, mental health workers, parents, and other personnel. It should help the new school professional become effective as quickly as possible. It should enable parents to better support the education of their children. It should facilitate school change in response to changing conditions and needs. Because the infusion of different or better trained staff into schools over the next thirty years will be slow, the best chance for significant changes in school practice in the near future is through in-service efforts.

In general, in-service training is less effective than it could be. The major reason is that it is frequently not a part of the program implementation, problem-solving apparatus of the school. Too often the in-service program is tacked on. Ideally the in-service program should be designed by the governance-management group that identifies key problems and opportunities, establishes specific programs and goals to address them, and mobilizes and develops available resources. The in-service program should be part of the resource development process. In this way the skills being taught have high relevance and priority. It is possible to broaden staff and parent interests after in-service programs have helped them meet highest priority needs.

When the governance-management body is representative of all involved in the work of the school (parents, teachers, administrators), there is a clear and compelling mandate for self-development and for school development. In such a situation, more than the most independent and secure among a staff are free to search and change where indicated. The mandate is all the more strong when the central administration strongly supports staff and individual school development through in-service program efforts. But non-specific and/or system-wide in-service programs are likely to miss the pressing task needs of staff and be tolerated or endured rather than beneficially exploited—unless such programs either introduce staff to or grow out of specific school-based needs.

In-service programs would be greatly strengthened by basing pay increases and promotions on in-service participation time and effort rather than on advanced degree acquisition. Programs could be developed in which university staff joined school staff in sponsoring such training. This would draw the university closer to the day-to-day life of the school and draw schools into the world of theory and research. The staff should include persons with instructional, administrative, and mental health expertise.

An in-service program should provide special assistance to new professional workers. It should support the continuing development of management, instructional, intra and interpersonal and environmental organization skills of all. While in-service curricula should be based on identified school needs, workshops, seminars, and other planned and informal instructional settings, it should utilize the full range of available instructional methods and technologies—television, role-playing, tension-reduction exercises. But they should be primarily in the service of addressing needs and not simply temporary stimulating, satisfying, even distracting, gimmicks or activities.

School-based in-service training should not eliminate system-wide in-service programs or input by local or national experts. Such programs should be used selectively to advance staff development goals determined at the central office and local school level. School staff can also benefit from the cross-fertilization and stimulation gained by attending regional and national professional meetings. But their best chance of utilizing what they learn at outside meetings exists when they have a chance to introduce it through the in-service program of their own well-managed, well-functioning school.

I would like to stress that curricula change in administrator, teacher, and mental health pre-service and in-service training should not take place abruptly or with missionary zeal. Carefully designed and evaluated experimental programs should be the basis for major program changes.

Nothing will ever be able to restore the natural mutually supportive and reinforcing relationships among community-home and school which existed a generation or two ago. Such a relationship is not necessary to build effective schools today. But trust and mutual respect among community-home and school can and must be restored; school staff can become powerful and influential in the lives of most students again. With appropriate emphasis on mental health and related managment skills school staff can be empowered to reduce the immature exercise of negative power by too many of today's students.

The pre-service and in-service programs, changes, and approaches I have outlined above should give school administrators, teachers and mental health personnel greater capacity to work cooperatively. Such skills would permit parents to relate better to schools and support the educational process. A school that is able to address student needs in an orderly way—first with attention to social and psychological comfort and trust and then through academic and intellectual growth—is in the best position to prepare students for successful living in the complex society of today and tomorrow.[8]

I agree with the argument that improved schools alone will not improve the life chances of large numbers of students; that improved training, management, and mental health techniques alone will not bring all schools to an optimal level of functioning. School programs are one part of a very complex set of problems, largely social, political, and economic.

A useful approach is to achieve success at some strategic area in the complex system and use it as leverage for total system change. After the family, the school is the most important developmental unit in modern social systems. By concentrating on ways to make this important unit function better, insights and leverage can be gained for making the complex larger system function more smoothly. Even without major political and economic change, many individuals, families, and groups gain power and influence through the knowledge, skills, and accreditation they acquire in the educational system. The needs of such people cannot be tossed aside in order to wait for the millenium. Many programs have demonstrated that much can be done to improve schools right now. Knowledge and techniques utilized in these programs should be used to improve more schools now—and eventually to improve the society.

Epilogue

1980–1992

After the 1979–1980 academic year our Yale Child Study Team discontinued our direct involvement in the King and Brennan project schools as planned, but earlier than scheduled. It was our original intent to help the schools institutionalize a self-sustaining, self-improvement process, and then concentrate on disseminating our approach throughout the New Haven School System, as well as elsewhere in Connecticut and the country. The project schools had institutionalized the basic process, but we wanted to learn more about the relationship of social skills to academic achievement among all students, particularly low income students from families outside the social mainstream. But the federal government attack on social programs gained momentum around this time, and we could not get financial support for our team.

In some ways the setback was a blessing in disguise. We would have learned more about the students in these two schools, but we would not have addressed the charge that the improvement was due to our presence or to the uniqueness of the parent, student, and staff populations at the two schools. And at that point there was still a general feeling in the society that it didn't matter so much if many young people did not do well in school—that they would find security at the bottom rungs of the economy; and that the world was unfolding as it should. Thus, there was not a great deal of enthusiasm for our model. At best there was cautious interest.

Also, for many reasons—some amusing had they not been tragic—there was, and still is, a determined need to believe that "those kids can't." A principal in a nearby school told me that we would not have the same success in his school as at the King School, because while the King parents were largely low income, they lived in single family homes, and his students were from a housing project. When I pointed out that the Brennan students, who *were* from housing projects, had had success, he countered, "Yes, but those are two-level dwellings; ours are multi-level dwellings." To his credit, once involved he came to believe that all kids can learn, and he helped his school make excellent gains. But he, like so many, was a victim of the kind of social and behavioral science research that points up the very real problems (life *is* difficult in multi-level, multi-family housing projects populated by large numbers of poor, non-mainstream, more often minority families) but doesn't leave anybody with a clue about why or how to improve the situation.

It had been clear to me since the 1950s that a new economy was coming that could not absorb the undereducated in a way that would enable them to take care of themselves and their families, with benefits for their communities and the society; the society was going to need to educate all its children to meet their adult tasks and responsibilities. We had just demonstrated that kids who according to "common knowledge" could not learn and behave well in face *could*. There was an urgent need to demonstrate that our work was not a fluke and that it could be repeated without exorbitant costs. And yet I probably underestimated the urgency and wanted to spend much more time learning and developing our model more fully.

The late Ron Edmonds and his colleagues—in important, pioneering work—studied schools that had served low income students successfully without special programs. They identified several correlates of success: safe and orderly environment, clear and focused school mission, strong instructional leadership, high expectations, opportunity to learn and adequate student time on task, frequent monitoring of student progress, and good home-school relations. Many people were beginning to try to create the identified conditions—called Effective Schools—with little or no knowledge about the processes involved in making these outcomes possible. Ron supported these efforts.

I was concerned lest the Effective Schools Movement, which was based on Ron's work, would promise more than could be delivered without a theoretical framework and knowledge gained from the study of these schools, as well as a number of field tests that would help explain the processes involved; and I feared that the baby of successful schools serving poor children would be thrown out with the bathwater of poor understanding, poor program implementation, and premature negative evaluation. But Ron was more urgently concerned that research literature of the day suggesting that schooling didn't matter was going to make it possible to write off poor, mostly minority kids before new research could establish that "poor kids can." He believed there was an immediate need to charge educators and schools with the responsibility of educating all students adequately even if we didn't fully understood the critical processes involved.[1]

A mutual friend arranged a meeting so that Ron and I could exchange views. He agreed that, through the use of our School Development Program, our project schools had become Effective Schools as defined by his correlates. He pointed out that while he had used child development and mental health concepts, more than anything else we had used common sense. But he felt that too many educators would argue they could not be held responsible because they did not have child development and mental health training; he held that it was important to change expectations first, and fully understand the most effective way to educate poor kids later. He encouraged me to develop our theoretical framework and field test our work further, but to give the work the visibility needed to make it clear that poor, minority children can achieve well under adequate school conditions. In retrospect, both approaches were necessary and complementary. We began to think more about dissemination and visibility, and toward these ends I renewed my effort to publish *School Power*.

We had been working on dissemination within New Haven. First, we worked directly with several other elementary schools. In 1979 the New Haven Superintendent of Schools, Dr. Gerald Tirozzi, began to develop an Urban Academy that involved key departments and people in the state system, some staff from the University of Connecticut, and our Child Study Center team in a school improvement plan for all the Title I or low income schools. Under this program our model was used as the primary intervention approach, but responsibility for intervention ultimately remained with the New Haven School System. Our staff provided workshops for the governance and management teams and the School System Department of Pupil Personnel. A steering committee made up of representatives from the three institutions governed and supervised this activity.

Unfortunately, a key component of the program—the paid parent in the classroom—was dropped because of financial and local political reasons. Parents participated as volunteers only. And there was no paid time for the meetings that would have been needed to give the process adequate attention. Schools had to squeeze time out of infrequent existing meeting times, or give volunteer time. Nonetheless, most of the schools made social and academic gains.

After Dr. Tirozzi was appointed Commissioner of Education of the State of Connecticut, the new superintendent, Dr. John Dow, reviewed the programs of the system and decided to use SDP (our School Development Program) as the key component of his improvement plan, Project Excel. But less than a third of the schools are now actually using the model as it was designed.

Dissemination

As a result of the publication of *School Power* in 1980, I received a call from the office of Federal Judge Douglas W. Hillman, who was handling a school desegregation case in Michigan; after considerable exploration, and as part of the case settlement, he ordered the Benton Harbor School District to use our model.

We had only the early dissemination experience in New Haven to draw on when we were invited to work in Benton Harbor, and we were not yet prepared to carry out a national dissemination effort. Our knowledge of organizational behavior suggested it would be wise to structure the intervention so that it would take form from within rather than be imposed from the outside. Thus, we decided to train as program coordinator a person from Benton Harbor to learn and implement the model. But I fell victim to the traditional notion of providing theoretical information rather than thinking about what we had found to be actually most effective in our own pilot project work: collaborative efforts that promoted a buy-in or acceptance of change. As a result, we made a major mistake in structuring the first out of town dissemination effort. But we probably learned our most important lesson from it—collaboration is critically important, as important as, perhaps more important than, individual effort; indeed it is a major reinforcement of individual effort.

Using criteria I had developed with then Benton Harbor Superintendent Dr. James Hawkins, he selected a project coordinator, Ms. Erma Mitchell, who was a very effective special education teacher with good knowledge of child development, a track record of successful work with students, parents, and peers, good organizational skills, and a strong commitment to creating conditions that would make it possible for *all* children to succeed in school.

Ms. Mitchell spent an academic year in New Haven learning our model and returned to implement it in Benton Harbor. She had an excellent understanding, but immediately ran into resistance from her colleagues: "You had that wonderful sabbatical year in New Haven, at *Yale*–now *you* do it." The problem was that our training did not help the coordinator promote collaboration. Eventually, Dr. Hawkins came to New Haven, observed, and convinced himself that our approach could work, and helped us understand the need to involve the intended collaborators. We then brought representatives from among all the adult players in the Benton Harbor system to New Haven for a two-and-a-half-day orientation to SDP concepts, direct observation of SDP schools, and discussions with parents and school-level and central office staff to help them get their own program off the ground.

We learned a second very important lesson—that no component of the process can work effectively in isolation; that an important sequence of activities must take place before the climate is right for collaboration and change, and that the governance and management function must be in place to implement the process of change systematically. And we learned again, as we did in our two initial pilot schools, that unless a "critical mass" of staff and parents buy into the ideas and begin to support them, resistance and conflict will develop or be heightened. The paid parent component was the only program that Mrs. Mitchell could implement, and these parents were soon acting in an organized, exploratory way that was threatening to the involved staff. Adversarial relationships developed. Eventually parents and staff overcame the ill effects of the troublesome start and made significant progress; but the system—like many urban districts under social stress—has since then been hampered by enormous community problems and related leadership changes.

In 1984, the new superintendent in Prince George's County, Maryland, Dr. John Murphy, contacted me. He had disaggregated the achievement test data in his district and identified a big gap between blacks and whites. He wanted to use our SDP model to help close the gap. This effort was also part of a desegregation settlement. We were asked to work with the schools close to the District of Columbia line, predominantly black and low income, that could not be easily desegregated.

Because Prince George's had only a small amount of money for this project, we had to find an efficient way to train the coordinator-trainer and simultaneously involve her colleagues

so that they would be reasonably knowledgeable and supportive. I discussed the criteria for the selection of the coordinator
with Dr. Joyce Thomas, who had been given responsibility for
implementing the program by Superintendent Murphy. They
carefully selected a coordinator, Jan Stocklinski.

We devised an immersion period in New Haven of one
month for the coordinator, and two and a half days for about 35
people, including principals and staff from the schools
involved as well as central office and parent representatives; in
short, representatives of all the adult groups with a stake in the
education process. In one year's time they put the process in
place in ten schools and generated good climates, and in three
years the ten schools dramatically outpaced the gains in the
rest of the District. In only three years, two of the schools went
from percentiles in the mid 50s on several California Academic
Achievement subtests to percentiles in the 90s. The most successful schools in the country received considerable attention
in regional and national media and have been made known to
government, business, and the general public. Because the orientation and training sessions they received appeared to help
make their success possible, we used the same basic approach
with the first ten or so school districts we worked with.

While I cite achievement test gains as evidence, we did not
believe, and do not believe, now, that they are the best indicators of school success. They do not indicate whether a student
is gaining the kind of cognitive, social, psychological, and
moral development needed to become successful citizens in an
open, democratic society—the purpose and goal of public
schools. But we knew that no approach would be taken seriously unless test scores were raised. So we paid attention to
test scores. Yet the very nature of our intervention—improved
home–school relationships and collaboration to support student development—addressed work and citizenship as well;
these aspects of schooling had generally been ignored.

Before I further describe our growing dissemination efforts
and results, I would like to give you a general description of
our second training and orientation program which was conducted for Prince George's County, and which became our standard approach until 1990.

First, I visited the Prince George's County School District, where I met and made presentations to the school board, central office staff, parents, teachers, and principals. The coordinator/trainer and eventually trainer of trainers, Jan Stocklinski, came to New Haven for a month's apprenticeship, where we had her accompany our staff coordinator, Dr. James Boger, as he worked with New Haven School System staff. She observed all of the components of our SDP approach. She also met initially and weekly with me to discuss the theory, our initial implementation experience, and current implementation activities, problems, and opportunities. In the last week of her stay she was joined for two and a half days by a representative group from Prince George's County for the orientation that would help her and them become collaborators.

The orientation was designed to address the following questions school people and parents generally raise at one level or another about change. First, "Why change? School worked for me when I was growing up"; or, "I'm okay and working hard"; or "Are you saying that I'm *not* working hard?" Second, "If I'm okay, what is the problem with today's kids and parents? And why are minority children and families disproportionately affected?" Third, "If I'm okay and they're okay, why are we not having more success?" Finally, "How can we have greater success?"

The discussion of the model during the orientation was designed to show that it is a response to what we found as the underlying causes of school underachievement: (1) economic and social stress that interferes with the ability of parents to give their children the kind of experiences that will enable them to meet expectations at school and achieve success there; (2) inability of school staff to create a climate and respond to students in a way that would support their development in school; (3) hierarchical and authoritarian school organization and management that in the past have made school change and adjustments almost impossible.[2]

Until these questions and underlying problems were addressed, even people who were disposed to change could still harbor assumptions and attitudes that interfered with their ability to help young people develop and learn in school. And even after these people heard the theory, it would help to have schools where it had been applied available as a demonstration. In asking professional people to change the way they were working, we were asking them to give up some of the attitudes and methods they had been taught during their own personal and professional development and had had sanctioned by their supervisors, peers, and others over the years. Among these was the suggestion that children from low income families marginal to the mainstream, most often minority, could not learn.

I developed an introductory presentation that ran along the same lines as Chapter 1 of this book. First, I described how science and technology were applied to every aspect of American life after World War II, changing the economy from one that required no or moderate education and skills for earning a living to one that now usually required a high school education or more. Simultaneously, scientific and technological changes in transportation and communication reduced the sense of community that supported the level of family and community functioning needed to prepare children for success in school and in life.

After the discussion of change I presented an overview of the basic principles of child development involved in growing up within a family, within a family's social network, and within the larger society: a child makes an emotional attachment and bonds to parents who are carriers of attitudes, values, and ways from their social network. The child imitates, identifies with, and internalizes the culture of the parent. In the process the parent is able to channel the aggressive energy that could be harmful to the child and others into the energy of learning, work, and play. Also, the parent helps the child grow along many developmental pathways, six closely related to academic learning—physical, social-interactive, psycho-emotional, moral, linguistic, intellectual-cognitive-academic. While education has focused on the linguistic and the intellectual-cognitive pathways almost exclusively, it is development along all six pathways that is important to prepare young people for academic learning.

I showed how children growing up in the average family are socialized and supported in their development in a way that prepares them to meet the expectations of mainstream institutions such as the school. I pointed out that children from non-mainstream families, often under economic and social stress, have a less good chance of meeting the expectations of school and ultimately succeeding there.

I pointed out that the pre-1945 school was successful for about one in five young people; but leaving or failure was not a real problem prior to this period, even up to the 1960s. Most people worked in factories and on farms, fished, or provided for themselves and their families in ways that did not require an education or required only a modest one. Today's economy, I said, requires a high school education of four and more persons out of five. As society has become more complex, there are more young people who do not belong to well-functioning, mainstream families, and it has become more difficult to provide adequate support for their development.

Despite the growing need, I said, education leaders and institutions did not adjust, nor begin to prepare future teachers and administrators to support the development of young people in a way that would enable them to have early success in school and a better chance to succeed in later school and in life. As a result, children from families that were locked out of the economic mainstream and suffering economic and social stress are now coming to school unprepared, and school people, through no fault of their own, are not prepared to support their development and successful learning in school. All young people are now at a greater risk of school underachievement and subsequent problems in functioning adequately as workers, family members, and citizens.

I emphasized that children who are underdeveloped or who developed differently from the way expected in school are viewed as "bad" and "dumb." The effort to control them and the low expectations held of them lead to a difficult interaction with the children and parents. Chaos or apathy, anger, alienation, and eventually a culture of social and academic failure follows, and minorities are even more adversely affected because of their more traumatic social history.

I compared the African-American experience with that of the European and Asian immigrants to show the critical economic, social, and political differences that led to disproportionately difficult economic and social outcomes in community and family for African-Americans, and in turn, led to underachievement in school. While Europeans experienced hard-ships during the century of immigration prior to 1915, they benefited from the organizing effects of cultural continuity. Their three generations of immigration and development paral-leled economic change and changing job market requirements: no education or skills before 1900, moderate until 1945, and increasingly high after 1945. Generation after generation of opportunity has promoted generation-to-generation transmis-sion of attitudes, values, and ways that facilitated adequate family and community functioning, support for child develop-ment, and preparation for academic learning.

African-Americans experienced abrupt and involuntary cul-tural disruption, the imposition of a slave culture, and exclusion from the political, educational, and economic mainstream through intimidation and terror until the 1960s—well into the era in which a high level of social development and education were needed to participate in the mainstream economy. While many blacks utilized the church and small town rural culture to undergo a similar pattern of family and community develop-ment, the absence of political and economic base of power was harmful to a disproportionate number, particularly after 1950, when education became increasingly important for participation in the primary job market. Generation after generation of politi-cal and economic exclusion and psychosocial, sometimes physi-cal, abuse have promoted generation-to-generation transmission of attitudes, values, and ways that have led to troublesome fam-ily and community functioning, weak support for child develop-ment, and poor preparation. (These dynamics are discussed in more detail in Chapter 2 and Chapter 3.)

As the presentation continued, I used my own experience of growing up in a low income, working class family living on the fringe of the highest socio-economic, predominantly white community as a way of understanding and demonstrating the difference between the black and European experience; and I made a comparison of my experience at home and at school, in a supportive social network, with that of three black classmates as a way of understanding the different outcomes among blacks. (I have described these different experiences in more detail in a book about my mother's effort to overcome extreme poverty and abuse, *Maggie's American Dream*.)[3]

My presentation did not blame school people nor parents, blacks nor whites. It made the point that all students are capable of achieving at the expected academic level. It showed that the underlying problem is social and economic change, and a social and education system adjustment that is too slow and often ineffective. This analysis suggests a school improvement approach that would provide children growing up in families marginal to the economic and social mainstream with many of the experiences that children from the mainstream receive in the ordinary course of growing up in their families.

My colleagues and I then described our outcomes in King and Brennan schools in the New Haven System, where the orientation was being given. Our outcomes showed that schools can be organized and managed in ways that make it possible for children from families under economic and social stress to achieve at a desirable social and academic level. When we began our work, the students at King School were 19 and 18 months below national norms in reading and math, respectively, on the Metropolitan Achievement Test. (The district changed to the Iowa Test of Basic Skills in 1978.) By 1981, shortly after *School Power* was first published, the students were at grade level. By 1984—four years after our Yale Child Study Center Team left the schools—the King students were a year above grade level on the Iowa in reading and math and the students at Brennan were seven months above grade level. The attendance was among the best in the city, and there were no serious behavior problems.[4]

Staff turnover has been low and staff attendance has been high in both schools, in fact among the best in the city. Many of the parents involved in the school program as paid part-time assistants graduated from our program to jobs they did not have the confidence to take before their school experience. At least seven of the parents involved during the 1975–1980 period returned to school themselves, went on to college, and are now professional people.

After describing the outcomes that our school improvement approach helped to make possible, I then described the SDP model—the School Development Program, often called affectionately by my colleagues the Comer Model, Program, or Process.

The process that helped to make these desired outcomes possible had been evolving over the years but had not been described as a model when *School Power* was published. In order to facilitate dissemination, we needed a way to help people conceptualize what we were doing. We eventually described the critical elements of our building level approach to school improvement as a nine-component model that includes three mechanisms, three operations, and three guidelines. The three mechanisms are the governance and management team, the parent's program, and the mental health team. The three operations are the development of a comprehensive school plan, staff development (needed to successfully implement the plan), and periodic assessment and modification of the school plan in response to identified needs. The three guidelines are a no-fault policy (with a focus on problem solving), consensus decision making (rather than voting and possible divisiveness), and collaboration (rather than power oriented leadership). Together, these approaches restructure the traditional school.

I described our governance and management (G&M) team. It was developed by us as an administrative team in 1968 and is now often called a school planning and management team, or called by other names in other places, but essentially it is a school based management mechanism. It is representative of all the adult stakeholders in a school and is the critical component of our model. It is made up of parents selected by the parent group, teachers selected by teacher colleagues, a representative from the professional support staff or mental health team, and a representative from the non-professional staff such as a clerk or custodian. The governance and management group is responsible for carrying out the three operations and acts within the guidelines of the school district and our model.

In developing the comprehensive school plan, the G&M team establishes a social and academic program in a school for the entire year. They may if they choose delegate this responsibility to a committee that reports to the team. The social program is designed to create a warm sense of community within the school and to help staff and parents interact well with each other; in turn, all are available to support positive growth and development of students. The team—made up of the same people who once lived in and created a sense of community around the school in a natural way—is now systematically organized to create these essential conditions in school. They facilitate the kind of child growth and development needed to promote teaching and learning in school.

Our initial project schools, and later some others, developed the "Social Skills Curriculum for Inner City Children," designed to help those children acquire the experiences and skills needed for success in later school and in life (see Chapter 11 for a detailed description). In New Haven it eventually led to a social development component in the system curriculum that addressed these issues from kindergarten through high school graduation; first through simulation, then through real world experiences in the workplace, government, public service activities, and social and cultural activities. Business people and others from these areas became involved in the work of schools. The idea was to give purpose and direction to learning; to make it meaningful and to promote community support.

I described this curriculum to our trainers and showed them how the needed climate is generated first within the G&M team and then permeates all the activities of a school, as those involved learn to live by the SDP guidelines—no fault, consensus, and collaboration. Staff development, assessment, and modification are straightforward management activities that promote efficient and effective operations. The G&M team provides the machinery for the coordination, communication, problem prevention, and problem solving, all of which make reasonably smooth program operation possible despite the complexity of the modern school.

The parent program serves to bring home and school together. The existing group in a school—PTA, PTO, or other—represents the parents develops the parent program; and a parent group is created if none exists. The parent group selects representatives to serve on the G&M team and develops activities, in cooperation with the staff, that address parent interests and needs and support the academic and social program of the school. Workshops by teachers and others on academic matters, child development, social service opportunities, career possibilities, and the like serve parent interests. Parents work with staff to create a year-long social calendar of activities that help to create a good feeling or climate within a school, and often integrate social and academic matters. The parent program departs from the traditional parent role in that the parents and their representatives are directly involved in program planning and implementation so that they sense ownership and responsibility. (The program is described in more detail in Chapter 8.)

I emphasized that these arrangements and activities serve to overcome distrust, anger, and alienation between home and school, enable parents and staff together to support the development of students in school, and enable students to feel supported. They also facilitate student imitation, identification, and internalization of the attitudes, values, and ways of the adults concerned about them. Desirable behavior and learning are being modeled and encouraged by the adults and internalized by students. The reduction in behavior problems and absences facilitates teaching and learning, good student social and academic self-concepts among students, and more learning. When the overall operation and climate of the school are good, ordinary problems are greatly reduced, and children with more serious problems and needs stand out. Moreover, mental health people are not tied up with operation- and climate-related problems and are available to help those most in need.

I described our mental health team. It is made up of the school psychologist, counselor, social worker, nurse, or any other helping professional in a building. In traditional schools these disciplines work individually and usually without much coordination among them; but in the SDP model they work as a team to promote communication, coordination, and cooperation. This prevents duplication and a fragmentation of services that is harmful to the student and staff alike. The team serves individual students, but more importantly focuses on prevention. In the process it shares its expertise in child development with teachers, administrators, and parents. (This work is described in more detail in Chapter 7.)

Because so many school improvement approaches have emerged in recent years, I next discussed how our program differs. First, most give specific attention to one major group within a school setting—either the students, or the teachers, or the parents; or to one program area—curriculum, or social skills, or artistic expression, etc. By contrast, we use a comprehensive approach in which all groups work in a collaborative fashion and *all* resources and programs are coordinated to establish and achieve school objectives and goals. Second, most programs are not driven by child development and relationship concepts at all, or at most utilize such concepts only in regard to the students. We differ from those because all aspects of our work are driven by relationship and child development imperatives, focusing most on institutional arrangements that hinder adequate functioning. Third, whereas many programs focus exclusively on academic achievement, ours attempts to first create a school climate that permits parents and staff to support the overall development of students in a way that makes academic achievement and desirable social behavior at an acceptable level possible and expected. We believe that such an approach has a much greater potential for improving students' chances to achieve school success, and decreasing their likelihood of being involved in problem behaviors—thereby, in turn, increasing their chances for life success.

All of the above concepts, procedures, and findings were presented during a morning session to those attending our orientation program in New Haven. The participants spent the next day and a half observing in King, Brennan, and the Jackie Robinson or Roberto Clemente middle schools. They usually observed a mental health team, sometimes a planning and management team in session, as well as the general school program. They spoke with the principal, teachers, parents, students and sometimes central office staff about their experiences with the model. They observed the social and physical conditions in the neighborhoods around the schools.

I met with these participants again in a "wrap-up" session in the last hour of the third morning and responded to questions and concerns. The district SDP or Comer Coordinator, and the representative group (which in future orientations sometimes included the superintendent) returned to their district and began the on-site implementation process. The question of how to begin was a part of the preparation of the coordinator.

After the New Haven session, our staff visited Prince George's County to support the implementation two or three times a year in the beginning, and we return at least once a year now. We have been available for telephone consultation on an ongoing basis. The district brought additional groups to New Haven for orientation as they expanded the number of schools involved. Jan Stocklinski and her staff eventually gave orientation sessions locally, and subsequently to other school districts. Again, the same training approach was used with all new districts until 1990. From time to time, coordinators, administrators, teachers, and parents from school districts that were farther along in implementing the process made presentations to new districts. In all we worked directly with eleven school districts outside of New Haven from 1990 to 1991.

Each school uses our nine basic components to create conditions which permit their own creativity and problem solving skills to flourish. As a result, all approach issues differently even though they are using the same nine-component School Development Program.

Middle Schools

In New Haven and Prince George's County, with the support of the Carnegie Corporation and the Committee of Successful Adolescent Development of the MacArthur Foundation, we have worked in about twenty middle schools. The PG middle class efforts show promise but are only in the second year. The New Haven middle school work was supported by the Carnegie Corporation. We contributed to and are using the guidelines presented in the Carnegie Report on middle schools, "Turning Points: Preparing American Youth for the Twenty-first Century."[5] Unfortunately, this work was hampered by real world problems—staff illness, transfers, administrative changes, and the rapid expansion of our program. Nonetheless, while there was no difference in achievement after two years between two schools using the SDP and two comparison schools, the schools using the SDP measured higher on collaborative decision making, as well as community and student-teacher relations; and the students scored significantly higher on the academic self-concept dimension of the Piers Harris

Self-Concept Scale. These findings have been predictive of significant academic gains in time in our past work.[6]

Evaluation and Research

As already mentioned, we followed our progress in the initial pilot schools primarily through monitoring academic achievement test results. One of our observers kept a diary during the first year; also, questionnaires were used regularly to help the school governance and management teams assess parent, staff, and student responses and to plan future social and academic activities. Attendance and behavioral problem data were kept and considered a proxy indicator of the social climate. After the first group of students who experienced improved performance graduated from our two pilot schools, we reviewed our mission and status to determine what type of evaluation and research would be most helpful. While longitudinal assessment would have been most interesting, we decided not to follow these students—first, because such studies are very expensive; and second, because doing so would not be in keeping with our primary interest and mission.

Our operational hypothesis, again, was that the early application of social and behavioral science principles to every aspect of a school program will improve the climate of relationships among all involved and will facilitate significant academic and social progress by the fourth grade among students from families under academic and social stress. We believe that a good climate of relationships enables parents, staff, and other adults to support the development of these students in school. Our interest was in further developing and disseminating the process that would make this possible; our mission was to demonstrate that it could be done, and to do it in as many schools as possible serving students from families under economic and social stress—and also to do it as soon as possible, before flawed evaluation and research established that it couldn't be done.

Also, for financial reasons, and because it was necessary to be opportunistic, we had to make compromises. Thus, while we believe that the presence of the paid parent in the class-room and adequate staff time for planning are extremely impor-tant, very few of the districts we worked with had these fea-tures; social climate and student development are more difficult to promote without them. The outcomes we report, while encouraging, are without two of the features we consider most important for program implementation.

Efforts to document the effects of the School Development Program have been consistent with our philosophy that educa-tional improvement embodies not only academic growth but social and personal growth as well. The program's effects have been assessed in various ways and on different outcomes, using diverse strategies and methods. In this section we briefly summarize some of the major evaluative research findings on the effects of the School Development Program regarding acad-emic effects, effects on behavior and school adjustment, and effects on students' self-concept.

Academic Effects

A trend analysis of achievement data among fourth graders in the two pilot SDP schools in New Haven conducted by our SDP research team indicated steady gains in mathematics and reading between 1969 and 1984. The grade equivalent scores for the two schools increased from about 3.0 in reading and mathematics in 1969 to 6.0 in reading and 5.0 in mathematics in 1984.[7]

Several experimental control group studies involving ran-domly selected students in carefully matched schools reported significant differences in academic achievement between stu-dents in SDP schools and students in non-SDP control schools. A study by Cauce, Comer and Schwartz reported that seventh grade students from SDP schools had significantly higher aver-ages in mathematics and overall grade point average than stu-dents from non-SDP schools.[8] Two studies by Haynes, Comer, and Hamilton-Lee reported that elementary school students in SDP schools in Benton Harbor, Michigan showed significantly greater one-year positive changes in grade equivalent scores in reading, mathematics, and language on the California Achievement Test when compared to students in non-SDP schools. SDP students also had significantly greater positive changes in classroom grades than non-SDP students.[9,10]

In a retrospective follow-up study, (Haynes, Comer, and Hamilton-Lee) assessed the performance of 92 sixth and eighth grade students. Fifty-seven (61%) were from a non-SDP elementary school and 35 (39%) were from a program school. The academic achievement of these students was measured by report card grades and by percentile scores on the Metropolitan Achievement Test. Significant differences in favor of the SDP students were found for sixth graders in mathematics, language, and total battery on the Metropolitan Achievement Test. SDP students obtained consistently higher scores on all other achievement measures, but these differences did not approach significance. At the eighth grade level the difference was not significant, but again SDP students consistently scored higher than non-SDP students.[11]

School level aggregated data analyses provide evidence of significant SDP effects on achievement. In 1986 an analysis of achievement data in the Benton Harbor, Michigan Area Schools showed significant average four-year gains—between 7.5 and 11.0 percentile points—in reading and mathematics at the second, fourth, fifth and sixth grades for SDP schools, exceeding gains reported for the school district as a whole. Program schools also registered higher gains in mathematics and reading than the district as a whole, with regard to the percentage of students obtaining 75% and above of the objectives on the Michigan Education Assessment Program (MEAP).[12]

An assessment of SDP effects conducted by the research office of the Prince George's County public schools in 1987 revealed that average percentile gains on the California Achievement Test between 1985 and 1987 were significantly greater for SDP schools than for the district as a whole. At the third grade level SDP schools gained about 18 percentile points in mathematics, 9 percentile points in reading, and 17 percentile points in language. The district as a whole registered gains of 11, 4, and 9 percentile points respectively in mathematics, reading, and language. At the fifth grade, program schools recorded gains of 21, 7, and 12 percentile points in mathematics, reading and language, compared to gains of 11, 4, and 7 percentile points for the district as a whole. Further analysis also revealed that academic gains were linked to the degree and quality of implementation of the SDP.[13]

Behavior and School Adjustment Effects

Measures of attendance, suspensions, classroom behavior, group participation, and attitude toward authority were used to assess students' school adjustment. Aggregated data analysis conducted in Benton Harbor, Michigan, indicated that over a four-year period between 1982 and 1985 SDP schools experienced significantly greater declines in suspension days, absent days, and number of corporal punishments recorded, when compared to the district as a whole. For example, SDP schools recorded a 19% decline in suspension days compared to a 34% increase in suspension days for the district as a whole. Similarly, for corporal punishments, SDP schools recorded a 100% decline compared to a 36% decline for the district as a whole.[14]

The experimental control studies of Haynes, Comer, and Hamilton-Lee already cited in New Haven indicate that SDP students, as compared to non-SDP students, experienced significantly greater positive changes in attendance, and in teacher ratings of classroom behavior, attitude toward authority, and group participation. The cited study by Cauce, Comer, and Schwartz[16] in New Haven found that SDP students reported significantly better perceived school competence and self-competence compared to a control group of non-SDP students.

Self-Concept

In a recent study,[17] Haynes and Comer compared SDP students in the fourth and sixth grades with non-SDP students using six self-concept dimensions on the Piers Harris Self-Concept Scale. Both groups of students were also compared with the national normative sample on total self-concept. Analysis of covariance was used to control for pre-test differences that existed between SDP and non-SDP students. On the post-test measures, SDP students scored significantly higher than the control group of non-SDP students on all six self-concept dimensions and significantly higher than the normative group on total self-concept. The two 1988 studies by Haynes, Comer, and Hamilton-Lee already cited[18] also indicated that SDP students showed significantly greater positive changes in self-concept when compared to non-SDP students.

Classroom and School Climate

In a 1989 quasi-experimental study conducted in New Haven and involving 288 students, students in SDP schools reported significantly more positive assessments of their classroom climate than students in non-SDP schools. Classroom climate was assessed using the Classroom Environment Scale. A school climate questionnaire designed by the researchers was completed by 155 parents and 147 teachers; in it, parents and teachers of students in SDP schools reported significantly more positive assessments of their schools' climate when compared to parents and teachers of children in non-SDP schools.[19]

Evaluation and Research Discussion

One of the unsettling realities of all indirectly managed intervention programs is that the success of the approach depends very heavily on the degree and quality of implementation carried out by the school staff. In a study of nine Norfolk SDP elementary schools, four had high mean implementation scores and were the higher achievers on the Iowa Test of Basic Skills; the two schools with the lowest implementation scores were among the lowest achievers; and three had mixed good implementation but low achievement.[20] A path analysis showed that good implementation contributed to a good school climate, and in turn to a good academic self-concept among students, decreased suspensions and absences, and improved academic performance in most cases.[21]

Even before the path analysis had been carried out, we observed in our pilot schools that good program implementation and improved climate had to be in place for two to five years before improved academic achievement occurred. This delay was usually due to curriculum instruction, and assessment content, method and management problems; it showed us that program evaluation was very difficult, virtually impossible, without some assessment of the adequacy of implementation of our SDP model as well as an assessment of the quality of the academic program.

Complicating matters even more is the fact that almost *anything* done in a school that enables the participants to feel valued and hopeful can have temporary positive effects—an athletic or academic competition championship, a new leader, a practice such as a note of praise to teachers when appropriate, indeed, a new intervention program. But unless the program of a school is systematically managed so that the participants feel valued and hopeful over time, the positive effects will be lost. Meanwhile the face that almost anything works temporarily makes evaluation difficult, particularly when it is done prematurely. This contributes to the cycle of hope and despair that confuses the public and makes school people cynical about new approaches to school improvement. Getting people to accept new approaches, even with positive evaluation and research findings, is difficult when everything works and nothing works. Thus an evaluator has a great responsibility for premature and simplistic evaluations can destroy potentially successful programs and keep alive temporary successes that we in the long run unworkable. On the other hand, evaluation findings can be very helpful. The documented success of the SDP schools without corporal punishment in Benton Harbor contributed to the elimination of the practice.

Also, we have observed, and are now trying to document, that schools serving low income, more often minority young people are more willing to change and address relationship issues than schools serving students of middle and above income, more often in heterogeneous racial and income settings. We believe this is the case because school staffs rely too heavily on aggregate test scores on standardized achievement tests. The academic performance of the most successful hides the existence and needs of academic underachievers. And the signs of social and psychological distress among students from all backgrounds are generally ignored or discounted as bad behavior, laziness, irresponsible conduct and the like—or simply as problems beyond the school's responsibility. In schools where almost nobody is succeeding, the staff and parents can be more easily motivated to try new ways of understanding and performing.

Further Dissemination and Development

In 1989 the Rockefeller Foundation expressed interest in making it possible for us to work with many more schools and school districts. We submitted a proposal to them entitled "A Plan to Expand Utilization of the School Development Program Principles," and in 1990 received a five-year grant to support this effort. The Melville Corporation also provided significant support for this work.

There are four major components to this effort. The ten school districts we began to work with from 1981 through 1990 are the direct service component. A second is an institute activity called the Comer Program for Change in Education (CPCE). A third component is a partnership program with other educational institutions and organizations. The fourth is a fourteen-part "how-to" videotape series entitled "For Kids Sake," and a supporting manual that shows how to implement our School Development Program.

We are involved in partnerships with 15 schools of education, universities, and state departments of education (as well as one mental health organization) in the U.S. North, South, East, West, and Midwest. These organizations participate in the institute, CPCE, along with the school district they are collaborating with in their local area; they learn the model together in a one-week session in New Haven, and then go home to implement the model together for six months, with telephone and on site support from our staff as indicated. They subsequently return to New Haven for a follow-up institute week at Yale. They are then expected to carry on their collaboration with diminishing support from our staff. The non-school district organizations will be in a position to support SDP development with other school districts if they so choose. This program is also designed to inform and support the teacher preparation program at the participating college or university.

Dr. Edward Joyner, our institute director, and Dr. Norris Haynes, our director of research, work together to prepare partners and district leaders in a way that helps them implement the SDP, and helps us assess the effectiveness of this approach. The program of the institute is developed under the leadership of Dr. Joyner, with the help and participation of our national faculty: Ms. Maria Martha Chavez-Brummell, Mr. Patrick Howley, Dr. Kimberly Kinsler, Dr. Robert Kranyik, Dr. Carmen I. Mercado, Dr. Frank Smith, Ms. Barbara Stern—and our staff. There are 34 preparatory modules: Action Research, Implications for Principals; Back Home Planning; Child Development and Mental Health; Child Development and Differential School Performance; A Challenge for Teachers in School Development Program Schools; Classroom Diversity; A Critical Factor for Supervisors; Creating the School Planning and Management Team—Shared Purpose, Collaboration, Consensus Building, and Role Development; Cross-Cultural Communications—Implications for SDP Collaboration; Cultural Diversity; Documenting Process and Outcomes; Effective Planning in the Real World; Effective Systems Planning; Fundamental Requisites of the Mental Health Team; Fundamental Requisites of the School Planning and Management Team; Historical Perspective—The Construction of a School Theory about "Schools"; Improving Your Leadership Effectiveness Through the Use of True Power; the Mental Health Team—Clinical Case Management and School-wide Prevention Strategies; The Miseducation of American Youth—The Problem of Education Malpractice; The Parents' Program; Person Centered Coaching; Planned Change—A Human Process; Planned Change and Systems Planning; The Role of Parents in the School Development Program: The Lincoln-Bassett Experience; The School as an Organization; School/Community Team Building; School Development Program Overview; Self-Analysis; Team Building—Roles, Communication and Decision Making; Team Building—Shared Purpose, Relationships, Group and Intergroup Dynamics; Team Building and the SDP—Task and Relationship Behaviors; Understanding Schools From an Organizational Perspective; Using Situational Leadership to Improve Schools; and What's Wrong with This School?"

Now that one full year has been completed, we can report subjective evidence that this program is off to a good start in thirteen of the fifteen districts involved.

The "how-to" videotape series and manual entitled *For Children's Sake: The Comer School Development Program* have been developed[22] to support the dissemination effort in school districts we are working with directly, through partnerships, and in school districts that are not directly or indirectly affiliated with our program. A newsletter is being used to facilitate communication among the participating districts and interested others. We also have an educational policy interest. In this regard a documentary entitled, "The Legacy of Maggie's American Dream," based on my biographical account already cited, has been shown on public television stations across the country. We are working with a number of groups with education policy interests.

We were always aware of the fact that our model—with a focus on relationships and child development—was only one part, albeit a critical part, of what was needed to improve American schools. The other areas in need of attention and change are curriculum and instruction, student assessment attitudes and methods, and technology utilization; and also staff preparation and system policies that will facilitate a child-centered schooling process. But as mentioned previously, we were not successful in finding an effective academic program leader in our early years. And also, we were concerned about stepping on the feet, if not the territory, of school people. And while some of our innovations brought child development principles to curriculum development, we did not address curriculum issues systematically and continually. This matter was addressed by the school districts.

The "Whole Person" curriculum, described in Chapter 11 and used in several schools, is based on an understanding that young children are first interested in the mysteries of their own bodies and then expand their interest to the people and things around them and beyond, and that they learn best when the curriculum is pegged to their interests. The "Social Skills Curriculum for Inner City Children," also described in Chapter 11, creates a realistic context for learning in the areas where children will need social and academic knowledge and skills to be successful as adults—government and politics, business and economics, health and nutrition, spiritual and leisure time activities. Through activities in simulated or authentic environments they study things that are immediately useful and meaningful to them, and are connected to the world around them.

On one occasion, members of the National Commission on the Welfare of Children visited a highly successful school in a very difficult neighborhood that was using our model. One astute observer told me that if we were making the point that improved climate and attention to child development alone could improve social and academic performance, we had made it resoundingly, but that we could have even greater success with instruction and curriculum approaches based on new research. Our intent is to demonstrate the critical relationship between adequate development and learning through the best curriculum program possible, and we were exploring opportunities to work with curriculum experts. But we believe that school improvement requires even more.

Our work over the years shows that curriculum and instruction are at the heart of the education enterprise, but that relationships must be such that young people can imitate, identify with, and internalize the attitudes, values, and ways of the meaningful adults around them in order to be motivated to learn academic material and, eventually, to become self-motivated, disciplined, self-directed learners capable of taking advantage of the resources of our society. Improving schooling requires giving attention to the four critical areas that can make these dynamics possible. The "America 2000" initiative—a state, federal government and private industry education improvement effort—gave us the opportunity to bring together the several groups and areas of expertise we have long felt must be joined in order to bring about school success for many more young people.

The New American Schools Development Corporation

(NASDC) competition led to our participation in a group that includes: (1) Ted Sizer at Brown University, whose work has been in curriculum and instruction; (2) Howard Gardner at Harvard University, who has been developing new student assessment techniques and new ways to understand child intelligence; (3) Janet Whitla of the Educational Development Corporation, whose work has been in technology development and utilization and teacher preparation; (4) our Yale Child Study Center SDP work, which addresses child development, parent and community support, and governance and management. Our successful proposal, "Authentic Teaching, Learning, and Assessment for all Students" (ATLAS Communities), will allow us to design education programs, in feeder patterns across grade levels in several school districts where we already have programs, in a way that will integrate our several perspectives.

We believe that ATLAS Communities can create the needed learning dynamic. In authentic communities, students and teachers will work together on essential questions and issues of significance within and outside school to develop lifelong "habits of mind, heart, and work." The curriculum will be integrated across disciplines and based on developmental principles. Authentic assessment will include the use of portfolios, performance examinations, and exhibitions. Technology will be used to link participants and as a learning tool. A governance and management mechanism will facilitate the learning process within school, bring family and community together in support of school, and promote policies flexible enough to be supportive.

One of our earliest concerns was the realization that many children are so far behind, or off course, in their development by the time they enter school that it is difficult for them to catch up, and that this creates problems for the child, the family, and the school. Because of the changing fortunes of the local Head Start Program, we were not able to collaborate with them. But also, we understood that many of the families could function more effectively if they were a valued part of a network of preparatory services—child and health care, welfare, recreation, employment, and the like.

Dr. Edward Zigler, my colleague at Yale and the first and

former director of the Office of Child Development, pioneered such a program called, "Schools of the Twenty-first Century." This program provides school-based, year-round care for children ages 3 through 5; school-based before-and-after-school, -holiday, and -vacation care for children ages 5 through 12; home-based parent education; support and training to family day care providers in the school neighborhood, and a school-based information and referral service. The program emphasizes high-quality day care, strong parental involvement, and a focus on developing the child as a whole person. With the support of the Carnegie Corporation we will collaborate with Dr. Zigler in a program that combines his approach with our SDP approach. Our pilot program is in Norfolk, Virginia, a district that is currently using our SDP very effectively.

Summary

In 1968 we set out to demonstrate that children from all backgrounds could achieve adequately in school if the setting supported their overall development. We applied the principles of the social and behavioral sciences to every aspect of elementary school programs, first locally and now nationwide, and in doing so we changed attitudes and behaviors of staff, parents, and students, and often enabled them to perform in ways that brought student social and academic achievement to acceptable levels. The effort is being extended to middle and high schools and shows promise.

Important components of the program—paid parents in the classroom and regular time for staff meetings—had to be dropped and need to be reinstated wherever and whenever they can be afforded. Also, while our model addresses the critical areas of relationships, child development, and systems management, it does not address instruction-curriculum-assessment issues. And it can only be effective when implemented fully. Thus, implementation, teaching, and curriculum factors must be considered in evaluations. Nonetheless, evaluations show that the SDP has contributed to significantly improved performance on standardized tests and important personal characteristics when compared to non-SDP schools in a number of places.

We are developing program ties with early childhood, family-enabling experts; elementary through high school curriculum-instruction-assessment, technology utilization experts; and also teacher and administrator preparation and support programs. In short, we have been steadily moving to develop intervention programs in all the areas that our theoretical constructs and empirical knowledge indicate should be helpful in improving schools and learning among all our children. But even if we could be successful in all these areas, and could greatly influence education policy, it would not be enough.

Many of our education problems are due primarily to the absence of economic opportunities and adequate family and community development policies. While educators can and must make adjustments that will help now, it is important to remember that the disposition for learning grows out of a family and cultural context that promotes it; and that a society must create the necessary conditions if it is to survive and thrive in the modern economic world.

Notes

Preface

1. David P. Gardner et al., *A Nation at Risk* (Washington, D.C.: National Commission on Excellence in Education), 1983; Harold Hodgkinson, "The Right Schools for the Right Kids," *Educational Leadership,* vol. 15, no. 5 (February 1988), pp. 10–11; Committee for Economic Development, *Investing in Our Children: Business and the Public Schools* (New York: CED, 1985); Carnegie Forum on the Education and the Economy, *A Nation Prepared: Teachers for the 21st Century* (New York: Carnegie Corporation, Report of the Task Force on Teaching as a Profession, 1986).

Chapter 1, pp. 3–26

1. United States Senate, Committee on the Judiciary, *Challenge for the Third Century: Education in a Safe Environment—Final Report on*

the *Nature and Prevention of School Violence and Vandalism*
(Washington, D.C.: Government Printing Office, 1977), p. 17.

2. Ibid., p. 18.

3. Ibid., p. 9.

4. Ibid., p. 9.

5. Ibid., p. 8.

6. Ibid., p. 14.

7. Ibid., p. 14.

8. Michael B. Katz, *Class Bureaucracy and Schools: The Illusion of
   Educational Change in America* (New York: Praeger, 1975), pp.
   3–55; Eleanor B. Leacock, *Teaching and Learning in City Schools*
   (New York: Basic Books, 1969), p. 146; R. L. Pounds and J. R.
   Bryner, *The School in American Society* (New York: Macmillan,
   1959), Chapter 3.

9. John Dewey, *The School and Society*, (Chicago, Illinois: University
   of Chicago Press, 1915), Chapter 1.

10. Erik Erikson, *Childhood and Society* (New York: Norton, 1950), pp.
    247–274; Sally Provence, Audrey Naylor, J. Patterson, *The Chal-
    lenge of Daycare* (New Haven: Yale University Press, 1977), pp.
    1–10; Jane Kessler, *Psychopathology of Childhood* (Englewood
    Cliffs, New Jersey: Prentice-Hall, 1966), p. 224.

11. Robert S. Lynd and Helen M. Lynd, *Middletown: A Study in Amer-
    ican Culture* (New York: Harcourt, Brace, 1929), pp. 478–495;
    Thornton Niven Wilder, *Our Town* (New York: Coward McMann,
    1938); Samuel Langhorne Clemens, *The Adventures of Tom Sawyer*
    (New York: Heritage Club, 1937).

12. Michael Anderson, *Sociology of the Family* (Baltimore: Penguin
    Books, 1971).

13. Alvin Toffler, *Future Shock* (New York, Random House, 1970);
    Lewis Mumford, *The City in History: Its Origins, Its Transforma-
    tions, and Its Prospects* (New York: Harcourt, Brace & World,
    1961), p. 30.

14. Mario D. Fantini, *What's Best for the Children: Resolving the Power
    Struggle Between Parents and Teachers* (Garden City, New York:
    Anchor Press/Doubleday, 1975), Introduction, Chapter 2.

15. Richard Adler and Douglas Cater, eds., *Television as a Cultural
    Force* (New York: Praeger, 1976), pp. 95–127; Lawrence A. Cremin,
    Traditions of American Education (New York: Basic Books, 1976),
    pp. 105–106.

16. James P. Comer, "What Has Happened to Our Children?" *New
    England Magazine of the Boston Sunday Globe*, November 13, 1977,
    p. 36.

17. Advisory Committee on Child Development, Assembly of Behavior-

al and Social Sciences, National Research Council, *Toward a National Policy for Children and Families* (Washington, D. C.: National Academy of Sciences, 1976), p. 3.

18. Kenneth Kenniston, and the Carnegie Council on Children, *All Our Children: The American Family under Pressure* (New York: Harcourt, Brace, Jovanovich, 1977), pp. 35–47.

19. Kenneth Kenniston, *Youth and Dissent: The Rise of a New Opposition* (New York: Harcourt, Brace, Jovanovich, 1971); "Communes Spread as Young Reject Old Values," *New York Times*, December 17, 1970.

20. James Comer and Alvin Poussaint, *Black Child Care* (New York: Simon and Schuster, 1975); August Meier and Elliot Rudnick, "Black Violence in the 20th Century: A Study in Rhetoric and Retaliation" in Graheim, H. D. and Gun, T. R., eds., *Violence in America*, pp. 380–392.

21. Seymour B. Sarason, *The Culture of the School and the Problem of Change*, (Boston, Mass.: Allyn and Bacon, 1971), p. 118.

22. Cremin, *Public Education*, p. 59.

23. James L. Hymes, *Effective Home-School Relations* (New York: Prentice-Hall, 1953), Chapters 2 and 3; Don Davies, ed., *Schools Where Parents Make a Difference* (Boston, Mass.: Institute for Responsive Education, 1976); Provence, Naylor, and Patterson, *The Challenge of Daycare.*

24. Sharon Lynn Kagan and Carol Malchman Schraft, *Bringing Parents and Schools Together: A Comparative Study of the Experiences of Low and Middle Income Parents in Two Urban Elementary Schools*, Yale University, 1979; Sara Lawrence Lightfoot, *Worlds Apart: Relationships Between Families and Schools* (New York: Basic Books, 1978).

25. Joan Costello, Marjorie Graham Janis, and Albert J. Solnit, "Overcoming Early School Difficulties: Three Aspects of Learning Inhibition," *The Elementary School Journal*, vol. 78, no. 2 (November, 1977), pp. 140–148.

26. "Reforms that Went Sour in Teaching the Three R's," *U. S. News and World Report*, vol. 76, May 20, 1974, pp. 65–66.

27. Arthur M. Ross "Rhetoric and Reality in Manpower" in Irving H. Siegel, ed., *Manpower Tomorrow: Prospects and Priorities* (New York: Agustus Kelley, 1967), pp. 55–71; "A Study of 5000 Mentally Retarded Workers in Government," prepared by U. S. Civil Service Commission in cooperation with the District of Columbia Department of Vocational Rehabilitation, 1970.

28. Charles E. Silberman, *Crisis in the Classroom: The Remaking of American Education* (New York: Random House, 1970), Chapter 2.

29. J. Victor Baldridge and Terence Deal, *Managing Change in Educational Organizations: Sociological Perspectives, Strategies and Case Studies* (Berkeley: McCutchan, 1975); Neal Gross, Joseph B. Giaquinta, and Marilyn Bernstein, *Implementing Organizational Innovations: A Sociological Analysis of Planned Educational Change* (New York: Basic Books, 1971); John Goodland, *The Dynamics of Educational Change: Toward Responsive Schools* (New York: McGraw-Hill, 1975).

30. Adolph Unruh and Harol Turner, *Supervision for Change and Innovation* (Boston: Houghton Mifflin, 1970), Chapters 4–5.

31. Lynd and Lynd, *Middletown*, p. 207; Martin Deutsch, "Early Social Environment: Its Influence on School Adaptation," in *Profile of the School Dropout*, ed. by Daniel Schreiber (New York: Vintage Books, 1967), p. 207.

32. Arthur T. Jersild, *When Teachers Face Themselves* (New York: Teachers College Press, 1955); Robert G. Owens, *Organizational Behavior in Schools* (New Jersey: Prentice-Hall, 1970), p. 14.

33. Kessler, *Psychopathology of Childhood*, p. 411; Seymour B. Sarason, *The Culture of the School*, pp. 111–150; Baldridge and Deal, *Managing Change*, Chapter 15.

34. James Deslonde, "Lincoln High: A Turn Around School, A Case Study of Violence and Vandalism in Schools," (paper prepared for Research Triangle, Inc., Research Triangle, N. C., 1977); Bel Kaufman, *Up the Down Staircase* (Englewood Cliffs, New Jersey: Prentice-Hall, 1964).

35. Gross, Giaquinta, and Bernstein, *Implementing Organizational Innovations*, p. 204.

36. Lynd and Lynd, *Middletown*, p. 207.

37. HEW Urban Task Force, *Urban School Crisis: The Problem and Solutions* (Washington, D. C.: National School Public Relations Association, 1970); National Advisory Commission on the Education of Disadvantaged Children, *Title I ESEA—A Review and Forward Look* (Washington, D. C.: Government Printing Office, 1969); National Academy of Sciences, *Fundamental Research and the Process of Education: A Report to The National Institute of Education*, December, 1977.

38. Gross, Giaquinta and Bernstein, *Implementing Organizational Innovations*, Chapters 2 and 3; Philip A. Cusick, *Inside High School: The Students World* (New York: Holt, Rinehart, and Winston, 1973), pp. 4–6; *Strategies and Case Studies* (Berkeley: McCutchan, 1975), Chapter 15.

39. Amatai Etzioni, *The Alternatives of Gradualism in Studies of Social Change* (New York: Holt, Rinehart and Winston, 1966), Chapter 3.

Chapter 2, pp. 27–41

1. Thomas Gordon, *Teacher Effectiveness Training* (New York: Wyden, 1974), Chapters VI, XI, XII; William Glasser, *Schools Without Failure* (New York: Harper and Row, 1969), pp. 1–11.

2. Marcus Foster, *Making Schools Work: Strategies for Changing Education* (Philadelphia: Westminster Press, 1971), p. 41–46; Maurice Berube and Marilyn Gittell, eds., *Confrontation at Ocean Hill-Brownsville: The New York School Strikes of 1968* (New York: Praeger, 1969).

3. Robert Coles, *The South Goes North, Vol. III—Children of Crisis* (Boston: Little, Brown, 1971), pp. 424–535; Seymour B. Sarason, *The Culture of the School and the Problem of Change* (Boston: Allyn and Bacon, 1971), pp. 115–118.

4. Martin Deutsch, ed., *The Disadvantaged Child: Selected Papers of Martin Deutsch and Associates* (New York: Basic Books, 1967), Chapter 4; Daniel A. Prescott, *Emotion and the Educative Process* (Washington: American Council on Education, 1938), p. 231.

5. James P. Comer, "Child Development and Social Change: Some Points of Controversy," *The Journal of Negro Education*, vol. 40, no. 3 (summer, 1971), pp. 266–276.

6. Susan Isaacs, *Intellectual Growth in Young Children* (London: Routelidge, 1930).

7. Harlem Youth Opportunities Unlimited, Inc., *Youth in the Ghetto* (New York: Haryou, 1964), pp. 203–244; Robert Rosenthal and Lenora Jacobson, *Pygmalion in the Classroom* (New York: Holt, Rinehart and Winston, 1968), Part 2, Chapter 5.

8. The aggressive behavior of many children is simply an adaptation of the normal energy used by all children to explore, learn and work. For discussion of this process, see Albert Solnit, "Some Adaptive Functions of Aggressive Behavior," *Psychoanalysis—A General Psychology* (New York: International Universities Press, Inc., 1966); Report of the Project on Classification of Exceptional Children, *The Futures of Children: Categories, Labels and Their Consequences*, Nicholas Hobbs, Project Director (Nashville, Tennessee: Vanderbilt University, 1974), pp. 34–42.

9. James Deslonde, "Bayside Junior High: In the Middle Going Down, A Case Study of Violence and Vandalism in Schools," (paper prepared for the Research Triangle Institute, Research Triangle, North Carolina, April 22, 1977), p. 25.

10. Daniel Schreiber, *Profile of the School Dropout* (New York: Vintage Books, 1967), pp. 198–234.

11. Westinghouse Learning Corporation, *The Impact of Head Start: An Evaluation of the Effects of Head Start on Children's Cognitive and Affective Development*, Final Report presented to the Office of Economic Opportunity (Athens, Ohio, 1969); M. Smith, "Innovation: Is The Bloom Wearing Off?" Report of the Ford Foundation School Improvement Program, Education Digest, vol. 38, March 1973, pp. 2–4.

12. Ivan Illich, *Deschooling Society* (New York: Harper & Row, 1971), pp. 66–67.

13. Christopher Jencks, *Inequality: A Reassessment of the Effect of Family and Schooling in America* (New York: Basic Books, 1972), pp. 253–64; John Ogbu, *Minority Education and the Caste* (New York: Academic Press, 1978).

14. Seymour B. Sarason, *The Creation of Settings and Future Societies* (San Francisco: Josey Bass), pp. 50–51; Culver and Hoban, eds., *The Power to Change: Issues for Innovative Education* (New York: McGraw-Hill, 1973); Adolph Unruh and Harold Turner, *Supervision For Change and Innovation* (Boston: Houghton Mifflin, 1970).

15. J. Victor Baldridge and Terence Deal, *Managing Change in Educational Organizations: Sociological Perspectives, Strategies and Case Studies* (Berkeley: McCutchan, 1975); Neal Gross, Joseph B. Giaquinta and Marilyn Bernstein, *Implementing Organizational Innovations: A Sociological Analysis of Planned Educational Change* (New York: Basic Books, 1971); John Goodland, *The Dynamics of Educational Change: Toward Responsive Schools* (New York: McGraw-Hill, 1975); Culver and Hoban, *The Power to Change*.

Chapter 3, pp. 42–54

1. Fred Powledge, *Model City: One Town's Efforts to Rebuild Itself* (New York: Simon and Schuster, 1970); David Birch, Reilly Atkinson, Sven Sanderstrom and Linda Stack, *Patterns of Urban Change: The New Haven Experience* (Lexington, Mass.: Lexington Books, 1974).

2. Fred Powledge, op. cit.

3. Robert Dahl, *Who Governs? Democracy and Power in an American City* (New Haven: Yale University Press, 1961), p. 120.

4. Rollin Gustav Osterweis, *Three Centuries of New Haven: 1638–1938* (New Haven: Yale University Press, 1953).

5. Robert Austin Warner, *New Haven Negroes: A Social History* (New York: Arno Press, 1940), pp. 66–68; John W. Barber, *A History of the Amistad Captive* (New Haven: E.L. & J.W. Barber, 1840).

6. U.S. Department of Commerce, Bureau of the Census, *Census of*

Population for 1900 and 1950, (Washington, D.C.: U. S. Government Printing Office, 1904 and 1952 respectively).

7. Rollin Osterweis, op. cit., chapter 26.

8. U.S. Department of Commerce, Bureau of the Census, *Census of Population* for 1900, 1930 and 1960 (Washington, D.C.: U. S. Government Printing Office, 1904, 1935 and 1961 respectively).

9. Robert Warner, op. cit.

10. Ibid., pp. 53–60

11. New Haven City Planning Department, *1970 Census Tracts— Neighborhoods*, 1972.

12. Statistics made available by the Office of Data Collection and Information, New Haven Education Department.

13. See Community Progress, Inc., *The Human Story* (1966) and *Ten Years of Human Renewal* (1972).

14. Samuel Nash, et al., "New Haven Connecticut: New Haven Chose to Desegregate," in M. Harris, N. Jackson, and C. Rydingsword, eds. *The Integration of American Schools* (Boston: Allyn and Bacon, 1975), chapter 5.

15. See Marilyn Levy, *Project Concern in Cheshire: A Preliminary Report* (Cheshire, Conn.: Department of Education, January, 1970); and *The New Haven Register*, June 13, 1968, p. 1.

16. Fred Powledge, op. cit., p. 92.

Chapter 4, pp. 57–75

1. For a complete discussion of the original program design, see Joan Costello, *A Summary and Integration of Evaluation Studies Conducted in the Baldwin-King School Program* (New Haven: Yale University Child Study Center, 1973).

Chapter 7, pp. 106–124

1. See James P. Comer and A. Smith, *Annual Report (1970–71): Model Schools Program* (Bridgehaven, 1971); and J. Costello, *Evaluation Report, Model Schools Program* (Bridgehaven, 1972).

Chapter 8, pp. 125–145

1. James P. Comer and Carol Schraft, "Working with Black Parents," in R. Abidin, Handbook of Parent Education (Springfield, Ill.: Charles C. Thomas Publishers, in press).

2. Diana Slaughter, "Maternal Antecedents of the Academic Achievement Behavior of Afro-American Head Start Children," *Education Horizons*, 1969, pp. 24–28.

3. Norman D. Comer, "An Analysis of Selected Racial Issues in Public Education as Perceived by Black School Administrators," unpublished dissertation (Loyola University, 1974).

4. S. L. Lightfoot, *Worlds Apart—Relationships Between Families and Schools* (New York: Basic Books, 1978).

Chapter 9, pp. 146–166

1. Charles W. Thomas, "Psychologists, Psychology, and the Black Community," in *Black Psychology* (New York: Harper and Row, Publishers, 1972), pp. 375–383; and Edmund Gordon and D. A. Wilkerson, *Compensatory Education for the Disadvantaged* (New York: College Entrance Examination Board, 1966).

2. Mary F. Berry, "The Teacher and the Rand Study," *Today's Education*, vol. 68, no. 2, April–May 1979, pp. 38–40.

3. Albert Solnit and Samuel Nash, *The New Schools Project*, proposal submitted to the Ford Foundation (New Haven: Yale University Child Study Center, 1967).

Chapter 10, pp. 167–188

1. Further discussion of issue in James P. Comer and Alvin F. Poussaint, *Black Child Care* (New York: Simon and Schuster, 1975), chapter 6.

2. Various descriptions taken from Marjorie G. Janis and Joan Costello, *The Discovery Room—Developing an Approach for Teachers to Help Children with Problems in Primary School*. Presentation at the Annual Meeting of the American Orthopsychiatric Association, March 1976.

3. For discussion of a wide range of situations and responses that are particularly appropriate with young black children, see Phyllis Harrison-Ross and Barbara Wyden, *The Black Child: A Parents' Guide* (New York: Wyden, 1973).

4. Joan Costello, Marjorie Janis and Albert Solnit, "Overcoming Early School Difficulties: Three Aspects of Learning Inhibition," *The Elementary School Journal*, vol. 78, no. 2, November 1977.

Chapter 11, pp. 189–210

1. Edward Zigler and Penelope Trickett, "IQ, Social Competence, and Evaluation of Early Childhood Intervention Programs,"*American Psychologist*, September 1978, pp. 789–798; Margaret Spencer, "The Social-Cognitive and Personality Development of the Black Preschool Child: An Exploratory Study of the Development Process," *Dissertation Abstracts International*, vol. 38, 1976, p. 970; and Asa Hilliard, *I'm Back! Children's Social Behavior: Assessment Criteria* (Westport, Conn.: Mediax Associates, 1978).

2. The new thrust that emerged, focusing attention on social skills, is described in detail in the proposal "A Social Skills Curriculum for Inner-City Children" prepared for the Minority Mental Health Center, National Institute of Mental Health (grant #MH27561-01-05), 1975. Abstract of Evaluation Reports appear in *Resources in Education*, ERIC Document 167668, ERIC Clearinghouse on Urban Education, 1979.

3. Child Study Center staff (James Comer and Carol Schraft) serve as consultants to the New Haven, Conn. public schools under grants from the Connecticut Justice Commission Program for Delinquency Prevention Planning and Programming for Positive Youth Development and the Rockefeller Foundation Program for School Development.

4. Specific work with kindergarten children is now taking place through the Social Skills Curriculum program in New Haven Public Schools, as described in note 2 above.

Chapter 12, pp. 213–230

1. The roles of various school personnel and their interactions are discussed in Seymour Sarason, *The Culture of the School and the Problem of Change* (Boston: Allyn and Bacon, 1971).

2. See P. B. Jacobson, et al., *The Principalship: New Perspectives* (Englewood Cliffs, New Jersey: Prentice-Hall, 1973).

3. Problems of current approaches to teacher education are discussed in K. Hinz and R. Saba, "The Training of Undergraduate Teacher Education Students in Interpersonal Skills and their Classroom Application," *Humanist Educator*, vol. 16, no. 2, December 1977, pp. 65–70.

4. Jean Carew and Sara Lawrence Lightfoot, "First Grade: A

Multi-Faceted View of Teachers and Children," (Washington, D. C.:
U. S. Office of Child Development, 1977).

5. Asa Hilliard, "The Pedagogy of Success," in Sylvia Sunderlin, *The
Most Enabling Environment* (Washington, D.C.: Association for
Childhood Education International, 1979), pp. 45–52; Bernard Wat-
son, *In Spite of the System* (Cambridge, Mass.: Ballinger, 1974).

6. By reviewing a sample of ten major graduate schools of social work
and psychology, the author found a very small number of required
courses which relate to any classroom situation or field training in
elementary or secondary schools. This tendency has not changed
over the past decade.

7. Several successful case studies are described in Don Davies, ed.,
Schools Where Parents Make a Difference (Boston: Institute for Responsive Education, 1976).

Chapter 13, pp. 231–247

1. James Coleman, et al., *Equality of Educational Opportunity*
(Washington, D.C.: U. S. Office of Education, 1966) and Christopher
Jencks, *Inequality: A Reassessment of the Effect of Family and
Schooling in America* (New York: Basic Books, 1972).

2. Fallacies in the "cultural deprivation" approach are clearly
addressed in Reginald Jones, "Labeling Children Culturally Deprived and Culturally Disadvantaged," in R. Jones, ed., *Black Psychology* (New York: Harper & Row, 1972), pp. 285–294; and Ronald
Edmonds, "Effective Schools for the Urban Poor," *Educational
Leadership*, vol. 3, no. 1 (October 1979), pp. 15–23.

3. James P. Comer, "Black Education: A Holistic View," *Urban
Review*, fall 1975, pp. 162–170; Patricia Gurin and Edgar Epps,
Black Consciousness, Identity and Achievement (New York: Wiley,
1975), chapter 5; and William Brazziel, "A Letter from the South,"
in R. Jones, ed., *Black Psychology* (New York: Harper & Row, 1972),
pp. 104–110. This approach of changing from negative to positive
expectations about low-income children's learning potentials also
serves as the foundation for the Push for Excellence program developed by Jesse Jackson. (For further information contact Push for
Excellence, Inc., Chicago, Illinois 60615.)

4. Comer and Schraft, 1979. (See note 1, chapter 8.)

5. George Weber, *Inner-City Children Can Be Taught to Read: Four
Successful Schools* (Washington, D. C.: Council for Basic Education, 1971); Michael Rutter, Barbara Maughan, Peter Mortimore,
and Janet Oustan, *Fifteen Thousand Hours* (Cambridge, Mass.:
Harvard Univ. Press, 1979).

6. See discussion of Leadership in the School (chapter 6) in Robert Owens, *Organizational Behavior in Schools* (Englewood Cliffs, New Jersey: Prentice-Hall, 1970).

7. See Sarason, *op. cit.*, chapter 7.

8. The issue of outside influences on schools and problems arising from them are discussed in Sarason, *op. cit.*, chapter 2.

9. Various levels of parent or citizen participation are presented in Sharry Arnstein, "Eight Rungs on the Ladder of Citizen Participation," in Edgar Cahn and Barry Passett, ed., *Citizen Participation: Effecting Community Change* (New York: Praeger, 1971), pp. 69–91.

10. Alvin Poussaint, "The Black Child's Image of the Future," in Alvin Toffler, ed. *Learning for Tomorrow* (New York: Random House, 1974), pp. 56–69.

Chapter 14, pp. 248–268

1. National Association of Secondary Schools in a Changing Society, *This We Believe: Secondary Schools in a Changing Society* (Reston, Virginia, 1975).

2. Kenneth B. Clark, "Education in the Ghetto: A Human Concern," in A. H. Passow, ed., *Urban Education in the 1970's* (New York: Teachers College Press, 1971), pp. 94–102.

3. V. K. Gilbert, et al., *Perceptions of Educational Leadership: A Study of the Needs and Training Opportunities for Educational Leadership in Ontario* (Toronto, Ontario, Canada: The Ontario Institute for Studies in Education, 1977).

4. Harris Shettel, et al., *Evaluation of the Impact of the Film Series "One to Grow On" on Selected Teachers and Students* (Washington, D.C.: American Institutes for Research in the Behavioral Sciences, 1975).

5. Lawrence Gary and Aaron Favors, eds., *Restructuring the Educational Process: A Black Perspective* (Washington, D.C.: Howard University Institute for Urban Affairs Research, 1975).

6. National Institute on Drug Abuse, Division of Resource Development, *Beyond The Three R's: Training Teachers for Affective Education* (Rockville, Md.: National Institute on Drug Abuse).

7. James Banks, "Cultural Pluralism: Implications for Curriculum Reform," in Melvin Tumin and Walter Plotch, eds., *Pluralism in a Democratic Society* (New York: Praeger, 1977), pp. 226–248.

8. Elizabeth G. Cohen, Jo Ann K. Intili and Susan Hurevitu Robbins, "Task and Authority: A Sociological View of Classroom Management" in *The 78th Yearbook of the National Society for the Study of Education*, Part II (Chicago: Univ. Chicago Press, 1979), pp. 116–143.

Epilogue

1. Kate O'Neil and Joan Shoemaker, eds., *A Conversation between James Comer and Ronald Edmonds: Fundamentals of Effective School Improvement* (Dubuque: Kendall/Hunt Publishing Company, 1989).

2. James P. Comer, *A Brief History and Summary of the School Development Program* (New Haven: Yale Child Study Center, 1991).

3. James P. Comer, *Maggie's American Dream: The Life and Times of a Black Family* (New York: New American Library, 1988).

4. James P. Comer, "Educating Poor Minority Children," *Scientific American*, vol. 259, no. 5 (1988), pp. 42–48.

5. *Turning Points: Preparing American Youth for the Twenty-First Century*, Report of the Task Force on Education of Young Adolescents (Washington: Carnegie Council on Adolescent Development, 1989).

6. Norris M. Haynes, *Summary of School Development Program Documentation and Research* (New Haven: Yale Child Study Center, 1991).

7. Norris M. Haynes, *Trend Analysis of Achievement in Two Original School Development Program Schools in New Haven* (New Haven: Yale Child Study Center, 1986).

8. Ana Mari Cauce, James P. Comer, and David Schwartz, "Long Term Effects of a Systems-Oriented School Prevention Program," *American Journal of Orthopsychiatry*, vol. 57, no. 1 (January, 1987), pp. 127–131.

9. Norris M. Haynes, James P. Comer, and Muriel Hamilton-Lee, "The Effects of Parental Involvement on Student Performance," *Educational and Psychological Research*, vol. 8, no. 4 (1988), pp. 291–299.

10. Norris M. Haynes, James P. Comer, and Muriel Hamilton-Lee, "The School Development Program: A Model for School Improvement," *Journal of Negro Education*, vol. 8, no. 1 (1988), pp. 11–21.

11. Norris M. Haynes, *School Development Program: New Haven Middle School Follow-up Study* (New Haven: Yale Child Study Center, 1988).

12. Norris M. Haynes, James P. Comer, and Muriel Hamilton-Lee (1988), op. cit.

13. Prince George's County Public Schools Research Office, *Report on Academic Achievement of Milliken Schools in Prince George's*

County (Upper Marlboro: Prince George's County Public Schools, spring 1988).

14. Norris M. Haynes, James P. Comer, and Muriel Hamilton-Lee (1988), op. cit.
15. James P. Comer, Norris M. Haynes, and Muriel Hamilton-Lee, "School Power: A Model for Improving Black Student Achievement," in W.D. Smith and E.W. Chunn, eds., *Black Education: A Quest for Equity and Excellence* (New Brunswick: Transaction Publishers, 1988), pp. 187–200.
16. Ana Mari Cauce, James P. Comer, and David Schwartz (1987), op. cit.
17. Norris M. Haynes and James P. Comer, "The Effects of a School Development Program on Self-Concept," *The Yale Journal of Biology and Medicine,* vol. 63, no. 4 (1990), pp. 275–283.
18. Cited in nn. 9 and 10 above.
19. Norris M. Haynes, James P. Comer, and Muriel Hamilton-Lee, "School Climate Enhancement Through Parental Involvement," *Journal of School Psychology,* vol. 27, no. 1 (1989), pp. 87–90.
20. James P. Comer, Norris M. Haynes, Khalipha M. Bility, Christine L. Emmons, and Sara Gebreyesus, *School Development Program Implementation and Outcomes: Norfolk, Virginia* (New Haven: Yale Child Study Center, 1992).
21. Ibid.
22. James P. Comer, Cynthia Savo, Margaret Spillane, et al., *For Children's Sake: The Comer School Development Program,* videotape series and manual subtitled *Discussion Leader's Guide* (New Haven: Yale Child Study Center, 1993).

Index